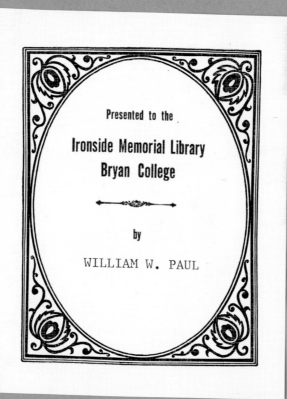

Foundations of
Historical Knowledge

Other Books by Morton White

THE ORIGIN OF DEWEY'S INSTRUMENTALISM

SOCIAL THOUGHT IN AMERICA: THE REVOLT AGAINST FORMALISM

THE AGE OF ANALYSIS (ed.)

TOWARD REUNION IN PHILOSOPHY

RELIGION, POLITICS AND THE HIGHER LEARNING

THE INTELLECTUAL VERSUS THE CITY (with Lucia White)

PATHS OF AMERICAN THOUGHT (ed., with Arthur Schlesinger, Jr.)

Foundations of
Historical Knowledge

by MORTON WHITE

 Harper & Row, Publishers

New York and London

For

ISAIAH BERLIN AND ARTHUR SCHLESINGER, JR.

CONTENTS

Acknowledgments

This book is based upon a course of lectures that I have been giving regularly at Harvard for several years. I therefore wish to express my appreciation to those assistants and students who have asked me searching questions and to those who have subjected my views to helpful criticism. I also wish to thank Professor Burton Dreben for carefully and generously reading my manuscript and for pointing the way to many improvements. My wife and sons have been helpful and encouraging to a degree that I acknowledge with gratitude and pleasure. Finally, I want to acknowledge the support of the American Council of Learned Societies, the Harvard Foundation for Advanced Study and Research, the Henry P. Kendall Foundation, and the Institute for Advanced Study in Princeton, New Jersey, where I prepared the major part of my final draft during the academic year 1962–1963.

M. W.

Cambridge, Massachusetts
April 1965

Foundations of
Historical Knowledge

CHAPTER I

Fact, Law, and Value
in History

This is a study in the philosophy of history, a discipline with a checkered past, a respectable present and, I hope, a brighter future. Once the philosophy of history was associated almost exclusively with grand speculation about the development of society, with pretentious volumes on the laws of civilization and its decay, and with futile debates about whether heroes, ideas, or material circumstances alone shape the course of human history. Idealists debated with materialists and monists with pluralists as they acted out their metaphysical differences in studies of the past: some pledged allegiance to Hegel's absolute idea, some to Marx's historical materialism, some to Vico and his cycles, some to gloomy Spengler, and some to the undaunted Toynbee. But all of this changed dramatically when philosophers —especially British and American philosophers—came to focus so much of their attention on the logic of language, the method of science, and the analysis of concepts. For better or worse—and I

1

But see
p. 12

think for the better—the speculative philosophy of history has not endured as a serious intellectual enterprise in the age of analysis. Among philosophers its place has been taken by an approach that is more closely linked with the philosophy of science and the theory of knowledge than it is with metaphysics. Instead of seeking to chart the development of epochs, cultures, and civilizations, the contemporary philosopher of history is more interested in analyzing historical thought and language. Instead of trying to advance or defend some general theory of the historical process itself, the contemporary philosopher of history who is not dominated by the aims of Marxism or by certain forms of theology is now primarily concerned with the logic of history, anxious to elucidate terms that are commonly employed by historians and historically minded thinkers, and eager to advance toward a clearer understanding of the chief intellectual activities of the historian.

Such an understanding is the main aim of the present study, which, unlike Hegel's course of lectures on the philosophy of history, can hardly be called what he thought his could be called: "A Philosophical History of the World." But its concerns are not only to be distinguished from Hegel's; they are also to be distinguished from those of authors of manuals on historical method, who describe the tools of textual criticism and outline the methods of dating documents and establishing authorship. Today's philosopher of history is not a metaphysical speculator, but neither is he a methodological consultant. Like the philosopher of natural science, the critical philosopher of history is theoretically oriented, primarily interested in analyzing historical language and achieving insight into history as a form of knowledge. The language of history, however, is as rich and varied as human speech itself. Virtually every form of statement made by the historian is made by the ordinary man as he conducts his business and his life, and so the philosopher who seeks to clarify historical discourse is faced with an embarrassment of riches. What aspect of historical language does he study? In answer to this question it is fair to say that he is primarily interested in analyzing the parts played by factual statements, lawful generalizations, and value judgments in historical investigation and writing.

Preoccupation with fact, law, and value has been constant for a century and a half during which philosophers and historians have argued about three dramatic theses. One thesis has often been identified with Ranke's much-quoted statement that the task of history is to say what really happened; another was advanced by Comte, Marx, and Mill, who thought that a science of history could formulate the laws of historical development; and a third was sponsored by idealists who insisted that the historian, unlike the natural scientist, inevitably makes or depends upon value judgments in his thinking and writing. Tradition has often identified history with disconnected factual statements of the form "George Washington slept here," "John Lackland passed here," or "Booth shot Lincoln," but as soon as we recognize that the historian engages in explanation and in selection, we must of course deepen and broaden our conception of historical investigation. Because the historian not only records but also explains events, he depends upon generalizations; and because he records certain events rather than others, he may depend upon value judgments that guide his selection. Unfortunately, however, the role of generalization and the role of value judgment have been exaggerated by different philosophers, and this has given rise to what Hegel might have called two moments in the epistemology of history: an earlier, positivistic moment represented by Hume, Comte, and Mill, and a later, idealistic one that may be associated with thinkers like Dilthey, Croce, and Collingwood. The positivists fixed upon the importance of lawful regularity and hence laid great stress on the logical connections between history and the social sciences, whereas the idealists, struck more by the role of value judgment in historical investigation, laid equal stress on the differences between history and science. Each group exaggerated a genuine aspect of historical investigation, for the simple truth is that history reports facts, employs general knowledge, and depends to some extent on value judgments consciously or unconsciously made. Therefore the philosopher of history need not identify himself either as a positivist or as an idealist, and may instead devote himself with greater profit to analyzing the interconnected roles of factual reporting, generalization, and value judgment in historical discourse.

To present such a description and analysis is the chief purpose of the present work, and in the remaining pages of this introductory chapter I shall set forth its main conclusions. They will be presented in brief and the arguments for them will hardly be complete, but the reader may find it useful to have before him an outline of the chain of reasoning he is about to encounter, as well as an indication of the author's point of view. The main theses of this book are best summarized by keeping in mind narration, the typical form of discourse employed by the historian, for a narrative consists primarily of singular explanatory statements, implies singular factual statements that are not explanatory in form, and rests to some extent on value judgments made by the historian.[1]

Leaving aside isolated statements that are not explanatory, a narrative, unlike a chronicle, is a conjunction of singular explanatory statements, and when it is the narrative of a single entity, like a person or a nation, it aims to present something that can best be characterized as the development of that thing. When I say that a narrative is primarily a conjunction of singular explanatory statements, I mean that for the most part it takes the form of asserting something like this: "Because so-and-so was true of nation s at t_1, such-and-such was true of s at t_2; and because such-and-such was true of s at t_2, this-and-that was true of s at t_3; and so on." It follows at once that a narrative implies singular statements of fact, like "The United States declared war on Germany in 1917," and therefore cannot be true unless such noncausal factual statements are true. They are the logical bricks with which a narrative is built, and if they crumble the narrative crumbles too.

Even though a narrative does not usually contain generaliza-

[1] Narration is analyzed at length in ch. VI.

tions that are laws, its conjuncts—singular explanatory statements—are connected with laws. They do not imply laws but, I
shall argue, they imply the existence of such laws, since a singular
explanatory statement like "The Civil War broke out partly because of the economic conflict between North and South" is true
if and only if there is an explanatory deductive argument which
contains the antecedent of the singular statement as a premise and
its consequent as conclusion.[2] It follows, as we shall see, that a
singular explanatory statement may be confirmed either by presenting a full-fledged deductive argument of the requisite kind or
by presenting good inductive reasons for thinking that such an
argument exists.[3] Generally speaking, the natural scientist is in a
better position to defend his singular explanatory statements deductively—by presenting a deductive argument—whereas the historian is likely to present only inductive evidence, some of it
statistical. However, even though a historian may appeal to statistical generalizations in the course of supporting his conviction
that certain explanatory deductive arguments exist, this does not
mean that he must offer what have been called statistical explanations, that is to say, explanations in which statistical generalizations rather than strict laws serve as premises.[4] So long as we do
not abandon determinism, we may hold that a singular explanatory statement implies that strict laws exist; and therefore when
we say that a country lost a war because it lacked raw materials,
we may mean by "because" just what we mean by it when we say
that a window was broken because a bullet was fired at the window, even if we can do no more than support the first explanation
by citing statistical correlations, whereas we can support the second by citing strict laws of physics and a deductive argument.

There is no a priori reason to think that the laws whose existence is implied by singular causal statements, or the statistical
generalizations which are cited in support of the belief that such

[2] This is argued in ch. III, pp. 56-61.
[3] See ch. III, pp. 84-91.
[4] See pp. 91-97.

strict laws exist, must suffer from the defects of the putative laws proposed by certain speculative philosophers of history.[5] Since the latter are often obscurely formulated and the number of examples upon which they rest are very small, they are more likely to be propped up (ineffectually) by appeals to metaphysics, epistemology, and cosmology. It is true that Hume and Mill combined a version of the regularity theory of causation with a belief in very general principles of human nature, but this belief must be distinguished from their philosophical analysis of causation. To assert that a singular explanatory statement implies the existence of a law is not to assert that the law must be as general as those that Hume and Mill had in mind when they spoke of laws of human nature. Moreover, as we shall see, it is perfectly possible for an advocate of the covering law theory of explanation to countenance laws about individuals.[6] The doctrine that I call existential regularism may be defended against many logical objections though it must be granted that the notion of law upon which it rests is in need of further clarification.[7]

So far I have summarized that part of my argument intended to meet some of the more general objections to the regularity, or covering law, theory of explanation, objections which purport to show that there is no logical link between singular explanatory statements and law. But I shall also criticize efforts to replace the notion of empirical law by the idea of rational principles of action.[8] Even though human beings whose actions are studied by historians may appeal to moral or normative principles in *defending* their actions, the historian who cites the agent's normative beliefs in causal *explanation* of the agent's actions does not make a logical appeal to those normative principles. The objector to the covering law theory at this point confuses the task of the historian with the task of the historical agent and, moreover, fails to see that an agent's belief may be causally related to another belief of

[5] See pp. 29-47.
[6] See pp. 47-53.
[7] See pp. 69-78.
[8] See ch. V.

his even though one proposition that he believes does not stand in a causal relationship to another proposition that he believes. Something analogous may be said about the link between belief and action. If a man does something because he believes that it is the right thing to do, his believing that it is the right thing to do may stand in a causal relationship to his action even though the proposition that it is the right thing to do does not cause the action. In short, a historian may construct a psychological explanation that parallels the agent's logical or ethical argumentation without becoming identical with it. The historian's psychological explanation may be analyzable in accordance with the regularity theory even though the historical agent's argument is not.

In that part of the study in which the above theme is developed, special attention will be paid to the problems of the intellectual historian, for they are in many ways analogous to the problems of the historian who reconstructs the practical arguments of historical agents.[9] The intellectual historian who engages in explanation is primarily concerned with the explanation of beliefs and attitudes, whereas other historians may be mainly concerned to explain actions, and yet both of them may engage in wholly factual investigations even though the subjects of their investigations engage in mathematics, theology, and practical argument. The historian may factually record and causally explain modes of reasoning which are themselves not causal.

Although a good part of my argument will be devoted to showing (1) that narratives contain singular causal statements which are factually true, (2) that they imply chronicles composed of noncausal singular statements which are factually true, (3) that they imply the existence of general statements which are factually true, and (4) that they do not involve an appeal to certain kinds of value judgments, the argument does not end there so far as the role of value judgment is concerned. For value judgments may play more complex parts in the assessment of a history. When a reader or a critic of a history asks himself the question, "What do

[9] See pp. 194-206.

I have to agree with the historian about in order to judge his history to be a good one?", his answer cannot always be, "Only about the truth of his factual statements, both causal and non-causal." There are many different kinds of extrafactual considerations that may enter into the assessment of a history.

In a large number of cases, when we assert one true explanatory statement rather than another and thereby treat it as a statement in which *the* cause, or the decisive cause, is presented, we assert it because we think that it refers to the fact that made the difference between something's behaving in a normal manner and its behaving abnormally.[10] But whether we say that the central subject of our narrative is behaving in an abnormal or an unusual way depends upon how we regard it or look at it; and sometimes that central subject will not, so to speak, force us to look at it in one particular way. On those occasions the decision to regard the subject of our inquiry in one way rather than another will determine which antecedent in the background of the behavior we will regard as the cause, and this decision may be based on a judgment of interest which in turn rests on a value judgment even though the value judgment is not logically implied by the statement of the cause. If we think of the behavior of a country as abnormal when compared with its own behavior just before the puzzling event, we may explain the puzzling event in one way; but if we think of that country as behaving abnormally by comparison with *other countries*, we may seize upon something else as the cause of its abnormal behavior. In places Mill implied that the investigator always selects *the* cause arbitrarily, and other students of the problem have held that the selection is made simply on the basis of the criterion of statistical abnormality. My own view is that sometimes a value judgment that determines the interest of the investigator may indirectly determine which explanatory statement he asserts in his narrative, and that this is compatible with the view that *the* cause is the abnormal contributory cause. If an historian is a political conservative who is averse to violent changes in so-

[10] See ch. IV.

ciety, he may be oriented toward seeking episodic causes in the background of the country, whereas if he is a radical, he may focus on a standing condition which, when regarded as the decisive cause of a certain kind of behavior, may point the way to revolutionary alteration of the country's social structure. Moreover—and this is crucial—a critic who reads these histories may prefer one to the other—call it superior—in accordance with his own value orientation. The ultimate grounds on which his preference of one true history as against another true history will rest, may be a value judgment about the wisdom of violent versus gradual social change.

We shall also see that a narrator will not only try to pick out *the* cause of an event, but that he may refer to something as *the* effect.[11] Here an element of value enters quite directly. Even if we are able to identify the cause of an event as its abnormal antecedent, we cannot analogously identify *the* effect of an event as the abnormal consequent of the event. Once again the decision as to which true statement to assert is dependent on an extrahistorical judgment which is not logically implied by the statement of the effect.

Finally, I shall argue, there are some uses of the expression "is the cause of" which are obviously moral in character and might well be abandoned in favor of other words that more clearly indicate that what is involved is a judgment of who is *to be held* responsible for a certain outcome.[12]

After arguing in the above manner about the historian's answer to the question "What is the decisive cause of what happened?" we shall examine his answer to the question "What happened?" in order to remark on another variety of value judgment that the historian may make in the course of constructing his narrative.[13] Here we shall see that when a historian characterizes one period in the career of his central subject as an "age of reason," a "renais-

[11] See pp. 234-237.
[12] See pp. 174-179.
[13] See ch. VI, esp. pp. 251-270.

sance," an "age of enlightenment," an "age of faith," an "age of
analysis," or as a period in which thinkers revolted against formalism, he may choose his description on the basis of a value judgment that he makes about events, men, and ideas. That judgment
may be there implicitly or explicitly, so that anyone who approves
of the particular historical reconstruction in which these descriptions and others appear may do so partly because he shares the
historian's value judgment about what the great deeds or ideas
of the nation's history are. At times these favorable assessments of
the historian's various descriptions will indicate convergence with
the historian which is partly evaluative even if the historian and
his favorable critic cannot disentangle the two elements. There
may be a resonance, so to speak, on two levels that are not easily
distinguished when both parties agree on the answer to the question "What happened?" For the same reason, a historian who
gives an account which is equally true but different may look at the
data differently and "work them up" differently just because his
value orientation is different. Any philosophical attempt to analyze
what is involved when the historian tries to say *what* happened
must therefore acknowledge the existence of this double vision,
vision that is partly historical and partly extrahistorical in character. Broadly speaking, the extrahistorical element in this vision is
dominated by the idea of memorability or worthiness to be recorded in a chronicle, and I know no way of eliminating this
factor in the construction and assessment of a history.

In dealing with this problem we shall be concerned with the
question "What is a superior narrative?" While we may say that a
narrative is true if and only if its components are true, such truth,
it may be argued, is not the only consideration in the historian's
estimate of a narrative. Often two historians will present two distinct histories of the United States of America, each of whose
components will be accepted by all parties as true, and yet historical critics will regard one narrative as superior to the other for
reasons which the philosopher of history must analyze. Here the
philosopher's main task is to discover whether the concept of a

superior narrative is radically different from the concept of a superior scientific theory, in particular whether the concept of a superior narrative is more value-laden and less objective than the concept of a superior scientific theory.

The historian Samuel Eliot Morison has said that sixty years ago it was difficult to find a general history of the United States that did not, as he put it, "present the Federalist-Whig-Republican point of view, or express a very dim view of all Democratic leaders except Grover Cleveland." But, according to Morison, by the middle of the twentieth century fashions had changed and it was then equally difficult to find a good history of the country "that did not follow the Jefferson-Jackson-Franklin D. Roosevelt line." Morison tells us that he was converted to the second line as a young man, when he discovered in his first researches on New England Federalism that "the 'wise and good and rich' whom Fisher Ames thought should rule the nation were stupid, narrowminded, and local in outlook."[14] We may therefore ask a series of questions of philosophical import about the grounds on which the historian chooses his line of narrative. Was Morison's earlier preference for the Federalist-Whig-Republican line dictated by a value judgment of the character and intelligence of certain people, a judgment which others did not share and which he later changed when he went over to the Jefferson-Jackson-Franklin D. Roosevelt line? Was his choice of line based on a view as to which Americans were good and broad-minded? Was his narrative of the American past determined exclusively by the so-called facts of the American past? And, more generally, is it true that the grounds on which a historian prefers one narrative will always be incompletely stated by him if he does not refer to implicit judgments of value like those to which Morison alludes?

The value judgments we have mentioned so far must be distinguished from explicit value judgments that a historian may make about the men and actions he talks about. The value judgments

[14] Samuel Eliot Morison, *By Land and By Sea: Essays and Addresses* (New York, 1953), pp. 356–57.

that may determine which cause a historian will seize upon as decisive or which true description of an era he will give, are likely to exist behind the arras of history-making as tools in the historian's workshop that he need not bring out into the open but may nevertheless use. By contrast, other value judgments may appear explicitly in the book he writes. These may be detachable obiter dicta that the reader may disregard while he reads the narrative, but sometimes the historian's moral judgments may not be detachable in this way: they may play a part in an explanation, as when he explains an action by referring to the goodness or badness of the agent's character. In both cases the critic of the history must, strictly speaking, accept certain value judgments if he is to accept the history as it is presented.

i.e., they may throw light upon his implicit value outlook.

Finally, as we shall see, the historian may judge that it is morally right to *make* moral judgments in certain circumstances and not in others.[15] Such a metamoral moral judgment will differ from the judgment of value that determines which cause a historian may select as *the* cause, the judgment of memorability that determines which chronicle he may select as *the* chronicle, and the moral judgments he makes about agents treated in his history. On this level we meet the dictum—as I construe it—that "right" and "wrong" imply "can." Once we are at this level of abstraction, we are considering a very broad moral principle that forms part of a historian's world view. Although the speculative philosophy of history may be defunct, and although the effort to deduce the laws of history from metaphysics, epistemology, and cosmology usually fails, there can be no denying that what a historian writes is dictated to some extent by his position on determinism, on the propriety of making moral judgments at all, and on the connection between moral judgment and voluntary action. His thinking on such matters will be of concern to us mainly because of the moral component in a world view so conceived, a component to which we are bound to call attention if we are trying to analyze the manner in which value judgment impinges on the writing of history.

II.

p.2

15 See ch. VII.

One of the most important things that will emerge from our study is that the historian must often distinguish two questions about a statement: "Is it true?" and "Should it, rather than another true statement, be made?" This becomes clear when he tries to pick out *the* cause of what happened from among many causes and is forced to say why he regards an event as unusual in one respect rather than as unusual in another; when he picks out *the* effect of an event from among many effects; and when he fixes on one description of what happened rather than another. A similar question arises when the historian makes or refrains from making a moral judgment out of concern for whether the agent did or did not act voluntarily. While clarifying the various grounds on which the historian attributes truth to statements and decides to make *them* rather than other true statements, we shall be presenting a systematic view of fact finding, generalization, and value judgment in history, and that, as I have said, is the main purpose of this book.

II

Explanatory Arguments

If we begin with the idea that a narrative, unlike a chronicle, is a conjunction primarily of explanatory statements like "The Moslem seizure of the Mediterranean Sea caused the breakdown of [what Pirenne calls] the Mediterranean Commonwealth of Europe," then one of the first problems to which we must address ourselves is the nature of the connection asserted in these explanatory statements. However, as I have already suggested and as we shall see in detail later on, this is not the only philosophical problem connected with narration. For if we think of a narrative as presenting a chain of linked statements about, say, a given country, then there are two fundamental problems that we may raise about that chain. First, we may inquire into the nature of the links in the chain; and then we may ask about the relationship between this chain as a whole and the thing of which it purports to be a history. The first inquiry is primarily an inquiry into the nature of statements made in answer to the question "Why did what happened happen?" and the second is primarily an inquiry into the nature of statements made in answer to the question "What happened?" We shall launch the first inquiry in this chapter, where we shall concentrate on the connection between the singular explanatory statements in a narrative and generalizations or laws.

It will be convenient to begin by considering what is sometimes called the covering law, or regularity, theory of historical explanation.[1] On this view an explanation of a war, a revolution, or an economic depression is similar in structure to an explanation of a fire. We may explain a particular fire, it is maintained, by deducing the statement that the fire has taken place from the statement that a spark has fallen into a wastebasket of dry paper surrounded by oxygen and from the law that whenever a spark falls into such a wastebasket under such conditions, a fire will take place. Some philosophers who accept this view contend that not only the truth of a singular explanatory statement in ordinary language, like "The lit cigarette caused the fire" or "The bent rail caused the derailment," but also that of a singular statement in history books, like "The Moslem seizure of the Mediterranean Sea caused the breakdown of the Mediterranean Commonwealth in Europe," is dependent on the truth of a law. Ever since Hume, such a theory has exerted a powerful hold on philosophers, even on those who recognize and emphasize the limits of historical speculation. The idea that we can intuitively see causal connections between historical events without appealing to inductively established laws, or that causes have unanalyzable powers to bring about their effects, has seemed indefensible to philosophers of an empirical turn of mind, and they have therefore been led to the view that causal statements are either disguised statements of laws or are in some way dependent upon them for their truth. Even though historians in their explanatory statements refer to particular events like the Civil War and the conflict between Northern and Southern economic interests, philosophers under the influence of Hume and

---

[1] See Carl G. Hempel, "The Function of General Laws in History," repr. *Theories of History*, ed. Patrick Gardiner (Glencoe, Ill., 1959), pp. 344–56; also Karl R. Popper, *The Open Society and its Enemies* repr. London, 1947), II, 248 ff., 342 ff.

Mill have maintained that such explanatory statements turn out upon analysis to imply, involve, presuppose, or depend on general laws.

Often one gets the impression from some advocates of the covering law, or regularity, theory of explanation that an explanation of an individual historical event is neither more nor less than a deductive argument of the kind previously illustrated in the case of the fire. It follows, at least on what I shall call the standard version of the covering law theory, that the singular causal statement made by the historian, or even that made by the man who says that the fire was caused by a spark falling into the wastebasket, is not, strictly speaking, an explanation. On such a view it may be an incomplete explanation or an explanation-sketch; it may be elliptical for, or an inferior version of, a deductive argument containing laws and so-called statements of initial conditions as premises, but it is not a full-fledged explanation.

Now in my opinion this standard way is not the best way to state the logical connection between generalizations and what are usually called historical explanations, and a considerable part of my argument in a later part of this study will be devoted to showing why and to presenting an alternative view of that connection. But since the standard version of the regularity theory has been staunchly advocated by many distinguished philosophers and also unfairly attacked, I want to present the standard version in this chapter and also to consider some ineffectual arguments that have been leveled against it. Then, in the next chapter, I shall show how the covering law theory should be modified so as to meet certain other objections without abandoning its basic philosophical aim. After presenting the standard version of the covering law, or regularity, theory, I shall consider three complaints about it: first, that any effort to analyze historical explanations as explanatory deductive arguments must lead to the formulation of generalizations that are so complex as to apply only to single instances, and hence to the formulation of generalizations that do not state lawful regularities; second, that the generalizations which the analyst cites in his explanatory deductive arguments are fundamentally similar to the shaky "laws" of speculative philosophers of history; and third, that the historian may explain the behavior of one individual on a given occasion without depending on knowledge of how other similar individuals behave.

THE STANDARD VERSION:
EXPLANATORY DEDUCTIVE ARGUMENTS

Because the regularity theory of explanation usually originates in the course of reflection on explanation in the natural sciences, most expositions of the theory begin by employing illustrations from natural science or illustrations from ordinary language in which the events explained are physical, chemical, or biological in character. Therefore, in order to make clear what that theory says, I shall illustrate it with explanations of such things as fires, cracking automobile radiators, explosions, and deaths. Whether one thinks that historical explanation is fundamentally similar to or fundamentally different from the explanation of natural events, one must have some notion of how the explanation of such natural events is carried out according to the standard version of the regularity theory. Moreover, the figure of exploding powder is probably the most common of those employed by historians who try to account for the occurrence of events; and therefore it is well to have in mind the logical structure of this constantly used scientific model or metaphor, to say nothing of that other favorite, the fertile soil that flowers when seeded.

According to the part of the regularity theory that bears most closely on the task of historians, the process of explanation typically begins after we ask why a certain event, such as the cracking of an automobile radiator during the night, has taken place. According to the standard version of the regularity theory,[2] in order to explain such a fact we present other facts expressed in statements of so-called initial conditions: that the car was left in the

[2] Hempel, op. cit., presents the illustration used in the text.

street all night, that its radiator was made of iron, that the radiator was completely filled with water, that the lid was screwed on tightly, that the temperature dropped from 39 degrees F. in the evening to 25 degrees F. in the morning, that the air pressure was normal, and that the bursting pressure of the radiator's material was such and such. But to complete the explanation, according to the regularist—as we shall call the advocate of the regularity theory—we must present laws which, together with the statements of initial conditions, logically imply the statement that the radiator cracked during the night. Such laws are: that water freezes below 32 degrees F. under normal atmospheric pressure, that below 39.2 degrees F. the pressure of a mass of water increases with decreasing temperature if the volume remains constant or decreases, and that when the water freezes, the pressure again increases. In addition, we need some quantitative laws connecting change of pressure with temperature and volume.

Leaving aside certain logical niceties, the idea behind the regularity theory of historical explanation is as follows: the statement of the historical fact to be explained will, in the simplest case, be a singular statement of the form "a is Q," where "a" denotes something concrete existing in space and time and "Q" expresses some property of such concrete items. And in order to explain the fact that a is Q, we must present true or well-supported statements of lawful connection and statements of so-called initial conditions which together logically imply the statement "a is Q." In other words, an explanation *is* a certain kind of deductive argument. In the simplest case we may present the two statements "All P is Q" and "a is P" in explanation of the fact expressed by "a is Q," but usually more than one such simple law and more than one statement of initial conditions appear in the argument.

Some regularists have emphasized that the law involved in an explanation employing only one such law will usually be quite complex, that its subject-term will not be like the "P" in "All P is Q," but rather that the law will often be of the form "All things

which are P and R and S and T are Q," where the subject-term is
a logical conjunction of terms. John Stuart Mill insisted very
strongly upon this kind of complexity. He says: "To certain facts,
certain facts always do, and, as we believe, will continue to, succeed. The invariable antecedent is termed the cause; the invariable
consequent, the effect."[3] But then he adds, "It is seldom, if ever,
between a consequent and a single antecedent that this invariable
sequence subsists. It is usually between a consequent and the sum
of several antecedents."[4] One of Mill's examples is that of a
person who eats of a particular dish and then dies. In connection
with such an example he says that "there certainly is, among the
circumstances which took place, some combination or other on
which death is invariably consequent; as, for instance, the act of
eating of the dish, combined with a particular bodily consitution, a
particular state of present health, and perhaps even a certain state
of the atmosphere." And therefore Mill says that "the real Cause
is the whole of these antecedents."[5] It is worth remarking here
that while Mill often writes as if an explanation will contain only
one law, it may, and usually does, contain several, as in the example about the cracked automobile radiator. There we have a
series of events that begins with the dropping of the temperature,
continues with the freezing of the water, goes on to the expansion
of the water, and finally concludes with the cracking of the radiator. Each step in the series is associated with a generalization
that plays a part in the regularist's reconstruction of an explanation of why a car's radiator cracked.

Furthermore, although sometimes a law, or the laws, appearing
in an explanation will connect events occurring or states prevailing
at different times, sometimes it will connect events and states that
do not occur or prevail at different times.[6] In an explanation we
may employ the law that a drop in the temperature of H_2O from

[3] *A System of Logic*, Bk. III, ch. V, sec. 2.
[4] Ibid., sec. 3.
[5] Ibid.
[6] See my "Historical Explanation," repr. Gardiner, op. cit., pp. 357–73.

anything above 32 degrees F. to anything below it, given an appropriate amount of pressure, will be followed, in time, by freezing; or we may employ the law that all sea water is salty. Although sometimes it is said that causes must be prior to effects, we can explain without citing causes so conceived. For example, we can *explain* the fact that a glass of liquid is salty by pointing out that it is sea water and that all sea water is salty, even though the liquid was not sea water before it was salty. Moreover, we can say in ordinary language that the liquid in the glass is salty *because* it is sea water, and even, with some awkwardness, that the cause of its being salty is the fact that it is sea water, without being forced into thinking that it was sea water before it was salty. In general, therefore, the law in an explanatory deductive argument may either link two simultaneously exhibited properties, like being sea water and being salty, or two properties exhibited at different times, like being subjected to a drop in temperature from something greater than 32 degrees F. to something less than 32, and being solid.

It is well to add a few other remarks that may ward off certain misunderstandings of the theory. First of all, the theory allows for what may be called the plurality of explanations, and this must be distinguished from the complexity of explanations. An illustration will bring out the point involved. Death may be explained in many different ways, each of them complex. When we explain the death of a man by drowning, our explanation will be different from our explanation of a death by stabbing. In other words, one explanatory deductive argument will contain a law of the form "Whenever P, Q, and R are present, death occurs," whereas the other will contain a law of the form "Whenever D, E, and F are present, death occurs." Both of these are different complex laws that may be used in different complex explanations of the deaths of different individuals.[7] It should be noted, too, that the theory does not

[7] Mill makes this clear as do H. L. A. Hart and A. M. Honoré, *Causation in the Law* (Oxford, 1959), p. 18.

exclude the (rare) case where a man is stabbed while drowning—a situation in which *concurrent* causes are said to be in operation.

Another thing to keep in mind is that according to the regularity theory, we must distinguish between the explanation of a fact like the death of a given man and an explanation of the fact that his death was brought about or caused by stabbing. In the first case, we tell why he died and not why stabbing led to or caused his death. On the basis of premises like "All P is Q" and "a is P," we explain the fact that a is Q and not the fact that a is Q because a is P; and yet some critics of the regularity theory seem to think that the regularist holds that such a deductive argument purports to explain the fact that a is Q because a is P.[8] One of these critics considers a case where the engine of his automobile "seizes up" and the garage mechanic says: "It's due to a leak in the oil reservoir." The critic then argues that the regularist is wrong because the regularist thinks that this explanation may be replaced by a deductive argument in which one of the premises is "Whenever an automobile's oil reservoir leaks, the engine seizes up"; and so the critic (irrelevantly) points out that such a regularistic explanation does not explain "why an oil leak should have *led to* the seizure."[9] But this is not what the garage mechanic was trying to explain, and the regularist is not analyzing the structure of such an explanation in the case in question. The mechanic was trying to explain why the engine seized up and not why the leakage *led to* or caused the seizure. Analogously, a man who tried to explain why Jones died by saying that he took arsenic would not be trying on that occasion to explain why Jones's death was brought on by taking arsenic. The regularist does have an additional theory about how to analyze explanations of "causal facts," i.e., facts referred to by singular causal statements, but it is

[8] See, for example, William Dray, *Laws and Explanation in History* (Oxford, 1957), p. 67.
[9] Ibid.

not relevant when the problem is how to analyze the explanation of noncausal facts like the seizing up of an automobile engine, the outbreak of a war, or the onset of a revolution.

Now we may examine the three complaints against the regularity theory that were mentioned earlier.

COMPLAINT 1: COMPLEX LAWS AND SINGLE EXAMPLES

Although regularists have usually insisted that the laws appearing in explanatory deductive arguments are complex, especially in historical explanations—which often require a great deal of qualification if they are to be accepted—this very complexity has been thought to create a grave difficulty for the regularity theory of explanation in history. It has been maintained[10] that if a historian takes seriously the idea that he must formulate true or well-established laws and makes the qualifications needed in order to arrive at such laws, he may pile condition upon condition into the subject-term of his law to the point where only one historical example is in fact covered by the law. And this, it is said, is fatal to the view that singular explanatory statements made by historians must be replaced by deductive arguments of the kind outlined earlier.

In order to deal with this objection in a concrete way, let us consider an argument that Pieter Geyl offers in criticism of Toynbee's law of challenge and response.[11] Geyl thinks that if one wishes to explain the success of Holland at a certain point in its history, one cannot attribute it merely to the fact that Holland rose magnificently to the harsh challenge of the sea. In other words, one cannot say simply that it achieved success because of this one factor. One must say rather that it achieved success because of a combination or conjunction of factors: the challenge of the sea, the excellence of Holland's soil, the assistance of the

---

[10] Ibid., pp. 39 ff.
[11] Pieter Geyl, "Toynbee's System of Civilizations," *Toynbee and History*, ed. M. F. Ashley Montagu (Boston, 1956), pp. 46–47.

surrounding forms of civilization—such as the assistance the Romans gave the Dutch when they instructed them in dyke-building—and the maritime situation of Holland. Geyl might therefore be prepared to assert a singular explanatory statement to this effect, one having the form "*a* is *Q* because *a* is *P, R, S*, and *T*." The logician who accepts the covering law theory will, in order to fit Geyl's explanation into the pattern described by that theory, presumably construct the following deductive argument:

> Whenever a nation is subjected to the challenge of the sea, has excellent soil, is assisted by its neighbors, and has an excellent maritime situation, it will rise to great heights of success.
> Holland had excellent soil.
> Holland was assisted by its neighbors.
> Holland was challenged by the sea.
> Holland had an excellent maritime situation.
> Therefore,
> Holland rose to great heights of success.

But now, it is said, the trouble for the regularist begins. Suppose he is asked what the evidence is for the first premise in this argument, the universal statement. He begins to look for confirming examples, but suppose that as soon as he does, he finds that Holland is the only nation he can produce which confirms the law that presides at the head of his deductive argument.

What is the trouble with this, according to the critic of the covering law theory? The trouble, he replies, is that the regularist's transformation of the explanation into a deductive argument in the interest of showing that the explanation contains a law, is otiose. For compare Geyl's explanation with an analogous explanation in natural science. If we say of a particular piece of litmus paper that it turned red because it was dipped into an acid, and the regularist reformulates that explanation in such a way as to make explicit our reliance on the law that all litmus paper turns red upon being immersed in acid, he not only reveals our reliance on a law when we give our explanation, but he also shows that we can confirm our explanation by presenting other examples of pieces of litmus paper turning red upon immersion in acid. Supposedly, the main point of the regularist's replacement of the singular explanatory statement by a deductive argument containing a law is to show that the explanation rests on evidence other than that which pertains to the particular item before us. And yet, presumably, in the case of Geyl's historical explanation when presented as a deductive argument, there are no nations other than Holland to whose behavior we are able to appeal in order to confirm our explanation. And so, the criticism of the regularity theory continues, does it not look as though the replacement of Geyl's singular explanatory statement by a deductive argument is otiose, superfluous, and misleading? If we can cite only one example in support of the universal statement "Whenever a nation is subjected to the challenge of the sea, has excellent soil, is assisted by its neighbors, and has an excellent maritime situation, it will rise to great heights of success"—and that is the very example about which we speak in our original singular explanatory statement "Holland rose to great heights of success because it was challenged by the sea, had excellent soil, was assisted by it neighbors, and had an excellent maritime situation"—then what is the point of the regularity theory in this case? How does it illuminate the singular explanatory statement by reference to *regularity* if we can produce no regularly recurring phenomenon in support of our law? Stated in another way the objection is that Geyl's singular explanatory statement is true even though it is not replaceable by a deductive argument that contains a genuine law as a premise, hence the standard version of the regularity theory of explanation seems to break down as a philosophical analysis or clarification of singular explanatory statements in history. It is concluded that Hume's theory of explanation is challenged seriously.

In fact, it is challenged in a way that may be illustrated by considering a generalization that Hume himself might have been tempted to assert and to use in a deductive explanation. In an effort to illustrate his belief that there are principles of human nature, he once said: "Were a man whom I know to be honest and opulent, and with whom I lived in intimate friendship, to come into my house, where I am surrounded with my servants, I rest assured that he is not to stab me before he leaves it in order to rob me of my silver standish."[12] On the basis of this statement we can easily construct a deductive argument that purports to explain why Hume's intimate friend, Adam Smith, did *not* on a certain occasion stab Hume in order to rob him of his silver standish. Suppose that Hume had been stabbed by someone else, who had made off with his silver standish, and suppose that an inquiring detective, who knew very little about Smith or about his relations with Hume, began to wonder whether Smith might have committed the crime, since Smith had been in the house on the night of the crime. One can imagine Hume explaining to the detective why the crime was not committed by Smith, and in his deductive argument Hume might have employed the generalization "For any pair of individuals x and y, if x is honest and opulent, and x and y have lived for years in intimate friendship, and x comes into the house of y, and y is surrounded by his servants, then x does not stab y in order to rob y of y's standish." But now suppose that when Hume is asked to give supporting instances of this generalization, he can only cite the case of Adam Smith and himself. That is to say, he cannot cite more than one case where two men who are related as x and y are in the subject-term of his law, are also related as x and y are in the predicate-term. After all, how many people who own silver standishes and are surrounded by servants, have more than one opulent, honest friend who periodically visits them?

The predicament we have been describing is not peculiar to history considered as a discipline dealing with human affairs. A person might on some occasion say that a particular match lit because it was dry, was struck, and was surrounded by a liter of

---

[12] David Hume, *An Inquiry Concerning Human Understanding*, Sec. VIII, pt. I. This statement occurs in a paragraph which appears only in the last corrected edition of 1777, sometimes referred to as "Edition O."

oxygen, and yet be able to mention only the particular match in his hand when asked to mention examples of the generalization "Whenever we strike a dry match that is surrounded by a liter of oxygen, it lights." One can imagine that the inventor of the match might have been in such a situation just after having gotten the first one to light.

In evaluating the criticism that is based upon such examples, we must distinguish two questions. The first is whether the regularity theory of explanation is refuted if we can show that a *given* explanation, upon being formulated as an explanatory deductive argument, contains a generalization that refers to only one example. The second is whether all historical explanations must have this feature.

It is important to realize that even though a universal statement *happens* to apply to a single individual, it may imply statements about other individuals. For example, when the inventor of the match says, "Whenever we strike a dry match that is surrounded by a liter of oxygen, it lights," and he can produce only one match, he implies that if another match were made, it would obey the law. Moreoever, at such time as the next manufactured match does not obey the generalization, the generalization is shown to be false. The same is true of the generalization employed in the regularist's formulation of Geyl's explanation, and of Hume's generalization. In other words, it is a contingent fact that the subject-term of the generalization should apply to only one example, and I cannot see how the critic of the regularity theory can deny this. He surely cannot prove that as we complicate the subject-term of the generalization, we *must*, in order to arrive at a true generalization, arrive at one which applies to only one example. Even if Holland should in fact be the only extant nation that ever faced a cruel sea while it had the advantages of a good soil, an excellent maritime situation, and neighborly assistance, it is not necessarily the only one—by which I mean that there is no contradiction in supposing that there is also another such nation.

Let us suppose, however, that for all we know there *is* only one such nation. What then? Then the explanation may be a very shaky one *if* its advocate can present no more evidence in its behalf. But in that case the reformulation urged by the regularist will have great virtue, simply because that reformulation will *bring out* the possible shakiness of the explanation. Can the critic seriously maintain that Geyl's explanation of the rise of Holland *is* acceptable even though we have *no* experience of other nations or other groups responding in a similar way in similar circumstances, and no other knowledge that will lend support to the explanation, and if there is no practical possibility of creating another similar instance artificially? I do not see how. The fact is that very often when we offer a deductive explanation whose generalization applies to only one example, there are other ways of supporting the generalization that will compensate for the paucity of inductive evidence. This is obvious in the illustration about the first match. If the inventor of the match should say, just after he has succeeded in getting the first match to light, that it lit because it was dry and struck in the presence of oxygen, he might defend his generalization "Any dry match when struck in the presence of oxygen will light" by deducing it from chemical laws concerning the behavior of sulphur and the statement that matches are made of sulphur. Moreover, Hume, in defense of his generalization, could have pointed out that honest men usually do not rob, that opulent men usually do not, that friends usually do not stab one, that people usually do not attack one in the presence of one's servants. Hume could have said that all of these facts together supply evidence for the *law* that no opulent, honest friend would ever stab one in the presence of one's servants in order to rob one, using the argument that if each one of these considerations points strongly to the conclusion, all of them together make it certain.

I repeat, however, that if, after a regularist transforms Geyl's explanation of the rise of Holland into a deductive argument whose generalization applies to only one example, the generalization is *not* given the sort of extra boost that the match man can give his or that Hume can give his, then the generalization is in trouble—*and so is Geyl's explanation*. It makes no difference that a historian should believe such an explanation with confidence if he cannot do more to support it. Nor will the "judgment" of which some antiregularists speak, help a historian unable to back up his explanation in the ways mentioned. His explanation is weak, and its weakness has been uncovered by translation into the terms advocated by the regularist. So far, then, from presenting an otiose account of historical explanation, the regularist may bring home to the historian the fragility of some of his explanations.

The question still remains, however, whether every historical explanation will, upon translation into the terms of the regularist, be seen to suffer the same fate. And I see no reason to think that the answer is in the affirmative. In other words, I see no reason to believe that generalizations employed in regularistic explanations of historical events always become so complicated as to apply to only a single example while they are not supported by other evidence. It is true that the historian may find himself in this predicament more frequently than the natural scientist does, but this merely says in a different form what we all know—that historical explanations are, generally speaking, less strongly supported than those in natural science. So far, then, from being generally unfaithful to the language of history, the regularity theory of explanation may be said to mirror one of its undeniable features by comparison to the language of science. Unfortunately, however, some philosophers of history operate on the basis of a different assessment of the powers of historians to offer convincing explanations. They seem to assume that on the whole explanations of individual historical events are just as solid and trustworthy as explanations of individual chemical events; and therefore, because the covering law theory when applied to historical explanations seems to expose the weakness of some historical explanations by comparison to scientific explanations, they wish on that score alone to reject the covering law theory. It is as if they believed that an analysis of historical explanation *must* yield the conclusion that historical explanations are, in general, just as solid, just as trust-worthy, just as well supported as scientific explanations. But this is obviously false. Historical explanations are, in general, more tenuously constructed, more debatable, more subject to doubt than the explanations of natural scientists, and one of the reasons for this is the fact that they *are* often based on complex generaliza-tions that apply to single instances while they are *not* supported by deduction from more fundamental truths—a fact which the cover-ing law theory reveals.

COMPLAINT 2: THE LAWS OF THE REGULARIST AND THE
LAWS OF THE SPECULATIVE PHILOSOPHER OF HISTORY

Although the "laws" of certain speculative philosophers of his-tory do not always turn out to apply to single examples, there is no doubt that they often apply to very few examples by compari-son to the laws of natural science, and this paucity of inductive evidence may lead some critics of the regularity theory of histori-cal explanation to complain that *any* law of the sort the regularist may employ in an explanatory deductive argument will resemble the allegedly bankrupt laws of the speculative theorist of history. Once again, however, it must be pointed out that there is no a priori reason to suppose that regularism involves an appeal to *indefensible* laws, and also that where a speculative theorist as-serts a law that is not supported by inductive evidence and he cannot compensate for that defect by, for example, deducing it from more fundamental statements, he is justly criticized. The fact that certain speculative philosophers of history assert faulty gen-eralizations is not an argument against the regularity theory of historical explanation. Indeed, just those thinkers who defend the regularity theory of explanation today are those who are likely to be most critical of the pretentious, unfounded theorizing of specu-lative philosophers of history. In this spirit I shall try to show how certain speculative philosophers of history fail to present sufficient inductive evidence for their laws and, as a consequence, are driven to serious philosophical mistakes. The point of this discussion will be not only to acknowledge and illustrate the errors that have been and may be committed in the name of law-seeking in history but also to point out that law-seeking *need not* drive a historian to such extremes when he offers an explanation.

One of the most instructive ways in which to illustrate the first point is to consider the views of certain Marxists. I do not wish to enter the question as to whether Marx himself fell into the predicament I am about to describe, but there can be no doubt that his disciples Lenin and Stalin did. Such Marxists first of all insist that by finding and formulating the laws of history they will be able not only to unearth facts about the past but also to come up with principles on the basis of which they can predict the future of man. But then, consciously or unconsciously, they sense the inductive fragility of some of their generalizations, the fact that they are based on a very small number of supporting instances, and they seek dubious deductive support for their foundering generalizations. By concentrating on their views we shall see how a thinker in search of historical laws can find himself with a dearth of inductive evidence and how he can be driven to the view that his laws may be supported by deduction from the general truths of philosophy. Thus we shall see how some Marxists come to the erroneous conclusion that epistemological realism or dialectical materialism can come to the rescue of historical materialism. For even if one conceives of general philosophy as going far beyond conceptual and linguistic analysis, as Marxists do, even if one conceives of it as supplying substantive philosophical truth about the world, general philosophy cannot come to the rescue of the speculative philosophy of history *in extremis*. To see how the Marxist view that it can, originates, and why the speculative philosophy of history comes away empty-handed after its appeal to general philosophy, we must enter a more detailed consideration of the concept of scientific law, i.e., the concept of law involved in the regularist's notion of an explanatory deductive argument.

In elementary logic, whether of the traditional or the modern variety, we are introduced to the notion of a statement which is universal in form, that is to say, one which begins with words like "all," "every," or "no." The traditional textbook example is "All men are mortal," and the well-drilled student of logic understandably finds it boring. But boring or exciting, it is a law of nature. It states a regularity; it implies that anything which is a man is also mortal; it permits one to predict with assurance that the next man one meets will die someday, will not live forever. In illustrating the concept of law, however, we need not restrict ourselves to this traditional example, for there are more interesting and more complex laws in all fields of scientific endeavor. Scientific laws are often expressed as equations which do not explicitly contain the words "all" or "every," but such laws may be rephrased or expanded so that they will be universal in form. Thus Galileo's law of freely falling bodies may be understood as saying that all terrestrial bodies which fall in a vacuum traverse a distance measured in feet that is equal to 16 times the square of the time of fall measured in seconds. The point to bear in mind is that the statement "All men are mortal" and Galileo's equation when expanded are both laws. They both assert that certain regularities hold.

However, a law of nature is not merely a true statement of universal form. A statement like "Every piece of paper on the desk this morning is white" is true and universal in form and yet is not a law of nature. It is very different in an important way from the statement that *every* piece of paper is inflammable, which—if it is true—is a law of nature. This second statement, for our present purposes, falls into the same category as the statement that all men are mortal and Galileo's law, whereas the statement about the pieces of paper on the desk this morning does not. In short, although all laws are universal statements, not all universal statements are laws.

Let us briefly summarize some of the ways in which the distinction between laws and nonlaws has been serviceably drawn.[13] For one thing, a law is able to support a corresponding contrary-to-fact conditional statement, whereas nonlaws cannot. Assuming it is true that all paper is inflammable, we are able to say of a theatre curtain made of asbestos that if it *were* paper, it *would be* inflammable.[14] By contrast, we cannot say on the strength of the fact that all of the pieces of paper on my desk this morning are white, that if the yellow piece of paper now on my filing cabinet were on my desk, *it* would be white. A law is a universal statement that is not logically replaceable by a conjunction of a finite number of singular statements. If the three pieces of paper on my desk this morning are named "1," "2," and "3," we may say that the entire content of my statement that every piece of paper on my desk this morning is white may be given in the statement "1 is white and 2 is white and 3 is white." But clearly no such conjunction is available for the translation of the law that all paper is inflammable, since this statement does not assert merely that all observed pieces of paper have been inflammable. It asserts something more.

The distinction between universal statements that are laws and those that are not is exemplified in the writings of speculative theorists of history, but rarely do they devote very much logical attention to it. A good example of a statement which is intended to assert a lawful connection is the statement of Marx that "the mode of production in material life determines the social, political and intellectual life processes in general."[15] As it stands, this statement does not begin with the word "every" or "all," but it is fair to say that Marx conceived of the relationship between mode of production and the social, political, and intellectual life processes much as Boyle conceived of the relationship between the volume and the pressure of a gas. Marx speaks as if he thought his

[13] For an illuminating discussion of this topic see Nelson Goodman, *Fact, Fiction and Forecast* (Cambridge, Mass., 1955), pp. 24–31.

[14] Ibid.; see also G. E. Moore, *Philosophical Studies* (London, 1922), p. 267.

[15] Karl Marx, Preface to *Contribution to the Critique of Political Economy* (1859), in *Selected Works* (Moscow and Leningrad, 1935), I, 356.

laws were fully as deterministic as certain laws of natural science.

On the other hand, Marx also made certain universal statements which he did not conceive of as laws; or perhaps it would be better to say that he made universal statements which he could not, in all consistency, have construed as laws. In the opening pages of the *Communist Manifesto* it is said: "The history of all hitherto existing society is the history of class struggles." Leaving aside the qualification that Marx and Engels make in a footnote —where they add that there was once a period of primitive, classless communism—one must observe that this statement is not intended to express a law in the sense in which "All paper is inflammable," Newton's law of gravitation, Galileo's law of freely falling bodies, Boyle's law of gases, and the law of the lever are intended to express laws. It is rather a summary statement of the fact, made explicit in a later passage of the *Communist Manifesto*, that in ancient Rome there were struggles involving patricians, knights, plebeians, and slaves; that in the Middle Ages there were struggles involving feudal lords, vassals, guild-masters, journeymen, apprentices, and serfs; and that in modern society there is a struggle between the bourgeoisie and the proletariat. Therefore, the Marxian universal statement about class struggles, like the statement "Every piece of paper on the desk this morning is white," may be replaced by a conjunction of finitely many— indeed very few—singular statements of fact: namely, "In ancient society there was a class struggle," "In medieval society there was a class struggle," and "In capitalist society there is a class struggle." Marx does not intend to say that the mere fact that something is a society requires that it be torn by a class struggle. The footnote of Marx and Engels on primitive communism, their prediction of a future communist society, and their use of the word "hitherto" in the statement that the history of all hitherto existing society is the history of class struggles—all show that Marx and Engels did not construe the assertion "Every society is divided by a class struggle" as a law of history. But they did regard Marx's "general result" in the Preface to the *Critique of Political Economy* as a law of history. For this reason, that general result and not the statement in the *Communist Manifesto* should be regarded as a paradigm of statements in the speculative philosophy of history.[16]

If the speculative philosophy of history is to be distinguished from history of a less ambitious variety, it should be distinguished because of its concern to establish those universal statements that are laws. By contrast to such laws, the assertion that ancient, medieval, and modern society have all been torn by class struggles is logically on a par with the singular statement "Caesar crossed the Rubicon" or with the assertion that all American presidents before Kennedy were Protestants. Furthermore, the speculative philosopher of history is not distinguished by the fact that he makes statements about entities like societies, even though it is true that he does. It is possible for a historian without speculative pretensions to make an assertion about one society—to say, for example, that its economy is capitalistic—without thereby asserting a law about all societies. What distinguishes a theoretical historian from his less theoretical confrere is not the fact that the theoretician talks about societies but the fact that he explicitly asserts *laws* about them, laws like Marx's general result.

So far I have spoken as if there were only two kinds of universal statements: laws and those that are like "All of the pieces of paper on the desk are white" or like "The history of all hitherto existing society is the history of class struggles." As a result I may have given the impression that the only way in which a universal statement can fall short of being a law is by being equivalent to a finitely long conjunction of specifiable singular statements like "Ancient society was torn by a class struggle, and medieval so-

---

[16] I realize, of course, that when Marx and Engels say that "the history of all hitherto existing society is the history of class struggles," they may mean to say more than that ancient, medieval, and modern societies were the scenes of class struggles. They may mean that in each of these periods the fact of the class struggle was the central, dominant feature of the three societies, or the feature which explains or illuminates these societies as no other feature does. And therefore it might be more circumspect to say that one plausible interpretation of their words is the one I have given.

ciety was, and modern society is." But it is important to observe that statements like "All crows are black" have also been regarded by some philosophers as nonlaws, and it is not obvious that such statements are equivalent to finite conjunctions of singular statements. Later we shall have occasion to pursue questions like this in greater detail; but here it is enough to observe that whatever the proper way to characterize puzzling examples of universal statements like "All crows are black," a law is thought of as asserting a *connection* and hence more than a fortuitous correlation. Marx certainly had this in mind when he spoke of the laws of history, and his critics have the same thing in mind when they express doubt about his laws.

The Paucity of Examples

Whatever the definition of the concept of law, it should be clear that a statement like "The history of all hitherto existing society is the history of class struggles" is not liable to all the complaints to which Marx's "general result" is liable. We may dispute the truth of Marx's characterization of ancient, medieval, and modern societies, just as we may dispute the truth of the statement about the three pieces of paper on the desk. But since in neither of these two cases is a lawful connection asserted, we have no ground for complaining that no such connection has been established. By contrast, Marx's general result, which does assert a connection, is subject to the complaint that it is not supported well enough, the point being that when you assert a connection you have to establish more than when you merely assert a singular proposition about the past, no matter how complex.

One of the main complaints leveled against the putative laws asserted by speculative thinkers like Marx and Toynbee arises out of the paucity of the instances that are usually cited by them in support of their "laws." According to some of their critics, when we assert that a lawful connection holds between the mode of production of a historical epoch and its intellectual life, and base this assertion on an examination of, say, three historical epochs, we are not supplying the so-called law with as much evidence as is required by ordinary scientific standards.

Just how devastating is this criticism? Let us suppose the Marxist can show that in ancient, medieval, and modern society, the mode of production was accompanied by what he can clearly identify as a corresponding mode of intellectual life; and by "accompanied" I mean simply that the mode of production and the mode of intellectual life both existed at the same time. This would be analogous to showing that three pieces of litmus paper turned red on being immersed in acid. But can we justify acceptance of Marx's "general result" on the basis of three supporting instances? In reply, it might be said that a law is often accepted on the basis of only a few supporting instances; in fact, that the law that acids turn litmus paper red is accepted in this way. Over a hundred years ago John Stuart Mill spoke directly to this point. He said: "When a chemist announces the existence and properties of a newly discovered substance, if we confide in his accuracy, we feel assured that the conclusions he has arrived at will hold universally, though the induction be founded but on a single instance. We do not withhold our assent, waiting for a repetition of the experiment; or if we do, it is from a doubt whether the one experiment was properly made, not whether, if properly made, it would be conclusive. Here, then, is a general law of nature, inferred without hesitation from a single instance; an universal proposition from a singular one." Mill then added: "Not all the instances which have been observed since the beginning of the world in support of the general proposition that all crows are black would be deemed a sufficient presumption of the truth of the proposition, to outweigh the testimony of one unexceptionable witness who should affirm that in some region of the earth not fully explored he had caught and examined a crow, and had found it to be grey."[17] Mill seems to doubt that there is a lawful connection between

[17] John Stuart Mill, *A System of Logic*, Bk. III, ch. III, sec. 3.

being a crow and being black, just as we refuse to say that there is a lawful connection between being a piece of paper on my desk and being white. In each case one is reluctant to say that if anything be a *P*, it must be a *Q*, and reluctant to say that if something not a *P* were to be a *P*, it would have to be a *Q*.

It would seem, then, that speculative theorists of history cannot be condemned simply because they assert what they regard as laws on the basis of only a few supporting instances. Sheer paucity of supporting instances is not enough to condemn an induction, nor is sheer abundance of them enough to certify it as valid. On the subject of what *does* distinguish the acceptable inductive sheep from the unacceptable goats, Mill wistfully reflected as follows: "Why is a single instance, in some cases, sufficient for a complete induction, while in others myriads of concurring instances, without a single exception known or presumed, go such a very little way towards establishing an universal proposition? Whoever can answer this question knows more of the philosophy of logic than the wisest of the ancients, and has solved the problem of Induction."[18] But even if one can present no general answer to Mill's question, one may argue that Marx's "general result" is, at best, more like Mill's statement about crows than it is like the laws of chemistry of which Mill speaks. For even if Marx could show that in an epoch of capitalist production something called capitalist philosophy prevailed, and so on for other epochs, one would hesitate to assert, on the basis of this evidence alone, a law linking mode of production and mode of intellectual life. Part of the reason for this, I think, is the fact that in the past similar inductions about epochs have been falsified, just as past experience shows that a given species of animal can have different colors and thus makes one hestitate to say that it is a law that all crows are black. In any case, Marxists themselves testify to a lack of confidence in the capacity of induction to establish their historical laws when they seek to deduce those laws from more fundamental principles.

[18] Ibid.

The Search For More Basic Principles

In doing so, Marxists follow a logical path described by Mill, for he was acutely aware of the shortcomings of induction in history. Along with Auguste Comte he explicitly urged speculative philosophers of history to recognize that their generalizations were in need of more support than induction could give them. Mill's view was that empiricism in history, meaning by that the notion that one can establish laws of history by the direct examination of instances falling under the law—civilizations, societies, and so on—was in general inadequate as a method for establishing the laws of history. For this reason Mill held that we should, in order to be confident that these generalizations are laws, try to deduce them from general principles regarding human nature. He thought that this deduction from general principles of human nature would perform the same logical service as deducing Kepler's laws from Newton's law of universal gravitation.[19]

In advancing this view Mill constructed a logical framework within which we may profitably view the thinking of Marxists, even though the fundamental principles to which they appeal are very different from Mill's laws of human nature. Marx was of course hostile to the view that there is an abiding human nature about which one could formulate universally applicable principles, and therefore he would not say with Mill that the speculative philosopher of history should ground his theory on psychology. But when one sees how some Marxists try to defend their theory of history, one cannot avoid the conclusion that they are grappling with a methodological problem like that which concerned Mill, and that they sense the need for moving in a direction like that in which Comte and Mill urged speculative philosophers of history to move, to derive laws of history from principles of a more funda-

[19] Ibid., Bk. VI, ch. IX, sec. 1. See also Mill, "On the Definition of Political Economy," in *Essays on Some Unsettled Questions of Political Economy*, pp. 142–43; Morton White, *Social Thought in America: The Revolt Against Formalism* (New York, 1949; Boston, 1957), p. 26; and R. P. Anschutz, *The Philosophy of J. S. Mill* (Oxford, 1953), pp. 73–77.

mental kind. However, the fundamental principles to which Marxists appeal when they try to support their laws of history are very different from those to which Mill appealed. The laws of historical materialism are not thought by Marxists to follow from psychological principles of human nature but rather from the philosophy of dialectical materialism. It must also be borne in mind that the laws of historical materialism are very different in important respects from the laws of natural science. Indeed, when we examine the laws of historical materialism carefully, we can see why a Marxist might well be misled into thinking that they can be deduced from a realistic epistemology and a materialistic metaphysics. The fact is that they are often so vaguely formulated that one might easily become confused about what they follow from or what follows from them.

Some expositors of Marx have suggested that his generalizations about history should be construed as analogous to the numerical laws of natural science, that in Marx's view "the economic structure of society and its changes were the independent variables of which all other cultural changes were a function."[20] We have seen, however, that such an assertion of functional dependence is as much an assertion of lawful connection as the statement that all men are mortal. From the functional formula of Galileo we may infer that the piece of paper I have just dropped out of my window would have fallen $16t^2$ feet in t seconds if it had fallen freely in a vacuum. And similarly, the Marxist who believes that for any historical epoch the ideology of that epoch is a function of the epoch's material conditions of life, implies that if the medieval epoch had been one in which capitalist methods of production had been used primarily, "bourgeois" philosophy would have dominated that epoch.

Let us proceed on the assumption that Marx's "general result" is a conjunction of functional laws of history, and let us see what logical problems arise when we construe it in this way. If we

[20] Sidney Hook, *Marx and the Marxists: The Ambiguous Legacy* (Princeton, 1955), p. 19.

designate philosophy as "*p*," art as "*a*," religion as "*r*," and material conditions of life as "*m*," then we may write down Marx's laws as follows:

$$(1) \qquad p=f(m)$$
$$(2) \qquad a=f(m)$$
$$(3) \qquad r=f(m)$$
and so on.

Each of these equations allegedly represents a law of society; and therefore, given the state of the material conditions of life, one should be able to tell what kind of philosophy the epoch will display, what kind of religion, what kind of art, and so on.[21]

One criticism that might be leveled against this version of historical materialism is that Marxists do not quantify in this context, that nothing in the Marxist case corresponds closely to saying that a body fell for 2 seconds and traversed 64 feet, or to saying that the pressure of a gas doubled when its volume was halved: no one has devised a scale on which Asiatic, ancient, feudal, and bourgeois production may be represented numerically. Nor, it might be added, has any one been able to reduce modern philosophy to a number on a scale which also assigns another number to medieval philosophy and still another to ancient philosophy. But in reply to such a criticism a Marxian functionalist might well say that a functional relationship is not always numerical and that therefore

[21] It is interesting to observe that Engels maintains in one place that on the basis of knowing the material conditions *alone*, we can explain the epoch's superstructure. In his preface to the English edition of the *Communist Manifesto* (pub. 1888) he maintains that the fundamental proposition of the *Manifesto* is "that in every historical epoch, the prevailing mode of economic production and exchange, and the social organisation necessarily following from it, form the basis upon which is built up, and from which alone can be explained the political and economic history of that epoch" (Karl Marx, *Selected Works*, I, 202). But then, writing only two years later, Engels says: "According to the materialist conception of history the determining element in history is *ultimately* the production and reproduction in real life. More than this neither Marx nor I have ever asserted. If therefore somebody twists this into the statement that the economic element is the *only* determining one, he transforms it into a meaningless, abstract and absurd phrase" ("Letter to Joseph Bloch, September 21, 1890," in Ibid., p. 381).

the absence of numerical determination is not a fatal objection to Marx's laws of history. The values of the variables in a functional equation need not be numbers. If Marx could state sufficiently clearly what the phrase "material conditions of life" means, what he means by a mode of philosophy or a mode of religion or a mode of art, and also state the relation holding between the former and each of the latter, he might be able to state nonnumerical functional laws of history. So construed, his laws would state that for each type of economic condition there is at most one kind of art that stands in a definite, specifiable relation to the type of economic condition. Marx's laws would then be functional even though not numerical. His laws need not be numerical in order to permit a reasonably clear characterization of the different values that all his variables may assume and of the functional relation itself. In theory Marx could present nonnumerical data corresponding to the various times of fall, the various lengths of fall, and to the functional relation of *being sixteen times the square of* in Galileo's example.

The serious question, however, is whether Marx or his followers present us with even nonnumerical directions for determining when epochs are characterized by different values of his variables and with directions for determining what the connection between the variables is. A physicist who tells us that the increase in length of a heated metal bar is a function of the change in temperature to which it has been subjected, can tell us how to measure the change in length and change in temperature on a given occasion and also tell us what the functional relationship between them is. The corresponding achievement of the Marxist would be a set of directions that would help us show that "the" philosophy of modern times is bourgeois and that its mode of production is bourgeois, and also a statement of what the functional relationship between mode of philosophy and mode of production is. For the Marxist historian to imitate the physicist in the formulation of empirical laws, he must at least be able to clarify his variables and specify the functional relationship between them: i.e., to clarify "*m*," "*a*," "*r*," and "*p*" in the above formulas and to tell us just what f is. But Marxists usually fail to do both these things in a satisfactory way. It is extremely difficult to find out how they define or identify *the* typical philosophy, religion, or art of a given period so that one can with confidence determine the values of their variables "p," "r," and "a." They do a little better with the values for "m," because modes of production may be more easily characterized and distinguished than modes of philosophy or styles of art; but even in their definition of their fundamental variable, Marxists encounter difficulties.

Those Marxists who employ the concept of functional law usually assert nothing beyond the fact that *some* functional relationship—they say not what—holds between the elements of ideology and the material conditions of life. Any further glimpses they give us into the nature of this functional relationship are too metaphorical to permit a scientific check of the laws of historical materialism. The elements of ideology are said to "reflect," to "express," and to have as their "foundation" the material conditions of life. But surely this way of speaking is not to be compared in clarity with that of the physicist who tells us that the functional relation of *being sixteen times the square of* holds between the space traversed in feet and the time taken in seconds by a freely falling body. In fact, Marxist metaphors can be positively misleading from a Marxist point of view because the relations of *being an expression of* and *being a superstructure on* are not, in their normal interpretations, functional relations. A functional relation is what the logician calls a one-many relation. In other words, if the formula "s is sixteen times the square of t" expresses a functional relation, then for any value of "t," say 2, there is at most one value of "s" which will turn the formula "$s = 16(2)^2$" into a true statement, namely 64. Similarly, if the mode of philosophy of a period is a function of the mode of economic production, then for any given mode of economic production there should be at most one mode of philosophy assigned to it by the function. But on a given foundation we may rear many different kinds of buildings or superstructures. Therefore, such metaphorical devices hardly help the Marxist who is bent on enunciating a functional relationship between ideology and the material conditions of life. On the contrary, they subvert his intention if he wishes to argue that the material conditions of life uniquely determine the ideology.

So far I have tried to make the following main points about the formulas of historical materialism: first, that they are intended as laws in the sense explained earlier; second, that they may express functional relations that are not numerical; third, that they are statements which even Marxists are not prepared to accept on the basis of only three or four supporting examples; fourth, that when one looks at the formulas closely, one finds that they do not expressly mention a functional relation as the laws of Galileo and Boyle do—they merely assert that *there exists* a functional relation between m and p, between m and a, between m and r; fifth, that this relation is metaphorically characterized by Marxists in a misleading way. Therefore, it is not only difficult to say that Marxists have established their functional laws by means of their three or four supporting instances, but it is also difficult to know what their functional laws are.

The last two difficulties may help explain why so many Marxists have tried to bolster their putative laws of historical materialism by claiming that they are derivable from philosophy. I do not mean to say that Marxists have always explicitly set themselves the task of deducing their laws from theories in the manner described by Mill and Comte. I mean rather that the paucity of the evidence they present for their formulas and the indeterminateness of the functional relation expressed by those formulas have often propelled Marxists, perhaps unconsciously, in the direction of general philosophy. Lacking sufficient inductive evidence for their laws of history and being unclear about what they were asserting in them—beyond the fact that ideology is determined in some way or other by the material conditions of life—they have rushed pell-mell to dialectical materialism and epistemological realism with the idea that a deduction of historical laws from them would more than make up for the historical laws' deficiencies in the way of inductive evidence and formulation.

Now I wish to examine part of this effort to derive the laws of history from general philosophy, but before doing so, it will be useful to observe that the historical materialist must accomplish two things if he is to make effective use of epistemological realism and dialectical materialism: (1) show that historical materialism follows from or is made plausible by them, and (2) show that both epistemological realism and dialectical materialism are true or highly probable. I shall devote most of my critical attention to part (1) of the Marxist's program. One might easily devote an entire book to criticizing part (2) of their efforts, to discussing difficulties in the epistemology and metaphysics to which Marxists have appealed while defending historical materialism, but fortunately that is not always necessary because it is often easy to show that the Marxists' philosophical premises do not imply their historical conclusions.

A number of very acute critics of Marxism have made my task easier, notably H. B. Acton, whose admirably lucid study of Marxist philosophy, *The Illusion of the Epoch*, has shown how unhelpful the appeal to dialectical materialism can be. According to Acton, the philosophy of Marxism, as distinct from its economics and its concrete historical studies, is composed of at least the following contentions: (1) the realistic view that material things exist independently of perception or thought about them, and that veridical perception and knowledge copy these independently existing things; and (2) the naturalistic view that matter existed before minds existed, and that minds have developed out of matter. But it does not take much effort to show that these doctrines do not support the load that some historical materialists have put upon them.

Because I do not propose to probe the elements of Marxist epistemology, I shall not enter into an analysis of the doctrine that physical objects exist independently of human consciousness. Assuming that it is a comprehensible doctrine and true, it is merely necessary to point out that it does not imply Marx's "general result" in the philosophy of history. Nor do we alter the situation when we add, in Lenin's words, that "matter is a philosophic category which refers to the objective reality given to man in his sensations,—a reality which is copied, photographed, and reflected by our sensations, but which exists independently of them."[22] First of all, as we have seen, the idea that ideology *reflects* the material conditions of life is at best a misleading metaphor when employed by Marx. But even if the word "reflects" were used literally, its literal meaning could hardly be that expressed in Lenin's remark about sensations reflecting objective reality. When, with Lenin, one holds a "copy theory of perception" or a "copy theory of truth," or a "reflection-theory," it is with a sense of the words "copy" or "reflect" in mind which is quite different from that in which the art of a period might be said to copy or reflect the productive relations or productive forces. Surely the Marxist does not want to hold that all art literally copies or reflects the mode of production of its epoch, for not all paintings of the feudal period are paintings of windmills and not all paintings of the capitalist period depict steam engines. The function connecting various elements of the Marxian superstructure with its substructure is quite hazy, but anything like a simple copy theory would clarify the doctrine to the point of absurdity.

It might be said by Marxists more philosophically subtle than Lenin that of course one should not expect to deduce a law of history from a theory of knowledge, any more than one should expect to deduce a law of physics from it. Hence, they might say, we ought not to take this derivation of historical materialism seriously. The really serious derivation is offered, they might argue, when Marxists appeal to their naturalism, their belief that mind sprang from matter. Such a derivation is offered in the following argument of Lenin's: "If materialism in general explains consciousness as the outcome of existence, and not conversely, then materialism as applied to the social life of mankind must explain *social* consciousness as the outcome of *social* existence." Against this Acton properly points out: "The matter that is 'primary' in

[22] V. I. Lenin, *Materialism and Empirio-Criticism, Collected Works,* XIII (New York, 1927), 101–2.

the doctrine of philosophical materialism is such things as gases, seas, and rocks, but 'the material life of society' consists of tools, inventions, and skills. The alleged *social* primacy of 'the material life of society,' therefore, is quite a different thing from the alleged primacy of matter over mind, for the 'material life of society' that determines the political and ideological forms itself contains mental components, whereas, on the Marxist view, it is from mindless matter that mind has sprung."[23] Therefore, if a combination of steam power and the profit system is to be called "material" by contrast to capitalist philosophy, the implied contrast between material and nonmaterial is quite different from the contrast between, say, the spiral nebula and the human mind. The capitalist mode of production is a mode of human social activity which in some sense involves thought, while the spiral nebula does not.

The main trouble with the attempt to derive historical materialism from the thesis that mind originated out of matter is that it relies on an equivocal use of the word "material," just as the effort to derive historical materialism from epistemological realism relies on an equivocal use of the word "copy." Because of such equivocation the deduction of historical materialism from metaphysical naturalism simply falls apart and it is left with very weak inductive support.

What moral may we draw from our examination of Marxism so far as the regularity theory of explanation is concerned? At most that some speculative philosophers of history have formulated so-called laws of history on the basis of a small number of instances, laws which have been sufficiently obscure to allow such philosophers to think that they could derive them from certain statements of epistemology, metaphysics, and cosmology. But—and this is crucial for the main argument of this chapter—I do not think it can be demonstrated that this failing of Marxism is characteristic of all efforts to generalize about human and social behavior, and hence that every explanatory deductive argument of the kind de-

[23] H. B. Acton, *The Illusion of the Epoch* (London, 1955), p. 142.

scribed by certain advocates of the covering law theory is bound to suffer the fate of historical materialism: paucity of inductive evidence and lack of any more fundamental support. I turn now to the third complaint mentioned at the beginning of this chapter.

COMPLAINT 3: LAWS ABOUT INDIVIDUALS

The objection we are now to examine revolves, like that in the first complaint, about the relationship between a law and a given individual. It will be recalled that the first complaint had to do with generalizations of the form "All things which are *P, R, S,* and *T* are *Q*," where only one item has the properties *P, R, S,* and *T*. But critics of the regularity theory have also called attention to the fact that not all explanations appeal to what they call laws that "apply to all times and places," by which they seem to mean laws that contain no individual names.[24] In effect they point out what a regularist can easily agree to, even though such critics seem to think that what they point out demolishes regularism; namely, that sometimes we explain why a man behaved in a certain way by maintaining that *he* always behaves in that way when in certain circumstances, and sometimes we explain why a nation or a society behaved in a certain way by maintaining that *it* always behaves in that way when in certain circumstances. Yet any puz-

[24] See, for example, Alan Donagan, "Explanation in History," in Gardiner, op. cit., pp. 428–43. The author refers to and relies upon related views of Gilbert Ryle and R. G. Collingwood. See also Dray, op. cit., p. 172, who points out in commenting on the views of J. Cohen in the latter's "Teleological Explanation," *Proceedings of the Aristotelian Society*, 1950–51, that not all covering law theorists would regard a law of a particular thing as a law. — It may be worth pointing out that the distinction between a law that contains individual names and one that does not, must be made in such a way as to survive Quine's device of removing *all* individual names from statements. See, for example, W. V. Quine, *From a Logical Point of View* (Cambridge, 1953), pp. 7–8, and *Methods of Logic* (New York, 1950), pp. 218–24. The matter is too technical to be treated here, but it will soon become evident that I am appealing to the difference between a statement like "Whoever wrote *Waverly* was Scotch" and "Whoever is a man is mortal," and that difference rests on the difference between nonlaws and laws.

zlement about how an explanation can depend on regularities even though it is based on a study of a single individual should disappear when one realizes that there are laws about individuals. When one says, "Jones always behaves in that way when under those circumstances" or "Russia always behaves in that way when under those circumstances," the juxtaposition of the proper name and the word "always" at the beginning of both statements signifies that we have to do here with a hybrid sort of statement; namely, one that is both singular and universal.

Before considering the role of such statements in historical explanation, we should be clear about the fact that they are quite different from the one-exampled generalizations discussed while we were considering the first complaint. It is one thing to assert a generalization that contains no individual names but which turns out as a matter of fact to refer to one individual at a given time (Holland, the first match, or the pair Smith and Hume in our earlier illustrations); it is another to assert a generalization which contains an individual name. And it is the second sort of generalization that we shall be concerned with now.

I cannot see how we can avoid the conclusion that a statement can be an explanatory law and a singular statement at the same time. A homely example of such a statement is "Whenever John eats spinach, John breaks out in a rash." It should be borne in mind that the force of "whenever" is such as to go beyond merely listing a series of times. In other words, the statement is not like the statement "All of the pieces of paper on my desk are white," which may be construed as equivalent to "1 is white and 2 is white and 3 is white" if there are only three pieces of paper on my desk, or like "All of John's children are asleep." The statement "Whenever John eats spinach, John breaks out in a rash" is more like "Every piece of paper is inflammable." It cannot be rendered simply as "John ate spinach on Monday and broke out in a rash on Tuesday, and John ate spinach on Wednesday and broke out in a rash on Thursday, and John ate spinach on Friday and broke out in a rash on Saturday" even if John ate spinach only three times in his life. Those three times might have been enough for

him, so he stopped eating spinach. He stopped because he saw
that there was a lawful connection between *his* eating spinach and
his developing a rash.

It is obvious, of course, that such a law about John will not
appear in a book of medical science, but that is irrelevant for our
purposes. We surely cannot be satisfied with a definition of the
word "law" which limits laws to statements that in fact appear in
books with the word "science" on their title pages. The law about
John is a law in the sense in which we have been employing it so
far. It will support a contrary-to-fact conditional and it may figure
as a premise in an explanatory deductive argument. For example,
his wife may say truly that if John had eaten the spinach put
before him at the Smith house the other night, he would have
broken out in a rash the next day. It can be used for prediction.
His wife can whisper to him as she watches him eating his spinach
at the Joneses—in order to keep up with them—that he will break
out in a rash tomorrow.

A little attention to elementary logic will show why it is that a
statement like this can be both singular and universal. It is singular insofar as it contains the name "John"; it is universal because
it contains the word "whenever." In logical terminology, the law
could be formulated so as to read "For every time t, if John eats
spinach at time t, then John breaks out in a rash at $t + 24$ hours."
Now I realize it might be said that John does not break out in a
rash upon eating spinach just because he's John. It might be said
that he breaks out in a rash because he is a man of a certain kind.
But this means only that our law about John might be derived
from other statements, or that in order to answer some *other*
question it must be. Sometimes when a man has a certain allergy,
we do not know *why* he has it. The question "Why does John
break out in a rash whenever he eats spinach?" is therefore quite
distinct from the question "Is it a law (in the above sense) that
John breaks out in a rash whenever he eats spinach?" and the
second question may be answered affirmatively even when the first
cannot be answered.

The universal statement about John may be used in a deductive explanatory argument. For example, we may ask why John broke out in a rash on Tuesday and be told that it was because he ate spinach on Monday. The argument may be set out deductively from the regularist's point of view. The law is, "Whenever John eats spinach at time t, he breaks out in a rash at $t + 24$ hours"; the statement of initial condition is that he ate spinach on Monday; the conclusion is that he broke out in a rash on Tuesday, which was to be explained. Now, of course, this is a simple law about John, and maybe most such laws about individuals, like laws in general, should have subject-terms more complex than "ate spinach at time t." But that is another matter.

It may well be that certain philosophers who defend the regularity theory are not willing to call statements about John "laws", but if they don't, they will be unable to answer certain objections to their theory, objections that are likely to be made by philosophers who rightly say that the historian may explain one thing about an individual by citing something else about that individual, about what *he* did and what *he* suffered. Acknowledging that there are laws about individuals makes it easy for the regularist to agree that historians do support some of their explanations by focusing on individuals in this way. An advocate of the regularity theory need only insist that the physician's explanation of why John broke out in a rash on Tuesday will have to appeal to some regularity—if only a regularity in the behavior of John.

Surely it cannot be denied that there are regularities in the behavior of a single person. Dickens gave comic expression to this truism when he recorded the following exchange in *Nicholas Nickleby*:

"Newman, I shouldn't be surprised if my brother were dead."
"I don't think you would," said Newman quietly.
"Why not, sir?" demanded Mr. Nickleby.
"You never are surprised," replied Newman, "that's all."

And if one wants nonfictional examples of the same point, he need only be reminded of the statement "Hitler hated all people he thought were Jews." A historian would certainly feel justified in saying that Hitler hated a certain person because Hitler thought that person was a Jew. And since one may reasonably define an anti-Semite as one who hates Jews, one can see that many deductive explanations in which the major premise attributes anti-Semitism to a certain person employ a logically disguised generaization about one individual as a premise in their argument. Many so-called dispositional explanations may be analyzed in this way. If the regularist wishes to go further and maintain that a law about an individual may be deduced from laws of a more general kind, that is a separate contention. The main point I wish to make is that regularism, as I conceive it, does not require its advocates to hold that the general laws offered in support of singular explanatory statements "apply to all times and places." Regularism is a theory bent merely on asserting that statements of causal connections may be logically analyzed by reference to laws and not on asserting that these laws must "apply to all time and places."

Once we conceive of the regularity theory in this broad way, we are able to understand other things more clearly. As I have said, our generalization about John is a simple one, and, no doubt, to be true it would have to include other terms in its subject. It may involve more than a reference to his eating spinach; so that in order to formulate a true law about him, we may have to incorporate a reference to the state in which he is when the spinach brings out the rash. The law would then read: "Whenever John is in state A and eats spinach, he breaks out in a rash." In such a case the subject-term of the law about John is conjunctive, and the number of possible singular, explanatory statements about John that the law may support will increase. As we shall see later, it may support not only "John broke out in a rash because John ate spinach" but also "John broke out in a rash because John was in state A."

Of course, if one uses a law about an individual in support of one's singular explanatory statement, and that individual is dead and buried, one does have a difficult problem on one's hands. For how does one *establish* a law about such a dead and buried individual? If one asserts a completely general law, one can usually support it by appealing to extant examples that fall under the same law, but one cannot do this if the individual about whom the law is asserted is dead and gone. For we are prevented from reviving him to see whether he will break out in a rash when given spinach. It is obvious that the generalization which asserts that Hitler hated all those he took to be Jews cannot *now* be established experimentally, if establishing it experimentally involves reviving Hitler, telling him that various persons are Jews, and then seeing whether he expresses hatred of them. But surely the regularist is not committed to the view that this is the only way in which we can find out whether a dead and buried individual like Hitler had a certain disposition.

The regularity theory allows for another way of supporting our belief that Hitler had a certain disposition. There is nothing to prevent us from explaining why an individual has a certain disposition by pointing out that he is an individual of a certain kind and that all persons of that kind have that disposition. To explain why Hitler hated Karl Marx by saying that Hitler took Marx to be a Jew and that Hitler hated all those he took to be Jews, is not to explain why Hitler hated all persons he took to be Jews—i.e., why he was an anti-Semite. That is another problem. But in explaining deductively why Hitler was an anti-Semite, we may appeal to generalizations about individuals of a certain class. There is no a priori reason for denying that there are laws of the form "All people having characteristics A, B, and C are anti-Semites"; and if we can find such a law and show that Hitler had characteristics A, B, and C, we can explain why Hitler was an anti-Semite and present deductive evidence in favor of the hypothesis that he was.

However, it is not essential for the regularist to maintain that such more general laws are discoverable or that they must be presented if we are to understand a given manifestation of Hitler's anti-Semitism. It is true that Hume and John Stuart Mill held that there are laws of human nature of a very general kind, and it is true that the school of social thought associated with Hume and Mill did seek such laws in its efforts to find explanations of historical phenomena. But one should not confuse the regularity theory of explanation, which is a theory about how to analyze explanation logically, with the speculative philosophy of history that Hume, Mill, and their followers in social science adopted. If they did not see that one can explain some aspects of a man's behavior by appealing to regularities in *his* behavior, regularities that were not general laws of human nature, then they were in error. But their mistake may easily be acknowledged by regularists who distinguish the problem of analyzing the logic of explanation from substantive problems in social science or the speculative philosophy of history. The fundamental drive of regularism, at least in our time, is not in the direction of a speculative philosophy of history but rather in the direction of analyzing explanation so as to avoid reference to mysterious powers and unanalyzed connections. In retrospect one may think of Hume and Mill as simultaneously representing two traditions: that of regularism and that of speculative history. Their regularism led them to a philosophical theory of explanation, whereas their speculative ambitions in social science led them to the idea that there were fundamental laws of human nature applying to all times and places. And one may defend the first without being driven to the second doctrine. Surely the use of the word "law" does not prevent us from speaking of laws of individuals. After all, so august a law as Galileo's refers to terrestrial bodies, i.e., bodies near the surface of an individual called the Earth. And while it is true that Galileo's law is deducible from other laws of physics, its deducibility from these other laws is not what makes it a law. In the same way, a law about Hitler may also be a law, and a law about Europe may also be a law, whether or not they are deducible from other laws or theories that explain them.

SUMMARY

Our main concern in this chapter has been to show that the standard version of the regularity theory of historical explanation cannot be refuted by arguing that the laws to which it refers must always be so complicated as to refer to the very individual about which the historian makes his unanalyzed singular explanatory statement; that it cannot be refuted by arguing that when such a law does refer to that individual, the reference to the law is always otiose; that it cannot be refuted by pointing to the grave defects of certain so-called laws in the speculative philosophy of history; and that it cannot be refuted by arguing that laws are never laws of individuals. If a law in an explanatory deductive argument does turn out, as a matter of fact, to refer to one individual or to very few individuals, it may be supported, for example, by deduction from more fundamental laws; and if it cannot be so defended, then certain singular explanatory statements may have to be abandoned. The regularity theory does not assert nor imply that all singular explanatory statements made by historians are true and well founded: on the contrary, it may on occasion lead us to see the shortcomings of such statements.

The regularist must be distinguished from the speculative philosopher of history who holds that there are principles of human nature, society, or the universe that lie at the heart of all historical explanation. That is a matter on which the regularist may be neutral. Although we have seen some of the difficulties that face the speculative philosopher of history who tries to formulate laws of history governing such things as civilizations, it by no means follows from our previous reflections that the concept of law has no connection with historical explanation. These reflections do not lead to the conclusion that it is impossible to formulate laws that will be both clear and true. They merely show that the generalizations of some theoretically minded historians are obscure and rest on lamentably few confirming instances. There is no a priori reason why generalizations about historical events need contain terms like Marx's "productive relations," "productive forces," "bourgeois philosophy," "reflects," "expresses," "rooted in," and "copies"; and therefore it may be argued plausibly that the effort to present historical laws is not shown to be absurd or impossible by calling attention to the shortcomings of Marxian views. If one could present historical generalizations that are clear and confirmed by many instances, one might not be led to take the route of Marxists and fruitlessly to seek support from metaphysics, epistemology, and cosmology. An advocate of the covering law theory of explanation may therefore readily grant that some inductive efforts to establish laws have been unsuccessful and may also grant that many compensatory deductive efforts to derive historical laws from metaphysics, epistemology, and cosmology have been strikingly unsuccessful. But this does not prevent the regularist from holding that when an ordinary historian tries to explain individual events or facts, his explanation is logically connected with generalizations. The question remains, however, as to what that logical connection is, and we shall see in the next chapter that there is more to it than meets the eye as one surveys the standard version of the regularity theory.

CHAPTER **III**

Explanatory Statements

Suppose it is granted that there are no valid a priori objections to the possibility of presenting explanatory deductive arguments, and that such arguments can sometimes be presented in full. Would it follow that only such arguments may be called explanations? No, because it is perfectly proper to say of certain singular causal statements that *they* are explanations too. For example, the following statement is an explanation: "Japan became a maritime nation after the beginning of the Meiji era because it had to import foodstuffs." In other words, there is a sense in which a *statement*, as opposed to a deductive argument, may be called an explanation. Having said this, however, I do not wish to argue that explanations in these two different senses have nothing to do with each other. On the contrary, one of my main concerns in this chapter will be to state what the connection between them is.

One wrong view of how they are related is that a singular causal statement is incomplete and that it must, in exact speech, be expanded into an explanatory deductive argument on the ground that only such a deductive argument is "really" an explanation. A philosopher who takes this view is likely to say that one can, of course, say in loose language that a statement like "Japan became a maritime nation because it had to import foodstuffs" is an explanation, but that strictly speaking it is not. Such a philosopher would argue that in saying Japan became a maritime nation because it had to import foodstuffs we are speaking elliptically and should, strictly speaking, expand our utterance into a deductive argument. However, this conception of how an explanatory deductive argument stands to a singular causal statement is inadequate for reasons that I shall present in this chapter. I shall also put forth an alternative view of the connection between singular explanatory statements and explanatory deductive arguments, a view which does greater justice to the thought and language of historians.[1]

It should be said at once that *sometimes* a philosopher may show that a certain form of ordinary speech is elliptical and hence recommend that it be expanded into something else, but we are not faced with such a situation in the case of the historian's singular causal statement or in the case of singular causal statements made in everyday conversation. A clear case of elliptical speech is what the traditional logician calls an enthymeme, a form of argument in which one premise of a syllogism is omitted. When one says "Socrates is a man, therefore Socrates is mortal" in ordinary language, one is presenting a defective version of the complete syllogism "All men are mortal; Socrates is a man; therefore Socrates is mortal," and the traditional logician may argue that one's enthymeme had best be replaced by the complete syllogism. Those who speak of the historian's singular causal statements as "explanation-sketches" as opposed to real explanations may be interpreted as holding them to be enthymemes in a widened sense. (I say "widened sense" so as to avoid the implication that the deduc-

[1] A similar point of view about singular explanatory statements, and much less sympathy for the regularity theory of historical explanation, are expressed by Michael Scriven, "Truisms and the Grounds for Historical Explanations," in *Theories of History*, ed. Patrick Gardiner (Glencoe, Ill., 1959), pp. 443–75.

tive argument which replaces the singular causal statement must be a syllogism.) On their view, the man who says "Because a is P, a is Q" is saying something which should be more properly expressed by a deductive argument like "Whatever is P, R, and S is Q; a is P; a is R; a is S; therefore, a is Q." However, the singular explanatory statements of historians and ordinary men are not enthymemes or incomplete arguments which need expansion in the way that "Socrates is a man, therefore Socrates is mortal" needs expansion. Singular causal statements are not arguments at all but statements. Like a singular causal statement, the *premises* and *conclusion* of a syllogism may be said to be either true or false, but the appropriate critical words to apply to a syllogism or any deductive argument are "valid" and "invalid" rather than "true" and "false."

Bearing this distinction in mind, we may say that whereas the utterance "Socrates is a man, therefore he is mortal" is an incomplete argument, the utterance "Because the North and South had conflicting economic interests, the Civil War broke out" is not. The person who reasons enthymematically will usually have in mind the omitted premise and supply it when he is taxed by a precisian, whereas historians do not usually have in mind all of the premises that would allow them to present an explanatory deductive argument. Moreover, even where they can present such an argument, the argument should not be thought of as the expansion or full expression of what is incompletely stated by the singular causal statement. The standard version of the regularity theory may be construed as requiring that every singular causal statement be expanded so as to *become* an explanatory deductive argument, on the theory that only such an argument is really an explanation, but this view may arise from a failure to see the difference between holding (a) that an expression like "This match lit because it was struck" is incomplete and must be *expanded* into an argument like "All dry matches light when struck in the presence of oxygen; this is a match; this was dry; this was struck in the presence of oxygen; therefore, this lit" and holding (b) that "This

match lit because it was struck" is *equivalent* to the statement that
a certain kind of explanatory deductive argument *exists*. The second is, as we shall see, a more plausible view.

Sometimes, of course, the philosophical analyst is obliged to
expand an elliptical expression, but because the singular causal
statements of historians are full statements as they stand, they are
not in need of expansion in the way that elliptical enthymemes
are. What the philosopher may try to do instead, therefore, is to
provide a clearer equivalent of the singular explanatory statements
made by historians.[1a] But once he acknowledges that he is trying
to find an equivalent for the singular explanatory statement, he will
see that a particular explanatory deductive argument is not such
an equivalent. Rather, the equivalent is the statement that a certain kind of explanatory deductive argument exists. If we begin
with a statement S whose equivalent we are seeking, at the end of
our philosophical labors we shall be able to say that S is true if
and only if an equivalent statement, T, is true. That is how it turns
out when we say that "Socrates is a man" is equivalent to "Socrates is a rational animal," or that "John Stuart Mill is a brother" is
equivalent to "John Stuart Mill is a male sibling." But if we begin
with the statement "The Civil War broke out because of the attack
on Fort Sumter" as our *analysandum*, can we link it analogously
to a particular explanatory deductive argument, which we may
call "E"? Can we say that "The Civil War broke out because of the
attack on Fort Sumter" is true if and only if E is true? Obviously
not, because we do not say of explanatory deductive arguments
that they are *true*. We say that they are valid, that they contain
true premises which logically imply their conclusions. Moreover,
the statement that the Civil War broke out because of the attack
on Fort Sumter is surely not *equival*ent to the statement that the
true premises of E logically imply that the Civil War broke out.
Therefore, in what follows I shall present a version of the regularity theory of historical explanation which will not force us to

---

[1a] On the difference between expanding and providing an equivalent see
J. L. Austin, *Philosophical Papers* (Oxford, 1961), p. 162.

say that a singular explanatory statement is equivalent either to an explanatory deductive argument or to a statement asserting the validity of such an argument. I call this version "Existential Regularism" for reasons that are already obvious.

EXISTENTIAL REGULARISM

It should be realized that what we are here trying to analyze or present an equivalent for is a statement of the form "A is a contributory cause of C" and not a statement of the form "A is the decisive contributory cause of C". Furthermore, the statement that the striking of match *a* was a contributory cause of its lighting is equivalent to the statement that *there are* conditions which the particular match satisfies and which, together with its having been struck, lead by some explanatory law (or laws) to the match's lighting. And this is in turn equivalent to the statement that there exists an explanatory deductive argument containing "*a* was struck" as a premise and "*a* lit" as conclusion. More generally, therefore, we may state the following thesis as a link between singular explanatory statements and explanatory deductive arguments:

> THESIS I: A statement of the form "A is a contributory cause of C" is true if and only if there is an explanatory deductive argument containing "A" as a premise and "C" as its conclusion.[2]

This thesis might license any one of the following statements: "Holland's having had excellent soil was a contributory cause of its success," "Holland's having been challenged by the sea was a contributory cause of its success," and so on. Moreover, we may

[2] It is assumed that no premise in the deductive argument is redundant, i.e., that we cannot deduce the conclusion from fewer than all of the premises in the argument. Moreover, the thesis may be interpreted in accordance with the ontological inclinations of the reader—be he nominalist or platonist. Therefore the argument which is said to exist may be construed either as a linguistic expression or as what that expression expresses. This is no place at which to enter that vexed question.

replace the expression "is a contributory cause of" simply by "is a cause of." If we adopt Thesis I as the analysis of singular explanatory statements, then a number of objections to the regularity or covering law theory may be met, although it must be acknowledged that several difficult problems are raised by Thesis I. In the remainder of this chapter I shall first show how Thesis I may be used to meet certain objections to the regularity theory and also used to avoid certain confusions about the connection between law and causality in history. After that, I shall turn to some of the problems and difficulties associated with Thesis I.

THE REPLY OF EXISTENTIAL REGULARISM TO CERTAIN OBJECTIONS TO THE REGULARITY THEORY

Existential regularism provides a way of linking singular explanatory statements and explanatory deductive arguments without treating the former as elliptical and without forcing us to say that only explanatory deductive arguments are explanations. It therefore allows us to meet certain objections to the standard version of the regularity theory. According to one of these objections, as we have seen, the regularist wrongly identifies such singular statements, or treats them as equivalent to, deductive arguments of a sort that historians rarely find themselves presenting; according to another, the regularist wrongly holds that singular explanatory statements imply laws which the historian cannot deduce from these singular statements.

The first objection may be met by pointing out that the fact that the truth of a singular explanatory statement implies the existence of an explanatory deductive argument of a certain kind does not mean that the singular explanatory statement is identical with or equivalent to the deductive argument. We can no more say this than we can say that because "*a* is a father" implies the existence of someone who is child of *a*, the father is identical with the child. For *a* to be a father he must have a child, but the child is distinct from the father. Moreover, the statement "James Mill is a father" is not elliptical for "James Mill begat someone." The former statement is complete although equivalent to the latter. Analogously, a singular explanatory statement of the kind analyzed in Thesis I is true if and only if a certain kind of explanatory argument exists, but the argument is distinct from the statement, and the statement is not elliptical for the argument.

The second objection may be met by pointing out that the statement "Jones is Q because Jones is P" does not imply the statement "All people who are P, R, S, and T are Q," even though the latter is a premise in a deductive expanatory argument that contains "Jones is P" as another premise and "Jones is Q" as conclusion. Thesis I does not assert that if the singular explanatory statement is true, then the statement "All people who are P, R, S, and T are Q" is true, or for that matter that any other universal statement like this is true. Anyone who is not familiar with certain formulations of and certain objections to the regularity theory of historical explanation may wonder why it is important to insist on what he may think is an excessively fine point. But some regularists have held that a singular explanatory statement implies a law, and their critics have tried to demolish the regularity theory by pointing out that we may accept a singular explanatory statement and yet deny the truth of any law of the kind presented by a regularist in his analysis or defense of the singular explanatory statement.[3]

According to Thesis I, however, statements of the form "a is Q because a is P" do not generally imply statements of the form "All P is Q" nor even more complex generalizations—whether those generalizations are false or true. It is particularly important to

---

[3] See, for example, H. L. A. Hart and A. M. Honoré, *Causation in the Law* (Oxford, 1959), pp. 13–14, where it is said: "Hume's insistence that constant conjunction or regular sequence between events is the essence of the notion of causation is represented by the doctrine that every singular causal statement implies, by its very meaning, a general proposition asserting a universal connexion between kinds of events"; see also p. 53 of the same work. William Dray, *Laws and Explanation in History* (Oxford, 1957), pp. 26 ff., attributes to the regularist the view that the singular explanatory statement may be *transformed* into a law.

note that the statement "A cause of a's being Q is a's being P" does not imply "All P is Q," which may be called the superficial generalization associated with the singular explanatory statement. Even if it is true that the wastebasket in my office caught fire yesterday because a lit match was thrown into it, it does not follow that all wastebaskets into which lit matches are thrown will catch fire. Even if it is true that the large-scale Scandinavian migrations in the ninth century began because of overpopulation, as Marc Bloch says they did, Bloch's statement does not imply the statement that whenever a country is overpopulated its inhabitants will migrate on the scale in question.[4] Such associated superficial generalizations will usually be false precisely because of what we have called the complexity of explanations, because of the need to say, for example, that the wastebasket contained certain materials, that enough oxygen was present, and so on. And if such generalizations are false, obviously they cannot be implied by singular explanatory statements that are true. Therefore, we should certainly not formulate the regularity theory in any way that requires us to say that every singular explanatory statement entails such a false generalization. I repeat, however, that even if a generalization is *true* and is also a premise in an explanatory deductive argument of the kind required for the truth of a singular explanatory statement, that generalization will not, in general, be implied by the singular explanatory statement whose equivalent is presented in Thesis I.

It is a virtue of Thesis I that it permits us to see how the regularist may meet certain objections presented by philosophers and also why certain arguments offered by historians under the influence of the regularity theory are invalid. It permits us to see how great is the temptation to think that a superficial generalization is implied by a singular explanatory statement, and also to see how failure to resist this temptation can give rise to two distinct modes of questionable argument. One of them is employed by philosophers who wish to refute the regularity theory of historical explanation, whereas the other is employed by historians who

[4] Marc Bloch, *Feudal Society* (Chicago, 1961), pp. 37–38.

wish to refute specific singular causal statements. The first, which we may call the argument of the misguided antiregularist, has been examined sufficiently, so we may turn to the second, the argument of the misguided regularist.

It is an irony of historiography that not only regularists and philosophers bent on refuting them have adopted a faulty view of the regularity theory. Even historians who are influenced by a simple-minded regularism sometimes operate with the same vulnerable conception of the relation between a singular explanatory statement and a generalization. Some of them seem to employ this conception in attacking certain efforts to explain the early triumph of democracy in America, as, for example, the explanation of Herbert Baxter Adams which appeals to the Germanic tradition in the background of American political life, the explanation of Turner which appeals to the frontier, and Charles Beard's explanation according to which the farmers and debtors were responsible. Against these explanations the following questionable arguments have been advanced: that the Germanic tradition has been present in Germany, which is hardly notorious for its democracy; that a frontier was present in many lands where democracy did not arise; and that Beard's farmers and debtors were a commonplace in western European countries which did not experience anything like the American democratic triumph in the early nineteenth century.[5] Yet all of these supposed refutations of singular explanatory statements are faulty if they proceed on the assumption that Herbert Baxter Adams, when he said that the presence of the Germanic tradition was responsible for American democratic institutions, necessarily implied that *wherever* the Germanic tradition is present, democracy arises; on the assumption that Turner necessarily implied that *wherever* there is a frontier, democracy arises; and on the assumption that Beard necessarily implied that *wherever* there are farmers and debtors, de-

---

[5] Louis Hartz, "The Rise of the Democratic Idea," in *Paths of American Thought*, ed. Arthur M. Schlesinger, Jr. and Morton White (Boston, 1963), p. 37.

mocracy arises. Each of these assumptions is in turn a special case of the erroneous assumption that a singular explanatory statement must imply the *superficial* generalization corresponding to it. But surely some of these eminent historians, if not all of them, must have realized that the generalizations underlying their singular causal statements were more complex. They must have realized, for example, that the presence of a frontier is not in general a sufficient condition for the rise of democracy and held, rather, that the presence of a frontier along with other features of the American scene at the time constituted such a sufficient condition even though these historians did not mention these other features in their singular causal statements.

J. B. Bury seems to have been guilty of a similar logical mistake when he summarily eliminated depopulation, the Christian religion, and the fiscal system as causes of the Roman Empire's dismemberment, by arguing: "If these or any of them were responsible for [the Empire's] dismemberment by the barbarians in the West, it may be asked how it was that in the East, where the same causes operated, the Empire survived much longer intact and united."[6] Such a negative argument as Bury's may proceed on the false assumption that if one says that an event of a certain kind is a contributory cause of an event of another kind, one implies that events of the first kind are always accompanied or followed by events of the kind to be explained.

Even Marc Bloch, who was so much more concerned with the logic of his discipline than most historians, seems to have been involved in a logical inconsistency in his treatment of two distinct explanatory statements, just because he seems to attack one by fallaciously arguing that it implies a false generalization but fails to use the same fallacious method of refutation on another. In his *Feudal Society* he considers as an explanation of the cessation of Scandinavian pillaging in the Middle Ages the fact that the Scandinavians were converted to Christianity, and apparently rejects

[6] J. B. Bury, *History of the Later Roman Empire* (New York, 1958), I, 308–9.

this explanation on the ground that it implies the false generalization that no Christian people would engage in pillaging. He says: "As we shall often have occasion to observe in the following pages, among the peoples of the West during the feudal era there was apparently no difficulty in reconciling ardent faith in the Christian mysteries with a taste for violence and plunder, nay even with the most conscious glorification of war."[7] On the other hand, when Bloch tries to explain the *beginning* of the Scandinavian invasions, he is prepared to accept as its explanation the fact that the Scandinavian countries were overpopulated at the time, though he surely would deny that the people of *every* overpopulated country invade in the manner of the medieval Scandinavians. What we have here is a kind of double standard. The statement "The invasions ceased because the Scandinavians were Christianized" is thought to imply the generalization "Every Christianized country ceases invading" and is therefore rejected because of the falsity of this generalization. But the statement "The invasions began because Scandinavia was overpopulated" is *not* said to imply—as it should, if the same sort of faulty logic were being employed—the false generalization "Every overpopulated country invades," and is *not* similarly rejected.

The conclusion we must draw is that even though it is hard for some antiregularists and some regularists to see that explanatory statements do *not* imply generalizations, especially superficial generalizations, we must hold tightly to this logical truth.

SOME DISTINCTIONS AND PROBLEMS

It is now time to turn to certain problems that are raised by Thesis I. They may be classified into three groups that overlap to some extent, as we shall see. We may ask certain important questions about the *analysandum*, i.e., the left-hand side of the "if and only if" in Thesis I; we may ask certain equally important questions about the *analysans*, or the right-hand side; and finally we may inquire into the "if and only if" itself.

[7] Bloch, op. cit., p. 35.

The Analysandum of Thesis I

There are several kinds of singular statements that differ from the kind under analysis in Thesis I, and it is well to mention them at this point in order to prevent any misunderstanding of what it is that the thesis asserts. Two of these kinds of statements may be thought of as logically stronger than "A is a contributory cause of C," i.e., to imply it without being implied by it. They are: "A is the whole cause of C" and "A is the decisive contributory cause of C." We shall consider both of them in detail later, but it is well to point out here that because they are stronger than the statement "A is a contributory cause of C," we must, when we analyze them, impose conditions for their truth that go beyond those stated in Thesis I. For example, the statement that A is *the decisive* contributory cause of C must not only satisfy the conditions laid down in Thesis I but must satisfy some further condition, and what that is we shall talk about in a later chapter. This extra requirement is represented by clause (2) in the following schema:

SCHEMA I: A is the decisive contributory cause of C if and only if:
　　　(1) A is a contributory cause of C, and
　　　(2) A has feature D.

This is called a "schema" because D is unspecified, and later one of our problems will be to try to specify it. One advantage of distinguishing Schema I from Thesis I, apart from the obvious one arising from the fact that the analyzed statements are different, is that some philosophers who might be willing to grant that "A is a contributory cause of C" is clear and empirical, might wish to deny that statements of the form "A is the cause of C" are clear or that they are empirical. Some of those philosophers who deny that statements of the form "A is the cause of C" are clear, argue, as we shall see, that there are no clear specifications for "D" in Schema I; while those who deny that "A is the cause of C" is empirical, argue that "D" will turn out, upon further analysis, to be a value-predicate rather than a descriptive predicate. In reply, some advocates of the regularity theory of explanation wish to assert two things: first of all, that Thesis I correctly analyzes the notion of being a contributory cause in such a way that singular statements employing it are factual, and second, that the selection of *the* cause or the decisive contributory cause is also made on purely factual grounds. But it should be clear that whatever the factual grounds for picking out *the* cause might be, they must be presented in *another* thesis of such a factually oriented regularist. For this reason alone Cartesian wisdom suggests that we "divide each of the difficulties under examination into as many parts as possible." Therefore the difficulty of identifying feature D will be treated in a later part of this study when we discuss the problem of filling in Schema I.

It is not only important to distinguish the logically *stronger* statements, "A is the whole cause of *C*" and "A is the decisive contributory cause of *C*," from the *analysandum* of Thesis I, but also important to bear in mind that some philosophers might be inclined to distinguish the *analysandum* of Thesis I from a statement which is, on their view, logically *weaker* than that *analysandum*. I have in mind a form of statement which is best expressed by the formula "A is one of the conditions jointly sufficient for *C*," and a kind of philosopher who might say that A could be—on a certain definition, of course—one of the conditions jointly sufficient for the presence of C and yet not be a contributory cause of C. Stated crudely, this view is that the presence of A may insure the presence of C but not explain it, and in the next section we shall examine this point of view more carefully because in one respect it forces us to face a very serious problem about the *analysans* of Thesis I, one having to do with what is meant by the phrase "*explanatory* deductive argument." In anticipation we may briefly point out what that problem is. It arises from the fact that the formula "A is one of the conditions jointly sufficient for *C*" may be defined as equivalent to the conjunctive statement that "A" is true, that "C" is true, and that there is a law which leads from "A" and other singular statements to "C." But then it might be argued that some laws are not, as it were, explanatory in character, i.e., that they might lead from "A" and other singular statements to "C" and yet not be such as to justify our saying that A is a contributory cause of C. On the contrary, it might be argued, such laws merely function as bridges that get us from the antecedent conditions to C without helping us to explain C. Since the existence of such laws justifies our saying that A is one of the conditions jointly sufficient for C but not our saying that A is a contributory cause of C, the problem is: how do we distinguish such laws from what may be called *explanatory* laws, i.e., those whose existence does justify us in certain cases in saying that A is a contributory cause of C?

We shall soon examine some simple illustrations that force reflection on this question and thereby bring us to probe more deeply into the notion of an explanatory deductive argument as referred to in Thesis I. But before turning to that notion in greater detail it is worth remarking that whereas the two statements "A is the whole cause of C" and "A is the decisive contributory cause of C" are stronger than "A is a contributory cause of C" because a whole cause and a decisive cause have properties that a mere contributory cause does not have, the statement "A is a contributory cause of C" will be called stronger than "A is one of the conditions jointly sufficient for C" because laws that support the former may have properties that laws supporting the latter do not have. For this reason if we wish to distinguish the decisive cause from a mere contributory cause, we must focus on what must be added in clause (2) of Schema I, whereas if we wish to distinguish a contributory cause from a condition which is merely one of the jointly sufficient conditions, we must distinguish the laws that appear in an explanatory deductive argument as it figures in the *analysans* of Thesis I, from the laws referred to in the definition of the phrase "is one of the conditions jointly sufficient for."

The Analysans of Thesis I

We have seen that universal statements in an explanatory deductive argument must at least be laws. And if a statement is equivalent to a conjunction of a finite number of singular statements, it will not, as we have seen in an earlier chapter, be a law. For example, we cannot explain the fact that a thing on the desk is white by arguing "All of the pieces of paper on the desk are white; this is a piece of paper on the desk; therefore, this is white." So the temptation might be to say that the universal statement in an explanatory deductive argument must have the form "Whatever was, is, or will be P, R, S, and T, was, is, or will be Q." But here we are confronted with something like Mill's example, "All crows are black," where it appears that we can say that "Whatever was, is, or will be a crow, was, is, or will be black," and yet feel that we do not explain a's being black by pointing out that a is a crow and that all crows are black. At this point one might think that one could avoid this sort of counterexample by saying that the universal statement in an explanatory deductive argument must support a contrary-to-fact conditional, i.e., that it must be such that we should be prepared to say, on the basis of it, that if a—which does *not* have the conjunction of properties P, R, S, and T—were to have that conjunction, a would be Q. This would be, according to some students of the problem, a test of whether the universal statement is a law of nature. It is obvious that such a characterization of a law of nature will not be helpful if we are trying to analyze the contrary-to-fact conditional statement,[8] but it might be thought that it will suffice if we are trying to analyze a singular statement of the form "A is a contributory cause of C" in the manner of Thesis I. Unfortunately, however, it is not altogether clear that such a singular statement is true if and only if there exists an explanatory deductive argument as described in Thesis I, if we define an explanatory deductive argument as one that contains, among other statements, at least one universal statement which merely supports a contrary-to-fact conditional statement.

Different sorts of counterexamples may be directed against this conception of an explanatory deductive argument. They are essen-

[8] For that would be circular. See Goodman, *Fact, Fiction and Forecast*, ch. 1, passim.

tially the examples that I spoke of earlier when I contrasted being a contributory cause of and being one of the jointly sufficient conditions for an event or state of affairs. The illustration of lightning and thunder will allow us to make some of the relevant points. Even if it is a law of nature that where there is thunder at time t_2, there has been lightning at an earlier time t_1, we would not present the following as an explanation of lightning in Boston at time t_1: (1) "Where there is thunder at t_2, there has been lightning at an earlier time t_1; (2) there was thunder in Boston at t_2; therefore (3) there was lightning in Boston at t_1." By contrast, however, we can say that the fact reported in (2) is a sufficient condition for that reported in (3). If it be thought that the only difficulty here is that the supposedly explained fact is earlier than the explaining fact, then it will be instructive to consider an argument containing the converse of the previous generalization, which is also a law: "Where there is lightning at time t_1, there is thunder at a later time t_2." Here the explaining fact is earlier than the fact to be explained. On the assumption that we understand by "lightning" the flash of light that we see at t_1 and that we understand by "thunder" the sound that we hear at t_2, and that both are different from the electrical disturbance that brings them both on, we surely will not *explain* the heard thunder by citing the seen lightning, even though the latter might be called a sufficient condition for the former if we impose no requirements on the relevant generalization other than that it be a law in the sense of a statement supporting a contrary-to-fact conditional. The remark that the lightning did not cause the thunder is quite in order here. William Dray[9] has made a similar point by using a hypothetical illustration when he says that even if it were a law of nature that every time the sky is red in the morning, it rains in the afternoon, we would not explain the fact that it is raining in the afternoon by pointing to this law of nature and the fact that the sky was red this morning.

If it be thought that the difficulty is simply dependent on a difference in time between the statement of initial condition and

[9] Dray, op. cit., pp. 61-62.

the explained fact, we may turn to an illustration of Sylvain Bromberger's[10] which in my opinion can be used to make the same point even though no time difference between explaining and explained fact is involved. Bromberger invites us to consider a case where we measure the angle A made with the ground by a straight line from the top of the Empire State Building to a point on the ground which is a known distance, d, from the base of the building. Given this angle, the distance d, and laws of physical geometry, we can deduce the height of the Empire State Building. Would we say that the Empire State Building is whatever height it is because the angle is A? Or because the distance is d? The basic point to be made in connection with the illustration about lightning, with Dray's illustration and with Bromberger's, is that the laws which figure in a deductive argument may support contrary-to-fact conditionals and yet we may hesitate to say that the deductive argument is explanatory. We may feel that a law which is to figure in an explanatory deductive argument must do more, so to speak, than support a contrary-to-fact conditional and do more than express a connection between subject and predicate. But what more?

We see more clearly now that our earlier problem about the difference between being one of a set of jointly sufficient conditions and being a contributory cause may point to a difference between two kinds of laws, explanatory and nonexplanatory. How shall we draw this distinction? When he faces this sort of question, Carl G. Hempel admits that sometimes an argument of the form "Whatever is P and R is Q; a is P; a is R; therefore, a is Q" will not be called an explanation of a's being Q even though the first premise is a law. Hempel, however, instead of regarding this as an objection to his analysis of an explanatory deductive argument, says that "ordinary usage appears to provide no clear general criterion for those arguments which are to be qualified as explanatory. This is not suprising, for our everyday conception of explanation

[10] Sylvain Bromberger, *The Concept of Explanation* (Unpublished Ph.D. dissertation, Harvard University, 1961), p. 104.

is strongly influenced by pre-analytic causal and teleological ideas; and these can hardly be expected to provide unequivocal guidance for a more general and precise analysis of scientific explanation and prediction."[11] In effect this leads Hempel to abandon the effort to disguish between explanatory deductive arguments and those deductive arguments that contain laws that are not explanatory, like "Whenever there is lightning, there is thunder very soon afterwards."

For a variety of reasons I am not convinced that this is a wise procedure. I am not convinced that philosophers have given enough attention to puzzling examples like those presented by Dray and Bromberger to conclude that they are the product of stone-age philosophy or that they are not governed by rules. I am also reminded that some positivistic philosophers—and they are most likely to be upset by the notion that more than a *mere* law is involved in an explanatory deductive argument—have spurned even the idea that an explanatory deductive argument involves *mere* laws[11a]. In fact, they have done so on grounds that are very much like those that Hempel uses when he abandons the distinction between two kinds of laws as a linguistic remnant of prescientific thinking.

I should make clear that I use the word "law" as Hempel uses it when he says that an explanatory deductive argument must contain laws,[12] and as Goodman uses it when he says that he does not know how to define it.[13] It would seem, then, that ordinary usage not only provides no clear general criterion for statements which are said to be *explanatory* laws, but it is equally deficient so far as *mere* laws are concerned. I realize, of course, that we can say that mere laws support contrary-to-fact conditional state-

---

[11] Carl G. Hempel, "Deductive-Nomological Versus Statistical Explanation," in *Minnesota Studies in the Philosophy of Science,* ed. Herbert Feigl and Grover Maxwell, III (Minneapolis, 1962), p. 110.

[11a] In other words they have not required that generalizations in an explanaatory argument be such as to support contrary-to-fact conditionals.

[12] Hempel, op. cit. pp. 99–110.

[13] Goodman, op. cit., p. 31.

ments, but then we can also say that explanatory laws, unlike nonexplanatory laws, can support statements of the form "A is a contributory cause of C." The point is that if the absence of an explicit analysis of the concept of explanatory law is what troubles a philosopher, he should be equally troubled by the concept of a mere law. On the other hand, if what the philosopher is worried about is our capacity to *pick out* explanatory laws by contrast to mere laws—without benefit of a definition or analysis or criterion —I venture to say that we can pick them out as well as we can pick out mere laws. The formula is simple: a mere law is a statement which supports contrary-to-fact conditional statements, whereas an explanatory law is one that supports statements of the form "A is a contributory cause of C." Furthermore the notion of a contrary-to-fact conditional statement is no clearer than that of contributory cause. Therefore, Hempel's situation seems to be this: he is willing to use the criterionless notion of law in his analysis of an explanatory deductive argument, but he is not willing to take the further step of employing the notion of *explanatory law* even though it seems to be in the same boat or very nearly the same boat. Naturally, one can sympathize with Hempel's unwillingness to define the notion of explanatory deductive argument in terms of the notion of explanatory law if that were to create a logical circle for him. But it is not obvious that it must create a circle and it is not obvious that it is a concept which is so hopelessly irregular in its application as to forbid further analysis.

Furthermore, it is not evident that Hempel can consistently take the view—sometimes taken by philosophers who wish to avoid the problem of analyzing the notion of explanatory law—that it is a "pragmatic" concept and hence beyond the purview of logical analysis. Although Hempel does not address himself to the question of how to analyze the notion of mere law, it is not at all clear that *it* is not a "pragmatic" concept, especially when one notes Hempel's sympathy with Goodman's treatment of this problem and then finds Goodman saying that one of the notions involved is that of a statement which "is acceptable independently of the determination of any given instance."[14] The idea of acceptability seems to go beyond syntax and semantics and to bring us to that sort of concept which is sometimes called pragmatic, and indeed it prompts us to ask whether the idea of law is not in some sense "normative."

For these various reasons, then, I am prepared to acknowledge that something like the notion of an explanatory law is involved in our conception of an explanatory deductive argument and hence in our conception of the truth-conditions for a singular statement of the form "A is a contributory cause of C." I also admit that we are still faced with a difficult problem when it comes to saying something illuminating about the notion of an explanatory law by contrast to the notion of a mere law. However, the fact that no one has as yet produced the requisite flash of insight does not mean that we must withdraw the contention that a singular statement of the form "A is a contributory cause of C" *implies* the existence of a *regularity*, or the contention that the existence of an appropriate explanatory deductive argument implies such a singular statement. Philosophy, like science, moves in a piecemeal way toward the truth, and there is no reason to spurn part of the truth because we do not possess all of it, that is to say, because we have not said what *kind* of regularity it is that figures in an explanatory deductive argument, because we have not yet been able to characterize an explanatory law in a satisfactory way. It is, of course, the absence of such a criterion that makes it easier for critics of the regularity theory to insist that an element of "judgment" enters into explanation, for perhaps judgment is employed in discovering whether a law is explanatory. But my own impulse is to grant that a mere law is not an explanatory law and then to try to say how one law differs from the other without repairing to the unanalyzed idea of "judgment."

Before leaving this problem I wish to call attention to the possibility that the notion of being an explanatory law might be relative in character and that recognizing it as such might help us in

[14] Ibid.

our effort to analyze it. One might argue that the expression "explanatory law" is elliptical for the expression "explanatory law for person or culture X," and that therefore our task is to analyze a *relation*. The following analogy may make the point clearer. One may hold, as some philosophers believe, that to prove a proposition is to deduce it from obvious axioms, and yet be forced to acknowledge that one and the same axiom might be obvious to one man and not to another. "Obvious," it might be said, is an elliptical expression, short for "obvious to person X." But if it is elliptical, we might be able to state a necessary and sufficient condition for the obtaining of this *relation* between a proposition and a person, and in that case present a criterion for obviousness in the relative sense. In an analogous manner we might some day be able to discover the features of a law that make it explanatory for a person or a culture. For this reason we need not, in my opinion, dismiss the notion of being explanatory as if it were some excrescence on a mere law that must resist philosophical characterization, anymore than we need dismiss the idea of *the decisive* contributory cause, as we shall see in a later chapter. There, as we shall see, illuminating results may be easier to come by, but the relevant linguistic habit is similar to that which leads one to distinguish mere laws from explanatory laws, and therefore the latter habit ought not to be dismissed as insufficiently pure for philosophers to analyze or as providing linguistic data which are so unruly as to defy the philosopher bent on extracting rules that govern them. I do not see why the philosopher of mind, if not the logician of science who conceives of his task more narrowly, should not acknowledge and try to analyze the sequence of different kinds of universal statements that lead from type A as illustrated by "All of the pieces of paper on the desk are white" or "All hitherto existing history has been the history of class struggles"; to type B, as illustrated by "All crows are black"; to type C, as illustrated by "Whenever there is lightning, there is thunder shortly afterward"; to type D, as illustrated by "Whenever it rains, the ground gets wet." Here we move from A, a mere summation of a finite number of facts, to a statement B about an indefinite number of items, which, like A, does not support a contrary-to-fact conditional even though it is universal in form, to a statement like C which supports a contrary-to-fact conditional but not a singular statement of contributory causation, to a statement like D which *does* support a singular statement of contributory causation.

Here I have merely speculated about whether the notion of an explanatory law as opposed to a mere law is relative and have pled for further analysis in this direction. What I have opposed is the idea that there is some clear inner logical core of the notion of explanation which may be analyzed without attention to what are sometimes dismissed as merely psychological or merely pragmatic overtones, and I have also opposed the even more questionable idea that we must give up our ordinary linguistic habits, allegedly because they are remnants of stone-age thinking. In a sense I have adopted a quasi-Humean approach to the problem, arguing that reference to more than law is required when we come to analyze an explanatory deductive argument and a singular explanatory statement, and that that extra something may well be *custom*. But it should be noticed that because custom may lead us to call some laws explanatory and others not, we need to know the way in which custom works—in other words, why it dignifies some laws by calling them explanatory. Moreover, if it is custom that decides, custom may decide differently in different cultures. For some men it might be perfectly acceptable to say that rain fell in the afternoon because the sky was red in the morning, because *they* regard the generalization "Red sky in the morning is always followed by rain in the afternoon" as explanatory. But the question is: on what grounds?

One thing is perfectly clear, and that is that we cannot expect to answer our question by focusing on the syntax of explanatory laws. It is also clear, I think, that semantics will not be helpful either. I mean that I do not think that we shall, by reflecting on the classes or properties referred to or expressed by the terms in a so-called explanatory law, discover why it is explanatory. That way is far too rationalistic. Indeed, it is precisely because the notion of an explanatory law is associated with extreme rationalism that many philosophers have given up the search for a criterion whereby we can distinguish explanatory and nonexplanatory laws. In the same way, some philosophers have decided to give up the search for a way of distinguishing mere extensional equivalence of terms from synonymy because they think of the notion of sameness of meaning as a remnant of rationalistic essentialism. And yet it seems to me that if we think of synonymy as a psychological notion which may yield to philosophical analysis, so we may think of the notion of an *explanatory* law as some day yielding similarly. Furthermore, just as it has been said that synonymy is a relative notion and that we should, when speaking exactly, say that two expressions are synonymous *for a certain person or culture*, so we should, if my earlier suggestion is sensible, say that a law is explanatory for a certain person or culture. There are striking similarities, as one might expect, between the problem of clarifying synonymy and that of clarifying the idea of explanatory law, which is so fundamental in the philosophy of science. In both cases we find that syntax and semantics are incapable of providing answers to our questions, in both cases a turn to psychology and pragmatics seems in order, in both cases the state of psychology and pragmatics makes things difficult for us. And yet, it seems to me, we must not take the easy way out and argue that the notions of synonymy and of explanatory law are necessarily meaningless or somehow unworthy of further philosophical study. For if we act on that counsel of despair, we shall not only remain unclear about synonymy and about the concept of explanatory law but also about the concept of mere law, as I have pointed out.

The Connection Between Analysandum and Analysans

Having talked so much about analysis, it will be useful to ask the metaphilosophical question, "What is the regularist trying to do when he offers a thesis like I?" What sort of statement is Thesis

I? Even if it is granted that Thesis I presents an equivalent of rather than an expansion of a singular causal statement, philosophers might disagree about the nature of that equivalence. Some philosophers might say that a doctrine like existential regularism represents an effort to analyze what a historian *means* when he makes statements like "New York became the foremost American city in the nineteenth century because of its excellent harbor." It would follow, of course, that Thesis I is what some philosophers call an analytic statement and that all statements of the form "A is a contributory cause of C" are *synonymous* with statements of the form "There exists an explanatory deductive argument in which 'A' is a premise and 'C' the conclusion."

What shall we say of this view? First of all, that it is not advisable to say that Thesis I is analytic, or is true by virtue of the meaning of its terms, even though there is a strong temptation to construe Thesis I as asserting a relationship which resembles that asserted in the following formula:

x is a grandparent of *y* if and only if
there is a *z* such that *x* is a parent of
z and *z* is a parent of *y*.

Now apart from philosophical doubts about the definition of synonymy, it seems quite all right to say that "grandparent of" is synonymous with "parent of a parent of." On the other hand, the relationship between the left-hand side and the right-hand side of the "if and only if" of Thesis I is somewhat different. If a man were to assert that John D. Rockefeller is not a grandparent of Nelson Rockefeller in spite of his being a parent of one of Nelson's parents, we might have reason to think that such a man meant something different by the term "grandparent" than we did. But there is enough plausibility in the criticism of certain versions of the regularity theory of explanation to make one hesitate to say that those why deny Thesis I must "mean" something different by the word "because." For this reason I hesitate to call Thesis I analytic in the sense in which "Whoever is a grandparent of a person is a

parent of a parent of that person" is analytic. The connection
between the left-hand and the right-hand sides of Thesis I is
different. It is therefore best construed as a statement of a necessary and sufficient condition for the truth of statements of the
form "A is a contributory cause of C," a statement *based* on the
fact that in a vast number of cases when a statement of the form
"A is a contributory cause of C" is regarded as true, there is an
explanatory deductive argument of the kind described in Thesis I
and conversely. In the light of this conclusion the philosopher who
is averse to postulating the mysterious ties between causes and
effects that bothered Hume and Mill recommends to the historian
that he accept Thesis I as a guide to the understanding of his
singular explanatory statements. In this respect the philosopher
behaves somewhat like a legislator who recommends that a certain
custom be raised to the level of an explicitly adopted statute that
will govern future explanatory language.

As I have already indicated, there is a very important similarity
between my treatment of an explanatory law and my treatment of
a philosophical thesis. We are faced with the problem of saying
what distinguishes each of them from a mere statement of extensional connection, and in both cases I have wished to avoid rationalistic or positivistic dogma at the expense of admitting that the
problem is unsolved. I do not find it illuminating to say with certain positivists that laws are merely universal statements of fact
about an indefinite number of things, and I do not find it illuminating to say with the rationalist that they express some mysterious
connection between their subjects and predicates. Similarly, I cannot accept the rationalistic view that Thesis I expresses the essence
of causal connection or the positivistic view that it is an analytic
statement. For this reason I feel that it is better to acknowledge
one's puzzlement and point to the direction in which one should
seek light, than to rest with the merely apparent security and clarity
of extant philosophical cant. The problem of scientific explanation
and the problem of philosophical explication are so intimately con-

nected that we can hope the great future philosopher who solves one of them will also solve, or indicate the way in which to solve, the other.

With this declaration of hope behind us let us try to sketch the experience concerning the use of language that underlies the recommendation that we adopt an analysis of explanation along the lines presented in Thesis I. If a man asserts the proposition "The striking of this match was a contributory cause of its lighting," he will accept as evidence in its favor the fact that we can produce an argument which contains a law like "All dry matches which are struck in the presence of oxygen light" and the statements "This match was dry," "This match was struck," and "This match was surrounded by oxygen." And if he can be persuaded that no explanatory deductive argument of this kind exists, he will deny the singular causal statement. Of course, showing that there is no such explanatory deductive argument is a very difficult task, for it involves showing in effect that the following statement is false: "There are properties of this match which, in conjunction with the property of being struck, lead by (explanatory) law to its being struck." But, as we all know, falsifying a singular causal statement *is* enormously difficult, and the very fact that Thesis I mirrors this difficulty by equating it with an existential statement is an argument in favor of Thesis I.

Those who think that Thesis I is false must argue that a singular causal statement can be true even if there are no explanatory deductive arguments of the kind specified in Thesis I, and I do not see how this can be maintained. Even if some philosophers are prepared to assert "This match lit because it was struck," while they deny any *given* law concerning matches, it is hard to suppose that they would maintain that the singular causal statement could be true while they denied the existence of *any* explanatory deductive arguments of the kind outlined in Thesis I. They might, as we have seen, hesitate to say that the left-hand side and the right-hand side of Thesis I "mean the same," but can they produce cases where statements of the form represented in the left-hand side are true and yet where their equivalents as represented in the right-hand side are false?

A person who asserts a singular explanatory statement will generally accept as support and as criticism of his statement the sort of support and criticism that we would all regard as relevant in the case of a statement which asserts the existence of an explanatory deductive argument. Suppose a man says that this match lit because it was struck. After he has made his explanatory statement, he may be asked how he knows that it is true. Suppose he replies that the match was struck, that it lit, and that all matches light when they are struck. His speaking in this way would not be conclusive evidence in favor of Thesis I, the *revised* version of the regularity theory, for it may show that the man takes his singular explanatory statement to be elliptical for this particular explanatory deductive argument, and hence replaceable by it. In other words, this response might be taken as support for the standard version of the regularity theory. But now suppose that a critic points out to the man that not *all* matches light when struck, even though this one did. If the man were to *identify* his explanation with the explanatory deductive argument he originally gave in support of his explanation, the critic would have decisively refuted the explanation since he would have refuted its major premise, and the man would be obliged to withdraw his statement that the match lit because it was struck. But I think it is fair to say that if such a person were criticized in this way, he would not regard his singular explanatory statement as *ipso facto* invalidated. Instead, he might still regard the explanatory statement as true and try to defend it in another way, particularly, if he was thinking of wet matches when realizing that not all matches light when struck, or if his critic called them to his attention. In that case, he might well present *another* explanatory deductive argument, one in which he asserted that all dry matches light when struck, that this match was dry and was struck, and that therefore this match lit. The point is that he is now advancing *another* explanatory deductive argument in behalf of the same, original singular explanatory statement. He still regards that explanatory statement as true, but he has exchanged one explanatory deductive argument for another in an effort to defend his singular explanatory statement without thinking that because he has shifted his argument he has come to defend an explanatory statement which has a different equivalent. And this shows that even though he presents a particular deductive argument in support of his singular explanatory statement, he does not think of that particular deductive argument as the equivalent of his explanation, as something which, when it falls, brings about the collapse of the singular explanatory statement.

It also shows, however, that he acts as if the invalidation of a given explanatory deductive argument does have some effect on his belief in the singular explanatory statement. If we interpret him as asserting that there are *some* properties of this match which, in conjunction with the property of being struck, are connected by *some* law or laws with its lighting, we can understand why he presents a deductive argument and why, when he fails to find one deductive argument, or one combination of properties and laws which will bear out what he says, he will look for another. And when his proposal of another is also punctured by the observation that not even all *dry* matches light when struck, and he dutifully goes on to assert that oxygen was present and that all dry matches light when struck in the presence of oxygen, he is illustrating the same refusal to identify the singular statement with the deductive argument and the same conviction that if his singular statement is true, then there is a relevant deductive argument which will back it up.

Finally, it is fairly obvious that if he could persuade himself that there is *no* explanatory deductive argument of the relevant kind, he would not keep on asserting that the match lit because it was struck. In other words, if he could be persuaded that it is not true to say that the struck match has a conjunction of properties which lead by some law or laws to its lighting, he would not assert that it lit because it was struck. *How* he might be persuaded of this is another question, and a difficult one, as we have seen.

In short, it would appear that the behavior of a man who has asserted a singular explanatory statement and who has been trying to meet objections of the kind we have outlined, indicates that he believes that his singular statement is true if and only if a certain kind of explanatory deductive argument exists. And what holds for "Because this match was struck, it lit" holds for many similar statements made by historians: for Herbert Baxter Adams' statement that the triumph of democracy in America may be explained by the Germanic tradition, for Turner's statement that it may be attributed to the frontier, for Pirenne's explanation of the collapse of the Mediterranean Commonwealth, for Beard's explanation of the Civil War, and for Marc Bloch's explanation of the Scandinavian migrations of the ninth century. These may all be formulated in singular causal statements which are analyzable in accordance with the theory of existential regularism, a theory which more faithfully reflects the linguistic behavior of historians than the standard version of the covering law theory, and which therefore commends itself on that ground for adoption, as well as on the ground that the alternative theory of a "mysterious tie" between cause and effect is no clarification of "because" at all. But, as we have seen, the regularist who wishes to distinguish himself from the proponent of mysterious ties must, admittedly, do more than he has done so far in clarification of the notion of a law and in clarification of an explanatory law. Thesis I may represent considerable philosophical progress, but it is not the last word on explanation.

THE EVIDENCE FOR SINGULAR EXPLANATORY STATEMENTS: DEDUCTIVE AND INDUCTIVE

Having outlined a necessary and sufficient condition for the truth of statements of the form "A is a contributory cause of C," we may now say a little more about how, in the light of our analysis, such statements may be supported and confirmed. It should be remembered that we are not concerned here with statements of the form "A is *the* cause of C" and hence are not now obliged to face the problem of distinguishing *the* cause from other contributory causes. We shall deal with that question in the next chapter.

It is obvious that one way in which the statement "A is a cause of C" may be supported is by producing a relevant explanatory deductive argument. But is it the only way allowed by Thesis I? If we suppose that a singular explanatory statement is true if and only if there exists an explanatory deductive argument of the kind described in Thesis I, how can we show that such an argument exists except by actually producing one? If we cannot defend such a statement except by presenting an explanatory deductive argument, then the insistence on the existential nature of the equivalent to the explanatory statement as presented in Thesis I will be academic. It would be like insisting that the statement "James Mill is a father" is equivalent to the statement "James Mill begat someone"; and yet saying that the only way in which we can support the statement that James Mill begat someone is by pointing to one of the begotten, i.e., John Stuart Mill or one of his siblings. We all know, however, that there are ways of supporting our conviction that a man is a father even when we cannot point to one of his children. His manner, his behavior, his speech may all give us good reason for thinking that he is. Let us take another example. If we assert that there are tigers in Asia, one way of demonstrating this conclusively is by going there and pointing to one. On the other hand, the fact that we have reports from reliable travelers is also good evidence for the existential statement. And what I wish to argue is that we may analogously view the statement that a certain kind of argument exists. It may be supported conclusively by the production of such an argument, or it may be supported by presenting inductive evidence, that is to say, by giving good, though not deductive, reasons for thinking that such an argument exists.

How can we give good, though not deductive, reasons for thinking that such an argument exists and hence good reasons for thinking that a singular causal statement is true? I do not propose to
answer this in a general way, but only to outline one way in which
we can inductively support a singular causal statement. In order to
do so, I shall describe a situation in which an investigator is, as we
might say, coming closer and closer to being able to present an
explanatory deductive argument and where the fact that he is
coming closer and closer gives him grounds for supposing that
such an argument exists. He begins by supposing that he can
assert "The fact that a is P is a contributory cause of a's being Q"
on the basis of the fact that a is P and a is Q, and that it is a law
that all P is Q; but then he discovers that while a is P and a is Q, it
is not a law that all P is Q. And so he examines the situation in
greater detail and discovers that the probability of a P being Q is
high enough to make him think that by further examination he
may discover some other feature of a—say R—which *will* get him
to a law, viz., "All P and R is Q." However, although a is R, he
does not discover a law of the hoped-for sort, but notices that the
probability that anything which is P and R is Q is greater than the
probability that anything which is P is Q. So he continues his
search and now discovers still another feature, S, which a has, and
which is such that the probability that anything which is P and R
and S is Q is greater than the previous probability.

This investigator, I suggest, has good reasons for thinking that
there is a strict explanatory law and that there are true singular
statements about a which, together with "a is P," logically imply
"a is Q" and hence make up a deductive argument of the kind
required by Thesis I.

One may, as we have seen, construe the singular explanatory
statement "The fact that a is P is a contributory cause of a's being
Q" as asserting that there are properties of a which, together with
P, lead by some law or laws to Q. We may think of the antecedent, "a is P," of the singular explanatory statement as a bridge-
pier on one side of a river, of the consequent, "a is Q," as a
bridge-pier on the other side of the river, and of the singular

statement as asserting that there is a bridge, or explanatory deductive argument, that links both piers. In the metaphor a bridge will consist of its piers and of the road that rests on them. Usually, though not always or necessarily, there will be more than one pier on the antecedent's side of the river, and each such pier will represent a property of the *a* mentioned in the statement "The fact that *a* is P is a contributory cause of *a*'s being Q." In terms of this metaphor, our investigator has done two things: he has introduced more and more bridge-piers on the left side of the river; and he has, by successive related qualifications of his universal statement, found stronger and stronger roads, i.e., statistical generalizations with greater and greater probability coefficients. Now, when a person defending a singular explanatory statement goes through such a progressive process in response either to a logician's prodding or to his own self-prodding, he may conclude that he has good reasons for believing that there *is* a deductive explanatory argument of the kind mentioned in Thesis I; that there are features of *a* which, together with its being P, are connected by *some* law or laws with its being Q. Since he has increased the strength of his road and found more and more piers on the left side on which to rest it, he has reason to believe that if he were to go on in this way he would strengthen the road even more and find further piers, hopefully to the point where he could present a full-fledged deductive argument, or perfectly strong bridge. But he need not *reach* that point. In other words, he need not *produce* the explanatory deductive argument whose existence he implies when he makes his singular explanatory statement. He may give good reasons for believing that there is a causal connection between "*a* is P" and "*a* is Q"; and since that is equivalent to showing that there are solid piers and a strong road that will together permit him to walk from "*a* is P" to "*a* is Q," he may give those good reasons by showing that he has been steadily adding more and more piers and strengthening his road. This gives him reason to think that *there is* a solid road and a set of piers—a bridge—that will get him across successfully.

In pointing this out, I do not wish to deny that the actual

production of a deductive argument will create even more confidence in the singular explanatory statement. If a historian, or a historian working in collaboration with a social or behavioral scientist, *can* produce an explanatory deductive argument of the kind prescribed by the standard version of the regularity theory, he will undoubtedly give us the best possible reason for believing the singular explanatory statement. But I am mainly concerned to affirm that there are other ways of establishing confidence in this statement, ways that are more typical of history. I am not fazed by the fact that historians who do not present deductive explanatory arguments support their explanations with less powerful evidence than they would have presented had they produced deductive arguments. As I have indicated earlier, I am not bent on showing that history has its own methods of arriving at explanations which are just as solidly based as those in the natural sciences. But I am eager to characterize the language of historians without forcing it into a logical bed originally construed for others. This is my chief reason for trying to show that singular explanatory statements are not incomplete or elliptical and that they *are* explanations. In this way I can accommodate the observation that we can rarely defend the historian's causal statements deductively without sacrificing a very important element of truth in the covering law theory and without abandoning the idea that the historian must supply evidence for his singular causal statements.

We may summarize the situation by saying that we can either give deductive evidence for such a statement by *producing* an explanatory deductive argument of the kind whose existence is asserted in Thesis I as the equivalent of "The fact that *a* is *P* is a contributory cause of *a*'s being *Q*," or we can supply inductive evidence of the kind just illustrated. If a historian can present inductive evidence of this kind, he presents what might be called indirect evidence for his singular causal statement, evidence that is in a certain respect like the evidence we present for the statement that a man is a father when we say that he behaves like a father, and unlike the evidence we present when we point to one of his children; like the evidence that we may present for saying that a person is a grandparent of another even though we cannot produce a person who is child of the first and parent of the second.

All of this is somewhat different from the view of Hempel on the problem of singular explanatory statements. He seems willing in one of his writings to grant that such statements imply the *existence* of what I have called an explanatory deductive argument but seems reluctant to call such a singular statement an explanation. And so he says: "To the extent that a statement of individual causation leaves the relevant antecedent conditions—and thus also the requisite explanatory laws—indefinite, it is like a note saying that there is a treasure hidden somewhere. Its significance and utility will increase as the location of the treasure is narrowed down, as the relevant conditions and the corresponding covering laws are made increasingly explicit. In some cases, such as that of barbiturate poisoning, this can be done quite satisfactorily; the covering law structure then emerges, and the statement of individual causal connection becomes amenable to test. When, on the other hand, the relevant conditions or laws remain largely indefinite, a statement of causal connection is rather in the nature of a program, or of a sketch, for an explanation in terms of causal laws; it might also be viewed as a 'working hypothesis' which may prove its worth by giving new, and fruitful, direction to further research."[15]

About this I wish to make the following comments. First, that I think there is as much reason to call certain singular statements "explanations" as there is to call explanatory deductive arguments "explanations." Second, that this *is* the usage that I think is employed by historians. Third, that Hempel seems to grant in this passage that so-called explanation-sketches are *statements* and not arguments. Furthermore, I should agree with Hempel that having an actual explanatory deductive argument in one's hand, so to speak, is a far better thing than merely having the knowledge that one exists. But it is not true to say, as Hempel *seems* to imply,

[15] Hempel, op. cit., pp. 105–6.

that the only way in which we can *test* a singular causal statement is to test the validity of an actual explanatory deductive argument.

I should also point out here that while Hempel is willing to assert that a singular explanatory statement implies the existence of a certain kind of explanatory deductive argument, he does not assert an *equivalence* like Thesis I. This may be because of the difficulties connected with explanatory arguments like that presented by Bromberger insofar as a deductive argument like the one produced by Bromberger might not be called explanatory. By contrast, I have in Thesis I asserted an equivalence on the assumption that the notion of explanatory law can be clarified. If, however, one does not require that an explanatory deductive argument contain more than what I have called a *mere* law, then he can assert Thesis I with only the usual reservations and worries about the concept of *mere* law. In any case, if one can defend Thesis I in either form, one can then go on to argue that anything which is evidence for the existence of an explanatory deductive argument of a certain kind is evidence for a singular explanatory statement of a certain kind.

This, as we have seen, opens up a new problem: the problem of developing a theory of how we inductively confirm statements asserting the *existence* of certain kinds of deductive arguments. Such a theory would be needed in any case for handling the confirmation of contrary-to-fact conditional statements since they, as Goodman has shown, are also intimately connected with statements asserting the existence of deductive arguments containing laws, i.e., connected with them in a way that would require us to show how such existential statements are inductively confirmed if we are to see how contrary-to-fact conditional statements are inductively confirmed. Moreover, this connection between contrary-to-fact conditional statements and deductive arguments shows, by analogy, how questionable it is to insist that an explanatory deductive argument *replaces* the singular explanatory statement, or how strange it is to say that the argument is *superior* to the statement except from some point of view that must be made explicit. Naturally, if a man *wants* to know *what* explanatory deductive argument can be offered in behalf of "*a* is *Q*," it will not satisfy him to be told that there is one, i.e., that *a*'s being *P* is a contributory cause of *a*'s being *Q*. But surely there are occasions when what he wants to assert is the singular causal *statement* and when he is not looking for a deductive argument. To be told, then, that he must press on to discover a deductive argument might strike him as impertinent—especially if he is a historian, and especially if deductive arguments are hard to come by, and especially if there is a nondeductive way of supporting his implied belief that relevant deductive arguments exist.

STATISTICAL SUPPORT AND STATISTICAL EXPLANATION

As we have seen, one of the main reasons for holding the view that a historical explanation is a singular causal statement equivalent to an existential statement of the kind described in Thesis I is that this view permits us to say that we have given an explanation even if we have not actually produced a full-blown explanatory deductive argument. In this way we can deal with certain objections to the regularty theory of historical explanation, namely, those which are based on the admitted difficulty of actually producing the kind of deductive argument required by the standard version of the regularity theory. But other regularists, like Hempel and Nagel, have tried to deal with this objection in a somewhat different way.[16] Instead of moving in the direction in which I have moved in order to escape the need to *produce* an explanatory deductive argument, they hold that an explanatory argument may take another form in history. Instead of insisting that a singular explanatory statement be regarded as elliptical for a deductive argument which contains what is sometimes called a strict deter-

[16] See, for example, Carl G. Hempel, "Explanation in Science and in History," in *Frontiers of Science and Philosophy*, ed. R. G. Colodny (Pittsburgh, 1962), pp. 7–33; and Ernest Nagel, *The Structure of Science* (New York, 1961), p. 558.

ministic law, some regularists seem to hold that it is elliptical for a parallel argument which, instead of containing a deterministic law, contains a probability or statistical law in its place—say, of the form "The probability is high that anything which is *P, R, S,* and *T* is *Q*"—and which contains the statement "*a* is probably *Q*" instead of "*a* is *Q*" as its conclusion.

What is to be said of this point of view? First of all, if it is based on the assumption that the singular causal statements of historians are elliptical and hence in need of expansion, it suffers from the same defects as the standard version of the regularity theory. I do not think that singular causal statements are elliptical for *any kind* of arguments. But the question arises, what about a revised version of the statistical theory, one which does not assert that singular causal statements are elliptical but rather takes the form of a statistical analogue of Thesis I, namely:

> THESIS I′: A is a contributory cause of *C* if
> and only if "*A*" is true, "*C*" is true,
> and there is a statistical explanatory
> argument in which "*A*" is a premise
> and the conclusion is "Probably *C*"?

Let me begin by saying that everything depends on what is claimed for such a thesis and what the reasons are for adopting it rather than Thesis I itself. If it is asserted that all singular explanatory statements in history books must be analyzed in this way because of the difficulties involved in producing explanatory deductive arguments, then it seems to me that one might respond as follows. First of all, it is not evident that whenever a historian uses an expression like "is a contributory cause of" he uses it in a way that is different from that in which an ordinary man uses it when he says that the striking of a window with a mallet is a contributory cause of its breaking. And yet the advocate of Thesis I′ is committed to the view that there is such a difference. He states truth-conditions for the historian's singular causal statements that differ from those he states for singular causal statements for which he can produce strict deterministic laws and explanatory deductive arguments. By contrast, Thesis I preserves the prima-facie uniformity of all such statements. It would seem that when Pirenne says that the Moslem seizure of the Mediterranean was a contributory cause of the breakdown of the Mediterranean Commonwealth, he takes himself to be using the phrase "a contributory cause of" just as it is used by the man who says that the dropping of the pebble was a contributory cause of the wave, and therefore it does seem peculiar to cast doubt on this identity of use by presenting two distinct theses, one of which presents the equivalent of the first statement in the statistical Thesis I′ and the other of which presents the equivalent of the second in the deterministic Thesis I. Moreover, the account in the preceding section of how we can, on some occasions, support a singular explanatory statement, gives statistics its due. Even though one asserts a singular causal statement which is equivalent, in accordance with Thesis I, to a statement asserting the existence of an explanatory deductive argument, one may employ statistics in supporting the statement. As it is sometimes said, a high statistical correlation may be evidence for a lawful connection.

Finally I want to direct a remark to those philosophers who, while they defend something like Thesis I′, do not wish to deny determinism in history. If they do not deny determinism in history, they at least allow for the *possibility* of finding explanations of the sort characterized in Thesis I. And this means that even if at a given moment they are not able to produce anything more than a statistical explanatory argument in defense of a given singular statement like "The conflict between Northern and Southern economic interests caused the Civil War," they are not prevented from asserting that there exists an explanatory deductive argument of the kind described in Thesis I. Another way of putting this point is to say that the fact that a is P is a contributory cause of a's being Q in the sense defined by Thesis I′ does not preclude the possibility that it is a contributory cause in the sense defined by Thesis I. It does not preclude the possibility unless Thesis I′ is thought to analyze those contexts of "is a contributory cause of" which are, so to speak, inherently statistical, that is to say explanatory statements which by their very nature cannot be supported by the production of an explanatory deductive argument. Now I can imagine a philosophical regularist defending Thesis I' as the analysis of all such singular explanatory statements, much as he might if he were dealing with singular explanatory statements made by quantum physicists. But so long as the regularist is not prepared to deny determinism in history, I do not see why he should adopt a two-thesis version of the regularity theory of explanation, one deterministic and the other statistical, even if he can, at a given moment, do no more than produce statistical generalizations in defense of his singular explanatory statements. It seems to me far more plausible to suppose that "because" and related words are used by historians as they are used by rock-throwers, that Thesis I is the basic formula for analyzing them, and that statistical arguments, when they are available, inductively point to the existence of explanatory deductive arguments. When a historian of Japan asserts (1) that the dropping of the atomic bomb on Hiroshima caused great physical destruction and (2) that it caused great social disorganization, he does not believe that the truth-conditions for the first causal statement are different *in form* from those of the second, even if it should be true that the "physical" statement of causal connection between the bomb and the physical destruction is supported by the production of an explanatory deductive argument, whereas the "historical" statement of causal connection between the bomb and the social disorganization is supported inductively. It would be more in keeping with linguistic practice and the historian's thoughts on such matters to say that in the statements "Because of the dropping of the atomic bomb, Japan suffered great physical destruction" and "Because of the dropping of the atomic bomb, Japan suffered great social disorganization" the word "because" is used in the same way, i.e., that the truth-conditions for statements (1) and (2) have the same form. Although Hume was addressing himself to a somewhat different question, I think that the following words of his eloquently support this point of view:

> . . . when we consider how aptly *natural* and *moral* evidence link together and form only one chain of argument, we shall make no scruple to allow that they are of the same nature and derived from the same principles. A prisoner who has neither money nor interest discovers the impossibility of his escape as well when he considers the obstinacy of the jailer as the walls and bars with which he is surrounded, and in all attempts for his freedom chooses rather to work upon the stone and iron of the one than the inflexible nature of the other.[17]

As I have said earlier, some philosophers who think that historical explanations are statistical arguments do not appear to be committed to the view that it is logically impossible to establish laws and to produce explanatory deductive arguments in history. They merely wish to record the difficulty of establishing such laws and producing such deductive arguments. Therefore it seems to me much more in keeping with their views to analyze the "because" of historians as we analyze the "because" of physicians and technologists who assert singular causal propositions. For suppose that, having decided to analyze the statement "The fact that a is P is a contributory cause of a's being Q" probabilistically, they then discover a *strict* explanatory deductive argument in which "a is P" is a premise and "a is Q" the conclusion. Will they now wish to say that the truth-conditions of the original singular explanatory statement have changed? I should have thought not, and for this reason the formulation of a probabilistic analogue to Thesis I seems to me an ill-advised move in response to the admitted difficulty of producing explanatory deductive arguments. It is better to think of the historian's "because" as analyzable in the same way as that of the physician, that of the technologist, and that of anyone who can establish his singular "because"-statements by the production of deductive arguments, but to point out

[17] David Hume, *An Inquiry Concerning Human Understanding*, Sec. VIII, pt. I.

that the historian's "because"-statements are more often established by the citation of statistics than by the production of explanatory deductive arguments.

Of course, the trouble with many singular explanatory statements in history is that they do not have the benefit of strong statistical support. It may be, as one historian of literature says, that American writers produced romances rather than novels in the early nineteenth century because America needed romances, but a historian who asserts such a proposition would be advised to try to produce relevant statistics that go beyond the false statistical generalization that nations usually get what they need in the way of literature. The man who first tries to connect striking matches with their lighting, then tries to connect striking dry matches with their lighting, and then tries to connect striking dry matches surrounded by oxygen with their lighting, uses a method that brings about greater confidence. Statistics do not replace singular explanatory statements, but, if properly used, they can certainly back them up.

It should be pointed out, of course, that in the analysis of singular causal statements presented in Thesis I, I have not taken into account the usage of quantum physicists who might make singular "because"-statements even though they can supposedly show that essentially statistical laws must appear in arguments used in support of such statements. In effect, I am offering a philosophical analysis of singular causal statements which explain events that we do not think are *not* determined, and I am arguing that an inability to present or to produce explanatory deductive arguments and a consequent appeal to statistical generalizations *faute de mieux* is not enough to justify a theory that "because" may have two distinct analyses for different contexts. On the other hand, it may well be that an effort to take into account the singular causal statements of quantum physicists would lead either to an amendment of Thesis I or to the proposal of two distinct definitions of "because," one for deterministic and another for indeterministic contexts. Although the language of quantum physics is well beyond the scope of this study, it is my impression that the considerations which might be adduced by a philosopher of quantum physics in favor of an amendment of Thesis I are quite different from those that might be used by a philosopher of history who does not deny determinism in human affairs but merely asserts the difficulty of establishing deterministic laws because of the complexity of human affairs. Such a philosopher may allow that we often offer statistical support for a singular explanatory statement which is equivalent to the statement that there is a *strict* explanatory deductive argument of the kind described in Thesis I.

If it be asked now whether I believe that there are *some* historical contexts of the form "A is a contributory cause of C" which *must* be analyzed in the manner of what I have called Thesis I', I must say that I do not know of any. I grant that in history a large number of singular explanatory statements—possibly all, for all I know—will be supported by the citation of statistical evidence, but then it is also true that in ordinary life at least a large number of singular explanatory statements about purely physical events will be supported by the citation of statistical evidence, as we saw in connection with the lighting of the match. But it does not follow from this that the truth-conditions of such singular statements must, so to speak, reflect that appeal to statistics in the manner of Thesis I'. Moreover if one thinks, as I do, that the expression "is a contributory cause of" is used univocally throughout ordinary and historical discourse, then it seems to me wiser to try to construe all contexts in which it occurs, after the fashion of Thesis I, and to account for the differences that other philosophers wish to convey in something like Thesis I' by calling attention to two different ways of supporting singular explanatory statements—deductive and inductive—and admitting that history is a domain in which the presentation of inductive evidence is most common.

JUDGMENT AND REGULARITY

However, whether we analyze singular explanatory statements in accordance with Thesis I or in accordance with its statistical analogue or in accordance with some combination of both, it is clear that even if historians cannot produce full-fledged deductive explanations, they can support their singular explanatory statements by appealing to certain *kinds* of generalizations and relevant conditions. It may well be that the most gifted and most distinguished historians have noses that lead them to good explanations of individual and social behavior, but the task of the historian is not only to discover explanations but also to defend them. In this respect he resembles the detective, and a detective, no matter how brilliant he may be in smelling out the culprit, must supply evidence to those who may not have his kind of talent. We may illustrate this point by considering the view that a historian uses his "judgment" in explanation, and that this dispenses with the need for appealing to regularities in human behavior.

It has been maintained, for example, that the historian Trevelyan rested on his judgment in the course of an explanation of the coming of the English Revolution, and it has been suggested that his use of judgment somehow eliminated the need to rely on general knowledge—even statistical knowledge—of how people behave under certain circumstances.[18] In order to support this view, emphasis has been laid on the fact that Trevelyan at a certain point in his book *The English Revolution, 1688–1689,* after presenting the background and antecedents of the Revolution and before describing the revolt, said: "The historian must now dive into the annals of conspiracy and weigh the prospects of revolt." The word "weigh" has been underscored in an effort to call attention to the employment of judgment rather than generalizations. With this in mind, let us examine the account given by Trevelyan.

The first thing that may strike us as we read Trevelyan's study

[18] Dray, op. cit., p. 51.

with this question in mind is his indirect appeal to statistical knowledge at the very beginning of his book. In discussing the appositeness of the term "glorious" as applied to the revolution of 1688, Trevelyan says: "There is nothing specially glorious in the victory which our ancestors managed to win, with the aid of foreign arms, over an ill-advised king who forced an issue with nine-tenths of his English subjects on the fundamentals of law, politics, and religion. To have been beaten at such odds would have been national ignominy indeed."[19] This strongly suggests that Trevelyan was prepared to assert that the English people successfully revolted against their king because he antagonized them legally, politically, and theologically and because they were able to enlist the aid of foreign arms. It also suggests that if asked to defend this singular explanatory statement, he might well have appealed to a statistical generalization about the probability (odds) that a people so related to its king would successfully overthrow him. Moreover, such an analysis of Trevelyan's account of the antecedents of the revolution would make it perfectly clear that when Trevelyan spoke of *weighing* the prospects of a successful revolt at a certain point in the story, he meant estimating the statistical probabilities that a revolt would occur, given the persistent Romanism of James II, his antagonizing of Parliament, the Trial of the Bishops, the birth of his son, the attitude of Louis XIV toward the English situation, and the attitude of William of Orange. Trevelyan concluded, I suggest, that the probability was high, and used this high probability in support of a singular explanatory statement as analyzed previously in Thesis I.

A similar analysis of Trevelyan's reasoning will illuminate other causal statements in his narrative. Consider, for example, his discussion of the effect of the so-called Trial of the Seven Bishops, one of the more decisive events in his story. Like so many other historians, Trevelyan prepares us for the event he wishes to explain by describing certain general features of the country just

---

[19] G. M. Trevelyan, *The English Revolution, 1688–1689* (New York, 1938; repr. 1954), p. 9.

before the Trial. He tells us that "in the early months of 1688, the union of classes, parties and churches against the King and his Jesuit advisers was obliterating all old landmarks and superseding the feuds of Whig and Tory, Church and Dissent. These old enemies, and the great middle mass of opinion not permanently attached to either faction, now formed a solid phalanx in defense of the Constitution and the Protestant religion of England. As much as any political movement recorded in our annals, it was a moral revival."[20] Trevelyan also tells us that "if principle was enlisted against James so too was prejudice. The violent anti-clerical passions of the English mob, easily aroused to burn the chapels of Puritan dissenters, regarded Jesuits and the Roman worship with even more furious hatred and fear."[21] And then, using a thermodynamic metaphor with which we are so familiar, Trevelyan says: "The political temperature of English opinion in the summer of 1688 would certainly have sufficed to restrain either Charles I or Charles II. But James II, obstinate in the belief that his father had fallen because he made concessions, and himself surrounded by flatterers who deceived him in order to cling to his offices, not only held his course but flung into the loaded mine the lighted match of the Trial of the Seven Bishops."[22]

What was this match and what was its effect? It will suffice to say that seven bishops of the Church of England were tried for failure to read in their churches James's Declaration of Indulgences, in which he suspended, among other things, all laws injurious to either Catholic or Protestant Dissenters. The trial's effect—the explosion—is reported in Trevelyan's statement that "the sight of seven prelates of blameless character and known loyalty to James (five of them were afterwards Jacobites!) entering the Tower as prisoners and standing in the dock as culprits, showed as nothing else would have done that the most revered and the most loyal subjects in the land would be broken if they refused

---

[20] Ibid., pp. 84–85.
[21] Ibid., p. 86.
[22] Ibid., pp. 86–87.

to become active parties to the King's illegal designs. If the Bishops suffered, who could hope to escape the royal vengeance?"[23]

Although reference to the loaded mine and the match is metaphorical, it would appear that Trevelyan thought that the logical relation between the situation as he describes it, the Trial, and the public response is the same as that between the mine, the match, and the explosion. Just as we need a law to get us logically from the loaded mine and the lighted match to the explosion, so we need one to get us from Trevelyan's background and the trial to the public's response. And if we turn to one of Trevelyan's more philosophical writings, we find him explicitly adopting a conception of explanation which is quite regularistic in tone. Speaking of Carlyle, he says: "His explanation of the Revolution is the simple one that, when people have been grossly misgoverned for centuries and their institutions are thoroughly rotten, there must be a terrific, blind explosion some day. That was a truth which Burke had not taken into account, a truth to be fully confirmed by the subsequent work of de Tocqueville, Taine, and others on the Ancien Regime."[24] One feels that Trevelyan would not have objected if his version of Carlyle's explanation had been presented in the singular explanatory statement "The French Revolution broke out because the French people had been grossly misgoverned for centuries within the framework of rotten institutions"; nor would he have had cause to object if a philosopher were to say that this singular statement is true if and only if there exists an explanatory deductive argument containing the statement "The French people had been grossly misgoverned for centuries within the framework of rotten institutions" as a premise and the statement "The French Revolution broke out" as conclusion.

It is possible to say, of course, that Trevelyan's explanation of the public reaction to the Trial of the Seven Bishops required judgment on his part, just as his weighing of the prospects of revolt did. But what does weighing the prospects consist of in such

[23] Ibid., p. 90.
[24] G. M. Trevelyan, "Bias in History," *History*, XXXII (N.S.), 8.

a case? Is it radically different from the case where we find a loaded mine, throw a match into it, and weigh the prospects of explosion? I think not and therefore feel that a reading of Trevelyan does not show that the regularity theory fails to cover his reasoning. "What would you expect in a situation of the kind I have described?" Trevelyan seems to ask. And when he asks, "What would you expect?" he does not mean to ask a psychological question about his reader. He means to ask him what ought to be predicted as the outcome of such a situation in the light of general knowledge. That the whole picture is more vague than it is in the case of the explosion or the cracked automobile radiator, I do not deny. But the intent of the historian in such cases is not radically different from that of the natural scientist who makes singular explanatory statements. Both of them make statements which imply the existence of explanatory deductive arguments, both of them try to produce evidence for the statement that such an argument exists. The historian ordinarily uses probability generalizations in support of his singular explanatory statements, but this, as I have pointed out, does not imply that he must analyze the word "because" differently in these contexts. It means, of course, that his evidence for his explanations is not as good as it would be if he were to produce a deductive argument, but this is what everyone feels about countless historical explanations, and it is a virtue of our analysis that it squares with this feeling.

SPECULATION REVISITED

Readers who still remember my sharp treatment of certain speculative philosophers of history will recall how I criticized a theorist like Marx, who asserted merely that *there exists* a functional relation between certain variables, who failed to state a historical law but merely gave us to understand that there was one connecting his variables. I compared Marx invidiously with Galileo, Boyle, Newton, and all the rest of the scientific greats because they not only told us *that* their variables were connected but also *how* they were connected. Yet I have maintained that the singular explanatory statements of sober, modest, unpretentious historians will be true if and only if *there are* explanatory deductive arguments of a certain kind: and I have said that a singular explanatory statement may be asserted as true even if laws cannot be produced. Is there any inconsistency here?

I do not think so. If a man says that he is presenting a law but does not, then he is more subject to criticism than a man who does *not* say that he is presenting a law and does not. When we examine the former's so-called laws and find that they are not laws at all, that they tell us, for example, that the material conditions of life are in general *connected* with the philosophy of a period without telling us how they are connected, we see that his laws are not adequate from the point of view of science. But if a person asserts a singular explanatory statement without producing a law and then presents no more than inductive evidence or good reasons in favor of the hypothesis that a law of the requisite kind exists, he is not misleading us into thinking that he can produce a knock-down, full-fledged deductive explanation of individual events of a certain kind. I do not mean to imply that all so-called modest historians, when they assert their singular explanatory statements, present enough inductive evidence of the kind that they ought to present, but there is a difference between failing to produce what is required for the establishment of one's singular explanatory statement and wrongly giving the impression that one can present the grand laws of the speculative philosophy of history. The historian's failure to produce evidence of the requisite kind for his singular explanatory statements may often be the result of his failure to see that he is committed to the existence of laws, and this is a criticizable lapse; but it should be distinguished from a pretentious claim to have formulated laws that turn out to be nonlaws.

Furthermore, the historian who takes seriously the views of the regularist is likely to use terms that are less opaque than the metaphorical expressions "copy," "mirror," "reflect," "is rooted in," "is reared upon." When such a historian comes to see that he is committed to the existence of laws, those laws, if they are discovered or approximated, are not likely to be couched in terms of unilluminating metaphors. And finally, the historian who absorbs the moral of regularism will be properly skeptical of the possibility of deducing historical laws from cosmology, metaphysics, or epistemology, because the aim of the regularist as regularist is not to construct another speculative system of history but to avoid mysterious ties, occult powers, rational connections, and the need for unchecked judgment.

IV

Causal Interpretation

Were we interested only in the notion of a contributory cause, our task of analyzing singular causal statements would be over by now. The doctrine of existential regularism, instead of serving as an introduction to the problem of analyzing such statements, would be close to the last word on the subject. However, it is not, if only because historians do not limit themselves to claiming that a given cause is merely contributory. They often elevate a contributory cause to special status, either by calling it the decisive contributory cause of the event or state of affairs they are trying to explain or by simply calling it *the* cause, and it is now our task to say something about this process of elevation. Since historians use many different terms when they single out a contributory cause, we must be clear about which sort of singling out we are trying to analyze. They may call a contributory cause the most important, the main, the principal, the chief, the real, or the decisive cause, and it is not obvious that all of these distinguishing phrases are used equivalently, or even that all of them are used with an established intention that might be expected to yield to philosophical analysis. For these reasons we shall focus on the terms "the cause," "the real cause," and "the decisive cause," for they seem to be used equivalently in many contexts and they do seem amenable to a kind of philosophical analysis that can withstand confrontation with actual historical usage.

Let us use the phrase "causal interpretation" in order to refer to the process of calling one contributory cause *the* cause or the decisive cause, and let us observe parenthetically that history is not the only discipline in which causal interpretation goes on. When a physician diagnoses the cause of a man's ailment and an engineer states the cause of an airplane crash, they, as much as the historian, engage in causal interpretation. In all such cases of causal interpretation we may raise a question as to the general grounds on which the interpreter defends his interpretation. More specifically, we may ask for the necessary and sufficient condition for being the decisive cause among contributory causes. In order to state this problem in more formal terms, we may return to the schema presented earlier in which "*D*" represents that necessary and sufficient condition:

SCHEMA I: A is the decisive cause of *C* if and only if:
  (1) A is a contributory cause of *C*, and
  (2) A has feature *D*.

If one looks at the problem in this way, one may ask a number of philosophical questions. First of all, is there exactly one distinguishing feature that figures in the defense of *all* statements of the form "A is the decisive cause of *C*"? And if there is more than one, is there one which is nevertheless employed in supporting the vast majority of such statements? If the answer to this last question is affirmative, what feature is most frequently employed? Furthermore, is it factual or evaluative—i.e., is it like "red," "crossed the Rubicon," and "English," or is it more like "good," "bad," "right," and "wrong?" We may also ask whether the distinguishing feature of *the* cause is absolute or relative, in other words whether it is like "to the right of" rather than like "5 inches long." If it is relative, clause (2) in Schema I, as we shall see, will have the form "A stands in relation D to m," and the *analysandum*, "A is the decisive cause of C," will have to be expanded so as to make explicit this relativity to another variable, "m." Finally, if the distinguishing feature or relation referred to in clause (2) is that which is used in the vast majority of cases in which *the* cause is singled out, we may ask what other properties are similarly employed and in what contexts they are employed.

It should be realized that we are now no longer concerned with the problem of what it is to be a contributory cause, and whatever the answers to the questions we have just asked, we shall have the ground provided by Thesis I beneath us. Apart from the doubts raised earlier about whether there is a difference between a law and an explanatory law, it is a factual task to decide whether a cause is contributory because it is a factual task to determine whether the kind of explanatory deductive argument described in Thesis I exists. Our main concern in this chapter will be the extent to which we can remain just as factual when we start choosing among the candidates provided by Thesis I. The nominating procedure outlined in Thesis I may be as factual as can be, but what about the electing procedure that historians go through when they pick out the decisive cause?

In order to present some conception of the issues involved as well as to present answers to some of the questions raised earlier, I shall in this chapter critically examine a number of defective theories of *the* cause and also defend what I think is a satisfactory theory. Briefly stated, that theory is that on most occasions when historians assert that a contributory cause is the (decisive) cause, (a) that cause is the abnormal contributory cause, (b) it is sometimes selected from a point of view which another investigator may not share, and (c) we cannot always establish on absolute grounds that one of these points of view is superior to others. Because of its stress on the abnormality of the selected contributory cause I shall call this doctrine "abnormalism." And although abnormalism has, in one form or another, been advanced by other thinkers, some of its advocates have not, in my opinion, laid sufficient stress on point (c) above.

In order to clarify what is involved in maintaining abnormalism I shall critically examine several other views, some of which are closer to it than others. I shall argue in section 1 against the view that the decisive cause is selected capriciously. In section 2 I shall present the case for abnormalism. In section 3 I shall show the defects of a variety of metaphysical absolutism, according to which the distinguishing feature of the cause is intrinsic to the cause. Specifically, I shall consider the view that the distinguishing feature consists in the cause's falling into some metaphysical category as traditionally conceived. In section 4 I shall consider the view that the distinguishing feature of the cause is the fact that it is a necessary condition in addition to being one of the conditions jointly sufficient for the event or state to be explained. In section 5 I shall criticize a psychological or epistemological view which, like abnormalism, appears to assert that the statement of the cause is factual and relative in character, but which is in other ways inadequate. In section 6 a similar argument will be leveled against what might be called a technological or pragmatic ground for singling out the cause. In section 7 I shall argue against one version of the view that the cause is selected because it has some value-property, where a value-property is distinguished by advocates of this view from a property whose presence is detected by factual investigation. This moralistic view, as it may be called, is different from abnormalism in a way that should not be obscured by the fact that according to abnormalism as I conceive it we sometimes make a value judgment in arriving at the point of view from which a certain selection of the cause is made. Finally, in section 8 I shall argue that whereas on some occasions when historians use the phrase "the cause" they may distinguish the cause on moral grounds, this is not a typical use of the phrase and might well be abandoned in the interests of candor and clarity.

1. THE ROAD TO CAPRICE

One of the most radical views on this subject is that the selection of the decisive cause is capricious and arbitrary. How have philosophers and historians come to this view? We can distinguish more than one road to this position, but one of the most influential takes its point of departure from the contention that as soon as we call a cause of an event *the* cause of that event, we speak inaccurately or falsify the facts. Such a view may be found at certain places in the writings of John Stuart Mill,[1] where he rests on the assumption that *the* cause of an event is what he called the *whole* cause, and where he says in effect that a person who presents *a* cause which is less than the whole cause and calls it *the* cause is speaking falsely. One of Mill's examples is that of a man who imbibes some mercury, goes out of doors, and catches a cold. Here Mill assumes that an explanatory deductive argument like the following exists:

> Whoever imbibes mercury and goes out of doors,
> catches cold.
> Jones imbibed mercury.
> Jones went out of doors.
> Therefore,
> Jones caught cold.

But, Mill continues, if such an argument is offered in support of our explanation as presented in a singular statement, it is, strictly speaking, false to say "The cause of Jones' catching cold was his going out of doors" and also false to say "The cause of Jones' catching cold was his having imbibed mercury." These statements are false because neither one of them presents the *whole* cause of Jones's catching cold, whereas the statement "The cause of Jones' catching cold was his going out of doors after having imbibed mercury" is true. We may say that on Mill's view both of the false

[1] *System of Logic*, Bk. III, ch. V. sec. 3.

statements involve interpretation, whereas the true one does not.

Having argued that interpretation involves falsification or inaccuracy, Mill then says that the decision to identify the cause of Jones's cold either as his imbibing of mercury or as his going out of doors is arbitrary and capricious. Mill points out first of all that men usually fail to state the whole cause in what he called "common parlance" by contrast to what he called "scientific discourse," and secondly, that when they use common parlance, they not only falsely speak *as if* something was *the* cause when it is not, but do so in accordance with no discernible rule. In order to appreciate this point of view one must realize that even if ordinary men always speak falsely when they call something *the* cause which is not the entire cause, they could conceivably speak falsely in accordance with a rule. There might be a method in the madness of their false and inaccurate speech. And yet it is precisely the existence of such a rule and method that Mill denies in one part of his writing on the subject. He says that when men in common parlance call *a* cause *the* cause, we cannot formulate a criterion on the basis of which they do so. He held that the decision to call *a* cause *the* cause of a given event will vary from person to person and from circumstance to circumstance in an unregulated way, so that the philosopher who studies the speech and writing of persons making such assertions will be unable to produce a rule that they follow. For example, Mill argues that we cannot say that men are governed in common parlance by the rule that they should select the causally relevant event that took place last—the going out of doors in the case of the man who caught the cold, or the taking of arsenic in the case of the man who died. Mill correctly points out that sometimes we select not an event but a so-called standing condition like the man's state of health when giving "the" cause of his death, and yet we do not always call a standing condition *the* cause either. On the basis of such considerations Mill argues that there is no factor which could not under some circumstance be called *the* cause of an event by some man or other. One person's interest, or what strikes him at the moment as the most conspicuous factor in the situation, might lead him to say that the cause of Jones's cold was his taking of mercury, whereas another person's interest might lead him to say that the cause of Jones's cold was his having gone out of doors. From the point of view of scientific discourse both would be speaking falsely, and if anyone were to try to give one of them the palm for speaking correctly in accordance with some commonly accepted rule that guided common parlance in these matters, he would not be able to formulate such a rule.

In order to understand the basic philosophical problem in- volved, we must distinguish the following questions: (1) Are all statements which rest on causal interpretation false? (2) Can different historians, without contradicting each other, interpret *the* cause of one historical event or state differently? I shall argue that the answer to the first question is negative by showing that Mill was wrong in identifying *the* cause as it is conceived in either ordinary language or history with *the whole* cause, and that the answer to the second question is affirmative. But having answered these questions in this way, I shall be obliged to face two that are more difficult: (3) How do we identify *the* cause if we refuse to identify it with the whole Millian cause? (4) Even if we adopt a view of *the* cause which is different from that of Mill, can we avoid the sort of caprice and arbitrariness of which he speaks if we also admit that what is *the* cause of an event to one historian can be its "mere condition" or occasion to another? In answering questions (3) and (4) I shall try to show that although causal interpretation is less anarchic and capricious than Mill supposed, we cannot eliminate a certain kind of relativity in many causal interpretations. The historian must always adopt a point of view in selecting the cause of an event, but his adoption of that point of view cannot always be justified by what some might call scientific considerations.

There is no doubt that historians sometimes speak as if they agreed with Mill in thinking that the only statements of *the* cause that are strictly true are those that speak the whole causal truth. As we have seen, Pieter Geyl has complained of the effort to explain the rise of Dutch prosperity by saying something like "Holland achieved success because it was challenged by a harsh environment." Geyl exclaims: " 'Oh land wrung from the waves!' Every Dutchman has heard innumerable times his people's sterling qualities explained from their age-long struggle with the water. And nobody will contest that here is one factor in the building up of our special type of society." But Geyl insists that this is only *one among many such factors*. He continues:

Within the Netherlands community the form peculiar to Holland (the Western seaboard province of which Toynbee is obviously thinking) cannot be regarded as original. If one looks a little more closely, one will observe that within the European and even within the Netherlands cultural area the rise of Holland was fairly late, and this no doubt as a result of these very conditions created by sea and rivers. If in the end it overcame these conditions, it was not without the assistance of the surrounding higher forms of civilization (even the Romans and their dyke-building had an important share in making the region habitable). But can even after that initial stage the continued struggle with the water be decisive in explaining the later prosperity and cultural fecundity of the country? Is it not indispensable to mention the excellence of the soil, once it had become possible to make use of it? and above all the situation, which promoted the rise of shipping and of a large international commerce? Was the case of Holland then *wholly due* [my italics] to hard conditions after all? Is it right to isolate that factor from among the multifarious complexity of reality and to suppress the favoring factors?[2]

Geyl's answer to his concluding rhetorical question is negative because, it would appear, he thinks that the only thing that may be called *the* cause or the decisive cause is the whole cause. What is to be said of this essentially Millian view of causation in history? Since our main concern is with historical causation, it is imperative to point out that even if one is sometimes able to state the whole Millian cause of a physical or chemical event, it is rare for a

[2] Pieter Geyl, "Toynbee's System of Civilizations," in *Toynbee and History*, ed. M. F. Ashley Montagu (Boston, 1956), pp. 46-47.

historian to be able to state it in the case of an event like the American Civil War, the English Civil War, the French Revolution, or the New Deal. Therefore, if Geyl is complaining about a failure to state the whole cause, he is applying a standard that a historian hardly ever meets. Let us leave aside Toynbee, who, of course, may think that a harsh challenge is in general sufficient in itself to bring about a successful response. If we concentrate on the views of a more cautious historian who might assert that *the* cause of Holland's success was the challenge of the sea, we must recognize that to accuse such an historian of speaking falsely simply because there are other factors that contributed to the rise of Holland is to use an argument which, if applied even to the explanation of natural phenomena, would lead us to label as false any explanation in which it was said, for example, that *the* cause of a particular explosion was the dropping of a spark. The fact is that ordinary men and historians in analogous situations often call an item *the* cause of an event even when they know that it is not the only factor contributing to the event. Moreover, they regard such statements of the cause as true and accurate.

Mill insists that *the* cause is the whole cause, but when we look at the language of those whose work Mill is logically analyzing, we find that his philosophical theory forces him to conclude that in an enormous number of cases in which historians use the concept he is analyzing they speak falsely. Can he maintain his philosophical theory in the face of results which are so much out of accord with our normal conception of historical language? No general theory will tell us how to answer such a question, but I think there is something wrong about a philosophical theory which forces us to say that virtually all explanatory statements that are made by historians are false. I conclude, therefore, that Mill and Geyl are wrong if they identify the relation of being *the* cause with the relation of being the whole cause. In order to give further support to this conclusion I shall try to show later how to identify *the* cause, but before doing so I shall first distinguish the whole cause and *a* cause of an event or state.

Thesis I states that A is a contributory cause of C if and only if there exists an explanatory deductive argument containing "A" as a premise and "C" as conclusion. But, it might be asked, what relation holds between the conjunction of *all* the statements of initial conditions in a supporting explanatory deductive argument and the statement "C?" The answer is that such a conjunction states the whole cause of C as Mill conceived it. Thus the ignition of a pile of TNT might be a contributory cause of its exploding, and so might the dryness of the TNT, whereas the ignition and dryness together might constitute the whole cause. But having distinguished these two relations—*being a cause of* and *being the whole cause of*—can we distinguish a third which is that of *being the cause of*? Mill's answer, as I understand it, is negative because he identifies *being the whole cause of* and *being the cause of*, whereas I believe that in historical language we can distinguish reference to a relation which lies, so to speak, in between *being a cause of* and *being the whole cause of*, and this intermediate relation may be called the relation of *being the cause of*. For example, when Alexander Stephens asserts that "the real cause of" the Civil War was the North's violation of the South's constitutional rights and that "slavery so-called" was merely the occasion or the "main exciting proximate cause,"[3] I think he meant that one of the contributory causes which was not the whole cause in Mill's sense was *the* cause of the Civil War. Hence the philosophical problem is to state what the distinguishing feature of such a contributory cause is. To return to our Schema I, our task is to say what feature or relation should be referred to in the second clause of "A is the (decisive) cause of C if and only if: (1) A is a contributory cause of C and (2) A has feature D," on the assumption that D is not the feature of being the whole cause as previously defined. Conceiving the problem of characterizing causal interpretation in this way, I now turn to one of the most plausible

[3] Quoted in H. K. Beale, "What Historians Have Said About the Causes of the Civil War," in *Theory and Practice in Historical Study*, Social Science Research Council, Bull. 54 (New York, 1946), p. 62.

efforts to solve it for a very large class of statements in which historians say that something is the cause of something else.

2. ABNORMALISM

The sociologist MacIver and the philosophical lawyers Hart and Honoré have argued that the cause of an event is what Mac-Iver calls an "interference with normal conditions."[4] On this view, we usually seek to explain facts that are abnormal or unusual, facts that are departures from the usual or normal course of events, like accidents, catastrophes, disasters. We try to explain a given train wreck because trains are not usually wrecked. If trains were commonly wrecked, this view seems to imply, we would not seek to explain the wreck of a particular train. And given the fact that a train wreck is unusual, we can see at once, it is argued, why the fact cited as the cause cannot be a normal or usual feature of the operation of trains or of some particular train. The basic point is that according to this theory the cause of an abnormal event is itself abnormal.

The plausibility of abnormalism may be seen more concretely by turning to the writings of a historian whom we have often mentioned. Pirenne's explanation of the collapse of what he calls the "Mediterranean Commonwealth" is one in which the Moslem invasion in the seventh and eighth centuries is said to be *the* cause. He thinks of this collapse as an unusual or abnormal event in the history of Europe, and for that reason thinks it demands explanation. Therefore, the opening chapter of Pirenne's *Medieval Cities* is devoted to showing the continuity in European life from ancient times down to the eighth century, when the overthrow occurred. Culturally, politically, and economically, he argues, an uninterrupted unity persisted on the shores of the Mediterranean, which was the center of gravity of European thought and culture. Moreover, one of Pirenne's most important efforts is to show that the

---

[4] R. M. MacIver, *Social Causation* (Boston, 1952), p. 186; H. L. A. Hart and A. M. Honoré, *Causation in the Law* (Oxford, 1959), pp. 31–38.

invasions of the barbaric tribes—which had, of course, preceded the Moslem invasion—did *not* destroy the civilization of antiquity. But what survived the Germans, he maintains, did not survive the Moslems. On the shores of the Mediterranean, he states:

Social life, in its fundamental characteristics, had been the same; religion, the same; customs and ideas, the same or very nearly so. The invasion of the barbarians from the North had modified nothing essential in that situation. But now, all of a sudden, the very lands where civilization had been born were torn away; the Cult of the Prophet was substituted for the Christian Faith, Moslem law for Roman law, the Arab tongue for the Greek and the Latin tongue. The Mediterranean had been a Roman lake; it now became, for the most part, a Moslem lake. From this time on it separated, instead of uniting, the East and the West of Europe. The tie which was still binding the Byzantine Empire to the Germanic kingdoms of the West was broken.[5]

Such an explanation has the same form as the very homely one in which a woman says that the cause of her husband's attack of indigestion was his eating parsnips.[6] The husband is the analogue of the Mediterranean Commonwealth, his indigestion is the analogue of the collapse of the Commonwealth, and his eating of parsnips is the analogue of the Moslem invasion. The indigestion and the collapse are unusual events and their causes are also unusual events. Thesis I permits us to say that a contributory cause of the man's indigestion was his eating of parsnips, and it also permits us to say that the Moslem invasion was a contributory cause of the collapse of the Mediterranean Commonwealth, on the assumption that appropriate explanatory deductive arguments exist. And if either the woman or Pirenne were to try, no doubt they would be able to present other items, each of which would be called a contributory cause—if not *the* cause—of the indigestion or the collapse of the Commonwealth. But when called upon to

[5] Henri Pirenne, *Medieval Cities* (3d rev. prntg.; Princeton, N.J., 1939), pp. 24–25.
[6] Hart and Honoré, op. cit., pp. 33–34.

distinguish the eating of parsnips from these other contributory causes, the woman—so the advocate of abnormalism maintains— would, if she understood what she was doing, say that it was the abnormal one among them, and Pirenne says the same thing about the Moslem invasion.

In addition to fitting the use of the expression "is the cause of," as employed by Pirenne in the above typical historical explanation, the doctrine of abnormalism leads us to view statements of the form "A is the cause of C" as supportable in a wholly empirical way, for it claims as against the ethical view to be examined later that statistical abnormality rather than departure from any moral norm properly identifies the cause. Abnormality so conceived is a descriptive characteristic of the cause, for when we say that the cause of the flowers' dying was the failure of the gardener to water them, we fix on his failure as the cause on the ground that he did not do what he usually does, or what gardeners usually do, and not on the ground that he violated a moral obligation, even though he may have violated a moral obligation.

The advocate of abnormalism is conscious of the need to protect his theory against the charge that *the* cause is picked out in a capricious way. And therefore a subtle defense of his theory requires an acknowledgment of the fact that sometimes there is a certain kind of relativity in the selection of *the* cause, that what one investigator properly cites as the cause of a given event may not be properly cited by another.[7] Although this might seem to be an admission that Mill was right, certain advocates of abnormalism correctly perceive that the acknowledgment of relativity is not necessarily an admission that the cause is picked out capriciously. Indeed they hold that the only way in which an objectionable sort of caprice may be eliminated is by making room for relativity.

But what is this kind of relativity that will allow us to say that sometimes one man's cause is another man's mere condition, and

[7] Ibid., p. 33.

yet not drive us back to the theory that the cause is picked out capriciously and arbitrarily? In trying to answer this question, we shall be led to see how the abnormalist may avoid saying that the cause is selected capriciously, but also how he cannot avoid the admission that a causal interpretation or statement of the cause is sometimes made from a *point of view* which cannot be justified by some criterion or standard beyond itself. The advocate of abnormalism is led to insist upon an element of relativity in his conception of the cause because he recognizes that when one says that the event to be explained is *abnormal*, one must say *in what way* it is abnormal, and similarly for the cause. Moreover, one and the same event, like the man's attack of indigestion, may be regarded as abnormal in different ways, and therefore will be given different explanations by different people who do regard it as abnormal in these different ways. Thus, "A woman married to a man who suffers from an ulcerated condition of the stomach might identify eating parsnips as the cause of his indigestion: a doctor might identify the ulcerated condition of his stomach as the cause and the meal as a mere occasion."[8] Here two different true conclusions about *the* cause of the indigestion are possible because of the different ways in which two people may regard the same man. The man's wife thinks of him as normally getting along without indigestion even though he has ulcers, and she therefore regards the eating of parsnips as the cause of his indigestion. But the physician, who is professionally interested in "diseases or deviations from the standard physical condition of human beings," will regard the ulcers as the cause.

Two analogously different approaches are possible in the case of the illustration from Pirenne. Another historian might offer an explanation of the collapse of the Mediterranean Commonwealth analogous to that which the physician gives. Such a historian might try to show what there was about the Mediterranean Com-

---

[8] Ibid. On the difference between cause and occasion see also Sidney Hook's contribution to *Theory and Practice in Historical Study*, p. 115.

monwealth which made it, or allowed it, to succumb to the Moslem invasion, and hence regard the cause of the collapse not as the Moslem invasion but as some feature of Europe analogous to the ulcerated condition of the man's stomach. Two such approaches are also possible when we try to explain the collapse of the Roman empire. Bury thought that a conjunction of several contingencies, as he called them, constituted the cause of the collapse; and this conjunction of contingencies resembles in logical status the Moslem invasion and the man's eating of parsnips. But another historian, or a sociologist, might well think that a certain feature of the Roman empire in that period constituted *the* cause of the collapse, and its being in decline he might regard as the counterpart of the man's having ulcers. In that case, the decline might be regarded as *the* cause of the collapse by a historian who would regard the contingencies to which Bury refers as like those that many "healthy" societies withstand all the time. In short, what the historian regards as the abnormal antecedent, and hence as the cause, may depend on the manner in which he looks at the subject under investigation.

Another kind of example of the same sort of relativity may be seen in the study of revolutions. Marxist historians think that revolutions come about as the result of the combination of two factors, a revolutionary situation and a revolutionary party. Therefore, a Marxist political leader who looks at a successful revolution in his own country may say that the cause of it was the activity of his own revolutionary party, whereas a visiting student of revolutions, whose head is filled with revolutions that failed when parties acted prematurely, may come to the conclusion that the cause of the revolution under consideration was the presence of a revolutionary situation. The first is thinking as the woman does about her husband's indigestion; the second is thinking along the logical lines of the physician and wondering what feature of the country distinguished it from other countries in which revolutionary parties failed to make revolutions. Abnormalism allows for both kinds of explanation.

This may be seen in abstract terms by thinking of the two singular statements of *the* cause as supported by one explanatory deductive argument which I shall call (B) for future reference:

(B): Whatever is P and R is Q.
    a is P.
    a is R.
    Therefore,
    a is Q.

Now the reason why one person may say truly that a's being P was the cause of a's being Q is that he may ask, "Why does a have the property Q when a is R and most R's are not Q?" The point is that a's being P is what makes the difference between a and most things which have R. And an analogous thing can be said in the case of the person who may say truly that a's being R was the cause of a's being Q. Throughout, of course, we assume that there is one "thing under inquiry," to use the phrase of Hart and Honoré—namely, a—and that "normal conditions . . . are those conditions which are present as part of the usual state or mode of operation of the thing under inquiry".[9] But—and this is crucial— we may in certain circumstances regard a either as a P or as an R. If we regard it as a P we think the cause of its possession of Q is its possession of R, whereas if we regard it as an R, we think of the cause of its possession of Q as its possession of P.

This possibility of viewing an individual in different ways is often present when the historian is considering a nation. When Marx sought an explanation of the triumph of Louis Bonaparte, he observed: "It is not enough to say, as the French do, that their nation has been taken by surprise. A nation and a woman are not forgiven the unguarded hour in which the first adventurer that came along could violate them. The riddle is not solved by such terms of speech, but merely formulated in another way. It remains to be explained how a nation of thirty-six millions can be surprised and delivered unresisting into captivity by three high-class

[9] Hart and Honoré, op. cit., p. 32.

swindlers."[10] Marx thought that an episode in the prior history of France was not the cause of the coup, but if countries like France in a statable respect had rarely been the scene of such coups, it would have been perfectly correct to refer to an episode as the unusual event that led to the coup. On the other hand, of course, Marx was justified in asking why France was led into captivity by three swindlers, when it was a nation of thirty-six millions, and when such nations are rarely led into captivity by three swindlers. In answer to *this* question one might point out how France was different from other nations in, say, social structure, or economy, or degree of political stability, and hence present a state rather than episode as the cause.

We may now ask two questions about this possibility of regarding more than one contributory cause as the cause and about this possibility of regarding the thing under inquiry in different ways. (1) How is *this* variety of *the* cause related to the variety of which Mill spoke? (2) Can one in general say of two ways of regarding the thing under inquiry, i.e., of two ways that lead to different statements of *the* cause, that one is absolutely superior to another? Let us consider these questions separately.

(1) Shall we say that Mill's view, according to which the selection of one antecedent as the cause is arbitrary and capricious, comes to the same thing as the theory which says that we appeal to the concept of abnormality in picking out *the* cause, because both allow the same amount of variety in the statement of *the* cause of a given event? Does abnormalism, even though it is distinguished from Mill's view by introducing the criterion of abnormality, permit us to come to essentially the same general conclusion as Mill does when he says that "however numerous the conditions may be, there is hardly any of them which may not, according to the purpose of our immediate discourse,"[11] be called *the* cause? For how, it may be asked, did it become possible for the doctor to say, and properly so, that the cause of the man's

---

[10] Karl Marx, *Selected Works*, (Moscow and Leningrad, 1935), II, 321.
[11] *System of Logic*, Bk. III, ch. V, sec. 3.

attack of indigestion was different from the cause that was properly given by the wife? The answer is that the doctor approached
the situation in a different way, which is to say that he took the
attack to be unusual in a way that permitted him to present his
different item as the cause. Well, the argument may run, given any
one of the contributory causes of an event, there will *always* be a
way of looking at the thing under inquiry which will allow us to
call that one of the contributory causes *the* cause, i.e., to view it as
the abnormal antecedent.

To answer this objection, let us suppose that the event or state
of affairs to be explained is the fact that *a* is *Q*. And let us suppose
that there exists an explanatory deductive argument of the form
(B) above. In order for the mentioned objection to be justified,
it should be correct, from some point of view, to present the fact
that *a* is *P*, and from another, the fact that *a* is *R* as *the* cause of
the fact that *a* is *Q in all cases of this kind*. But consider what this
implies. It implies that for every explanatory deductive argument
like (B), there is a way of regarding *a*, say as *P*, such that most
P's are not *Q*, but such that all things that are *P* and *R* are *Q*; and
also that there is a way of regarding *a*, say as *R*, such that most
R's are not *Q*. Thus, we should be able to ask, "Why did *a*—a dry
stick of dynamite—explode when most dry sticks of dynamite do
not explode?" and get as the answer: "The cause—the difference-
maker—was the fact that *a* was brought into contact with a lit
match." And we should also be able to ask, "Why did *a*—a thing
brought into contact with a lit match—explode when most things
brought into contact with lit matches do not explode?" and get as
the answer: "The cause—the difference-maker—was the fact that
a was a dry stick of dynamite." And we should be able to say
something like this about *all* such explanatory deductive arguments, in which case any statement of the initial conditions in the
argument might be regarded as a statement of *the* cause of the
event to be explained.

Can this be shown generally? I do not think so. If we imagine
that the singular statement of the cause is supported by the exist-

ence of exactly one explanatory deductive argument which we can produce, we can see why it is not always possible to be so free in the selection of *the* cause as might be thought by the objector who argues that abnormalism and Mill's doctrine come to the same thing in the end. For suppose that the supporting explanatory deductive argument has the form of (B) above. It may well be the case that whereas most P's are not Q, i.e., that it is unusual for a P to be Q, it is simply not true that most R's are not Q. In that case we may well ask, "Why does a have property Q when a is P and most P's are not Q?" and get as an answer, "Because a is R." On the other hand, if it is false to say that most R's are not Q, we cannot ask the question, "Why does a have the property Q, when a is R and most R's are not Q?" The point is that only sometimes will a given explanatory deductive argument allow an option as to the manner in which the subject of inquiry may be regarded as abnormal, and hence an option as to which of the statements of initial conditions may be thought of as stating the cause. Yet it is only when such an option is possible that one has a choice as to the manner in which the subject, a, may be regarded, and hence a choice as to which statement of initial conditions shall be regarded as stating *the* cause of the fact that a is Q.

This is a convenient place to call attention to an illuminating relationship between the view that the cause is always identical with the whole cause in Mill's sense, and the view that it is the abnormal antecedent. The argument that I have labeled (B) a few pages back may be construed as having a universal premise which reads: "For every x, if x is P and R, x is Q." The purpose of formulating it in this way is to call attention to the fact that "x" may be thought of as ranging over a large class of entities called the universe of discourse, and in the present case we may think of the universe of discourse as the class of all physical objects. Now, in order to show the similarity and difference between the view that *the cause* of a's being Q is the whole cause of a's being Q, and the view that the cause may, as it were, be less than the whole cause, it is well to bear in mind that it is probably always possible from the point of view of abnormalism to ask the question, "Why does *a* have the property *Q*, when *a* is a member of the class of physical objects and most physical objects are not *Q*?" It is probably always possible because of the enormity of the class of physical objects by comparison to the classes corresponding to terms like "*Q*" whose applicability to object *a* we might wish to explain. For example, most physical objects do not explode, so it seems perfectly all right from a very abstract point of view to ask of *a:* "Why did *a* explode when *a* is a physical object and most physical objects do not explode?" and get an answer which refers to what Mill conceives of as the whole cause. The physical object *a* exploded because it was TNT, dry, and ignited, it might be said.

Once we see this connection between *the* cause and the *whole* cause we can also see why the notion that they are identical in all contexts is excessively restrictive. The statement of the cause which is appropriate when the subject under inquiry is viewed as a member of the class of physical objects is only one statement of the cause among many that are possible. Moreover, historians are rarely interested in finding out the cause of the behavior of an entity when the entity is regarded merely as a member of the universe of discourse so conceived, and that is why the cause is for them rarely the whole cause. In any case, regarding the subject of inquiry, *a*, merely as a physical object is only one among many ways of regarding *a*, and presenting the whole cause is merely a special case of presenting *the* cause.

(2) Once we see that on some occasions more than one fact may be cited as *the* cause, depending on how we regard the thing under inquiry, the question arises as to whether a historian may say on some absolute basis that one way of *regarding* the individual under inquiry is superior to another that leads to another statement of the cause. In reply I must say that I see no way of supporting the conclusion that one is absolutely superior to the other, i.e., no way that reflects our actual mode of speech on these matters. Where the fact to be explained may be regarded as unusual in two different ways because the behavior of the thing under

inquiry may be (truthfully) regarded as unusual in two different ways, then I know no absolute ground on which to support the contention that a statement of the cause which is arrived at when we regard the thing under inquiry in one way is superior to that which is arrived at when we regard the thing in another way. For example, I can see no absolute ground for saying that Pirenne's effort to find the *episode* in the career of Europe which brought about the collapse of the Mediterranean Commonwealth was an effort based on a way of regarding Europe that was inferior or superior to that employed by a historian who tried to discover what *standing condition* of Europe, by contrast to other societies, brought about the collapse of the Commonwealth. Even though the medical knowledge of a physician exceeds that of the patient's wife, I know no basis on which one can say that the question that leads him to diagnose the patient as having ulcers indicates that he is regarding the patient from a point of view that is superior to that of the wife, in that it will elicit *the* cause of the attack of indigestion whereas her question will elicit something inferior. It may be said, of course, that the diagnosis of ulcers might lead to the removal of ulcers; but then the diagnosis of parsnips might lead to the elimination of parsnips from the man's diet. The point is that there are basic differences of interest, basic differences in concern and curiosity, which may lead historians to ask different questions; and in answer to these different questions they will call different things the cause of a given event. I see no way of eliminating the possibility of this sort of variety. In particular, I see no way of appealing to something called the task or the essence of history in order to establish a hierarchy. Different historians may give different causal interpretations in certain situations because they regard the subject of their investigations differently, but there is no "criterion" that I know of for deciding that one point of view reveals *the true* cause. Moreover, there does not even seem to be a point of view which is *normally* taken by historians when the facts, so to speak, present them with a choice of point of view. And historical language is in this respect like the ordinary man's language.

Within history one finds the same possibility of variety as one finds in ordinary language, and the ordinary man, I submit, does not employ a criterion that allows him to say that operating from one point of view will elicit the "really real" cause of an event whereas operating from another will not, in cases where the facts allow two interpretations.

In order to give more formal expression to the main positive thesis of this chapter, we may think of the statements we have been analyzing as elliptical for statements of the form "A is the decisive cause of C from point of view m."[12] The proposed analysis of this expanded statement would then reflect the relational character of clause (2) of Schema I as follows:

> THESIS II: A is the decisive contributory cause of
> C from point of view m if and only if:
> (1) A is a contributory cause of C, and
> (2) A is the abnormal cause—the
> difference-maker—from the point of
> view of the historian who regards the
> subject of his inquiry in manner m.

According to such an analysis the historian who asserts a proposition to the effect that something is the cause of something else from point of view m is asserting an empirical proposition since neither clause (1) nor clause (2) refers to extraempirical matters. We have seen what it means to say that an investigator regards the subject of his inquiry in manner m. It means, for example, that he regards it as either a P or an R when the law in the supporting deductive argument has the form "Whatever is P and R is Q." But while every statement of the form "A is the decisive cause of C from point of view m" is empirical, the historian's decision to regard a as P rather than as Q—when he has a choice—may rest

---

[12] Sidney Hook (in *Theory and Practice in Historical Study*, p. 114) has argued that a statement that A is the decisive cause of C is, in effect, elliptical for a relational statement of the form "A is the decisive cause of C relative to y," but "y" in his analysis does not range over points of view or ways of regarding the subject of inquiry.

on an interest which in turn rests on a value judgment. This value judgment is not logically implied by the statement having the form "A is the cause of C from point of view *m*," but the fact that the historian chooses to look at the subject of inquiry in manner *m* rather than in manner *m'* may reflect or rest upon a value orientation that is not debatable. Therefore the different conclusions of two historians, one of whom asserts that A is the cause of C because he has viewed the subject of inquiry in manner *m*, and the other of whom asserts that A' is the cause of C because *he* has viewed the subject in manner *m'*, may rest on an inarbitrable difference in their interests.

The difference here is not unlike the difference between two observers of the epistemological penny, one of whom says that it looks elliptical to him and the other who says that it looks round to *him*. It is, of course, an objective fact that the penny will look round from one point of view and elliptical from another, but we may come to one conclusion rather than another as to the shape of the penny precisely because we prefer to look at it from one angle rather than another. Therefore, if two observers come to two different conclusions as to the look of the penny, we may prefer one conclusion precisely because it is the conclusion that would be arrived at by looking at the penny in our favorite way rather than another's. Of course, some philosophers might hold that looking straight down on the penny from above is the statistically *normal* way of looking at the penny, and hence conclude that the penny's look from that angle is its real look. But even if one is inclined to accept this way of invidiously contrasting the circular look and the elliptical look, I do not think that one can make an analogous point in the case of all alternative statements of *the* cause. I repeat that I do not think that one can order manners of looking at the subject of inquiry in a causal inquiry on the basis of their statistical normality or degree of approximation to such normality, even if one *might* say that manners of approaching the penny get closer and closer to the real shape as they get closer and closer to looking at it from an angle of 90 degrees. I emphasize "might" here to indicate that I am not happy with the doctrine of the real or normal look, but since I do not wish to argue that issue here, I shall merely say that even if one were able to defend such a doctrine in the theory of perception, he could not successfully defend its analogue in the theory of causation.

Anticipating the theme of a later part of this study in which narration is examined, we may say that the question "What is the cause?" is subject to a similar relativity as the question "What happened?" And this is contrary to ancient doctrine on both of these subjects; namely, (1) that there is always such a thing as *the* efficient cause of an event, which is absolute and independent of the "why" question asked and the interests of the person who asks it, and (2) that there is such a thing as the essence of an individual event which is absolute and independent of the "what" question asked and the interests of the person who asks it. The question "What happened?" (the counterpart of the question "What is the essence or formal cause of this individual?") and the question "What is the cause of what happened?" (the counterpart of the question "What is the efficient cause?") give the impression that answers to them can be both unique and absolute, but they are not. And although we can say that answers to them are factual once we fix the points of view from which we ask them—as we do in the case of the traditional question "What is the efficient cause?" when we interpret it in accordance with abnormalism—there is no Archimedean point from which points of view may always be assessed, no essence of history which dictates what point of view must always be adopted in order to pick out the correct answer either to the question "What is the cause of what happened?" or, as we shall see in a later part of this study, to the question "What happened?" The possibility of this much relativity we must allow if—as can be expected—different historians will often have different values, hence different interests, hence often come to different conclusions as to what the cause of a given event is.

It must be pointed out, however, that some writers on this subject seem to think that one can devise scales of importance on the basis of which one can decide that one cause or factor in a historical situation is *more important* than another in a way that allows for no "subjective" differences of the kind permitted by the version of abnormalism presented above. Before turning to such views I should repeat that abnormalism as I conceive it allows the possibility that *sometimes* the cause is uniquely and absolutely determined without reference to the historian's interest. If our supporting deductive argument is of the form (B) above, and if most *P*'s are not *Q* but it is not true that most *R*'s are not *Q*, then by this objective and absolute fact about the components of the law that presides over the explanatory deductive argument, it is determined that the cause of *a*'s being *Q* is *a*'s being *R*. In such a case we are deprived of our option of saying that *a*'s being *P* is the cause precisely because we cannot even frame the question that will elicit as an answer "The cause of *a*'s being *Q* is *a*'s being *P*." By contrast, however, some writers on this subject seem to think that all uses of the phrase "more important cause" or "most important cause"—and by implication the phrase "the decisive cause"—may be analyzed in absolute terms and hence that there is no interest-determined selection of the kind to which I have called attention. In a sense these writers are at the opposite pole from Mill, whereas my version of abnormalism is somewhere in between theirs and Mill's. I have tried, in effect, to vindicate Mill's view for a limited number of cases, namely those cases where the so-called facts do not uniquely determine what *the* cause is by eliminating one way of regarding the subject of inquiry, whereas the philosophers I have in mind seem to want to blot out *all* relativity of the kind that Mill called attention to.[12a]

Ernest Nagel has dealt with this problem with as much care as

[12a] In a fuller statement on the matter we should also make reference to the relativity involved in fixing on *one* explanatory argument, as in the above illustrations.

anyone has devoted to it, and therefore we shall find it profitable to examine something he says about it.[13] He has put forward a number of interesting suggestions as to how to analyze the notion of greater importance of historical causes or factors, and all of them seem motivated by the desire to eliminate the element of "subjectivity" in picking out the cause. Although Nagel's exposition involves reference to what he calls "contingently necessary conditions," I shall neglect that component of his view, for one thing because I do not, as will be evident later, think that the factors whose relative importance are to be compared should be described as contingently necessary conditions in Nagel's sense, and for another because Nagel's idea that such conditions are to be compared is not crucial for the issue now before us. Therefore, in accordance with our previous analysis we may think of the factors to be compared as different conditions that are jointly sufficient for the event or state in question. With this in mind let us turn to Nagel's point of view as illustrated by one of his efforts to rank factors.

Nagel considers a case in which a strong dislike of foreigners and an acute need for additional economic markets are both, _ex hypothesi_, contributory factors in an industrial nation's adoption of an imperialist foreign policy. In order to accomodate his illustration to the previous analysis of a singular statement of _the_ cause, let us assume that we can present an explanatory deductive argument like the following (alternatively, one may think of the first premise in what follows as a statistical statement, since that would be in closer accord with Nagel's view of historical explanation):

(1) Whenever an industrial country has a strong dislike of foreigners and an acute need for additional markets, it will adopt an imperialist foreign policy.

(2) Ruritania is an industrial country.

(3) Ruritania strongly dislikes foreigners at time t_1.

[13] Ernest Nagel, _The Structure of Science_ (New York, 1961), pp. 584 ff.

(4) Ruritania has an acute need for additional markets at t_1. Therefore,

(5) Ruritania adopts an imperialist foreign policy at t_1.

Now, as I understand Nagel, one of his efforts to analyze the notion of more important cause or determinant would lead him to hold that if and only if Ruritania's xenophobia is fairly constant and its need for markets varies considerably, may we say that the more important factor in Ruritania's adoption of an imperialist foreign policy at time t_1 was Ruritania's acute need of markets at time t_1. His point is that Ruritania's high degree of xenophobia is a value of a variable which varies slightly (whether in the case of Ruritania alone or in the case of all industrial countries is not clear from what he says, but let us assume that he means the former), whereas Ruritania's acute need for markets is a value of a variable that fluctuates widely, and this constancy of the value of one *variable* plus the changeability of the other *variable* is what makes Ruritania's acute need for markets the most important factor in bringing about its adoption of an imperialist policy at a given time.

Now I do not wish to deny that one can *distinguish* the factor reported in statement (4) in this way, but I do think it worthwhile to point out that such an analysis of what it is to be a more important cause is perfectly compatible with the kind of relativity of *the* cause to which I have been calling attention. For clearly, if it be true that most industrial countries which have a strong dislike of foreigners do not adopt imperialist foreign policies, and if most industrial countries which acutely need additional markets do not adopt imperialist foreign policies, then it would be possible to fix *either* on Ruritania's xenophobia *or* on Ruritania's need for markets as *the* cause of its adoption of an imperialist foreign policy at a certain time. In such a case a historian might well acknowledge the difference between a variable like the degree of xenophobia, which maintains a constant value in a given country, and a variable like economic need, which does not, and nevertheless say that from a certain point of view *the* cause of the country's adoption of an imperialist foreign policy on a certain occasion was the (admittedly constant) degree of xenophobia in the country.

Nagel's basic point may be seen by reflecting on a more old-fashioned sort of illustration. When Mill said that death might be brought on by a combination of several factors—the constitution of a man, his state of health, the state of atmosphere, and his having imbibed poison—Mill did not think of his underlying law as relating variables, but it is clear that we might treat the law that Mill had in mind as related to one connecting variables. We might say that whenever a human being has a constitution of strength a, and degree of health b, and is living in an atmosphere whose pressure is c, and imbibes an amount of arsenic d, he dies. Now this law is the parallel of the one that asserts that a lot of xenophobia and an acute need for markets will together bring on an active imperialist policy in an industrial country. So the question arises in the case of Jones's death: is it true that we are forced to say that Jones's having taken amount of arsenic d was *the* cause of his death just because *all his life* his constitution had been of degree a, his health of degree b, and the atmospheric pressure in which he lives of degree c, whereas he has imbibed *various* amounts of arsenic at different times? I do not think so. For clearly, an investigator who knew that Jones's constitution and health and that the pressure impinging on him had all been virtually constant for his whole life might ask, if he knew that not every man who has taken amount d of arsenic dies, "Why did Jones, who took amount d of arsenic die, when most men who take that amount do not die?" and get as an answer: "The cause was his having a constitution of degree a, his having health of degree b, and his having lived under pressure of degree c."

I repeat that I have no intention of denying that sometimes historians *may* rank factors as Nagel says they do, but it should be clear that this sort of ranking in no way prevents us from acknowledging the role of interest, and, if you like, subjectivity, in the selection of *the* cause on some occasions. The issue raised by

Nagel's ranking of factors is similar to one that we shall consider in the next section, where we shall examine the views of those whose hankering after an absolute metaphysical criterion for picking out *the* cause leads them to say that the cause is always a state or "standing condition." For after all, the xenophobia of Ruritania *is* what is sometimes called a standing condition, unlike its acute need for markets, and so is Jones's constitution. So let us turn to more traditional attempts to eliminate altogether the role of the historian's interest in the selection of *the* cause. Although they are far less sophisticated than Nagel's, they too rest on the assumption that by examining the facts alone we can always decide which among several contributory causes is *the* cause or the more important cause of a given event or state of affairs.

3. METAPHYSICAL ABSOLUTISM AND THE CAUSE

Some writers on causation maintain that a contributory cause is said to be the decisive cause only because it falls into a certain metaphysical category, and that therefore we never pick out *the* cause with reference to a point of view that can vary from historian to historian. Some writers, for example, maintain that the cause is what they call an underlying cause, and this is construed by them to be a *state* in contrast to a historical *event* or *episode* that takes place in a relatively short period of time. For this reason it is interesting to observe that when Mill devoted himself to showing that in common parlance the cause need not be an event, he thought that there was a widespread mistaken tendency in his time to think that the cause is always an event. By contrast, some present-day writers on historical causation insist that an event cannot be the cause and that only a state can be. In a sense, therefore, the corrective tendency initiated by Mill has gone too far. Mill had to work hard to show that a state could be a cause, whereas now some commentators on historical explanation insist that nothing else could be a cause. The truth is, however, that causes may be either events or states, and therefore this categorial basis for distinguishing between causes and noncauses among the conditions jointly sufficient to bring about an event is inadequate.[14]

Underlying States

In order to see what might prompt a historian to think that historical causes are always states, we may examine the view of the historian Louis Gottschalk. He begins his discussion of this topic by telling us that historians distinguish between the immediate cause of a historical event and its underlying causes. Thus, he says, the immediate cause of the First World War was the assassination of the archduke, and the immediate cause of the Second World War was the German invasion of Poland, whereas the underlying causes "included power politics, world anarchy, commercial rivalries, national aspirations, mutual fear, and territorial ambitions."[15] It is fair to say that in this passage Gottschalk identifies immediate causes as events and underlying causes as states. If Gottschalk had said nothing more than this, we might think he was merely presenting a useful and familiar classification of causes. But he soon abandons the suggestion that he is simply classifying contributory causes and says that an " 'immediate cause' is not *really* [my italics] a cause. . . . It is the precipitating event that serves as the dropping of a match in a combustible pile or the tripping of a hammer on an explosive. As such it is a good lead toward the antecedents that may be more satisfactorily described as 'causes.' "[16] In the same vein, Sidney B. Fay speaks of "the truer explanation" involved in alliances, armaments, and secret diplomacy, by contrast to explanations in which the actions of individuals are cited.[17]

As I have said, at this point one encounters a complete reversal of the position which Mill felt obliged to criticize, for now it

[14] Mill, op. cit., Bk. III, ch. V, sec. 3.
[15] Louis Gottschalk, *Understanding History* (New York, 1954), p. 209.
[16] Ibid., p. 210.
[17] Sidney B. Fay, *The Origins of the World War* (New York, 1931), I, 2.

looks as though we are being told that *only* the underlying state can really be the historical cause, or "more satisfactorily described as" the cause. Curiously enough, Gottschalk, in spite of regarding the precipitating event in history as analogous to the dropping of a match into a combustible pile, does not allow that a precipitating event might be the cause of an event. He uses the very analogy that one might suppose might lead him in the opposite direction as a basis for arguing that an event is *never* the historical cause of an event. In other words, he would say that none of the following statements could ever present *the* cause of a historical event:

The Lutheran Revolt broke out because of the posting of the Ninety-Five Theses.

The Lutheran Revolt broke out because of the Disputation with Eck.

The American Revolution broke out because of the imposition of the Stamp Tax.

The French Revolution broke out because of the swearing of the Tennis Court Oath.

The French Revolution broke out because of the calling of the Estates General.

The French Revolution broke out because of the formation of the National Assembly.

The American Civil War broke out because of the election of 1860.

The American Civil War broke out because of the firing on Fort Sumter.

On the contrary, Gottschalk seems to hold, historians should identify as *the* causes of events only states or conditions like the territorial ambitions of powers, their commercial rivalries, their alliances, their economic conditions, and so on. A medical counterpart to such a thesis would be that we should never say that the cause of Jones's death was his imbibing of arsenic but should always say that the cause of his death was something like his bodily constitution or the weakness of his heart, even though the eating of the arsenic precipitated his death. But can one defend a general view of the historical cause whose analogue in everyday language is obviously indefensible?

It must be realized that a certain kind of regularist need not face such a question. For if a regularist takes the extreme view that we present explanations when and only when we present explanatory deductive arguments, he may hold that although some statements of initial conditions are statements about events ("The temperature dropped below freezing last night") and others are about states ("The car's radiator is made of iron"), the distinction is of no interest to him so far as the problem of explanation is concerned. For he holds that only the whole deductive argument presents an explanation and that nothing of the sort that we call a singular explanatory statement presents an explanation. Therefore, the extreme regularist is not obliged to say whether the antecedent of a singular explanatory statement must refer to a state or an event. The question does not arise for him. But what should be said by the historian for whom the question does have such an interest? Should he, with an eye on his own language and that of his colleagues, say that the cause is always a state? Naturally, a historian might find it more interesting to seek out antecedents of this kind. At one point in his argument Gottschalk implies that the so-called underlying cause "may be more satisfactorily described as" the cause, and there he might merely mean that they are for a variety of reasons more interesting to ferret out. But to say this is different from saying, as Gottschalk says earlier, that "the immediate cause is not really a cause."

The point is that Gottschalk is wrong if he means that historians always use the phrase "the cause" so as to refer to a state or standing condition. In order to see this we need only examine J. B. Bury's explanation of the collapse of the Roman empire. It is an effort at explanation, and surely no philosophical analysis of historical explanation can be correct if it forces us to say that Bury was not even making an effort at explanation. Bury says: "An amazing sequence of events had surprised the Empire after the death of Theodosius the Great. Provinces had been seized by barbarous invaders, and the very soil of Italy desecrated by German violence. The sight of Rome herself stricken and insulted, no longer able to speak the language of a mistress but compelled to bargain with the intruders on her own territory, could not fail to make men ask, 'What is the cause of these disasters?' "[18] After considering a number of answers that he regards as inadequate, Bury says in effect that the disasters were caused by events rather than states. He denies that either depopulation, the Christian religion, or the fiscal system can be regarded as causes of the collapse that took place in the days of Honorius. Using the term "general considerations" to designate what we have called states and what Gottschalk would call "underlying causes," Bury says: "The truth is that the success of the barbarians in penetrating and founding states in the western provinces cannot be explained by any general considerations. It is accounted for by the actual events and would be clearer if the story were known more fully. The gradual collapse of the Roman power in this section of the Empire was the consequence of *a series of contingent events.*"[19] The contingent events were the "irruption of the Huns into Europe," the defeat of an emperor through faults of his own, the death of another emperor, the passing of the succession to a feeble-minded boy.

If so distinguished a historian as Bury can offer this kind of explanation, we must certainly surrender the view that historians always seize upon states rather than episodes or events in their explanation of events. Of course, this does not mean that Bury supports the contrary view, or that we should generalize from this and say that every historical explanation cites an episode as the cause. Bury himself implies that some explanations cite nonepisodes as causes when he says:

The "sterility of the human harvest" in Italy and Greece affected the history of the Empire from its very beginning, but does not explain the collapse in the fifth century. The truth is that there are two distinct

[18] J. B. Bury, *History of the Later Roman Empire* (New York, 1958), I, 301.
[19] Ibid., p. 311.

questions which have been confused. It is one thing to seek the causes which changed the Roman State from what it was in the best days of the Republic to what it had become in the age of Theodosius the Great—a change which from certain points of view may be called a "decline." It is quite another thing to ask why the State which could resist its enemies on many frontiers in the days of Diocletian and Constantine and Julian suddenly gave way in the days of Honorius.[20]

It is obvious on the basis of this passage that Bury would grant that some historical explanations refer to underlying causes or states or general considerations, but he rightly refuses to say that all historical explanations do. In this respect Bury illustrates the correct view that causes are not distinguished merely on the basis of a categorial criterion according to which they must be either states or events. They may be either.

We may see that historians sometimes treat events as causes by considering Pirenne's statement that the cause of the destruction of the economic unity of antiquity was the invasion of Islam, which was "thrown across the path of history with the elemental force of a cosmic cataclysm" and whose "sudden thrust had destroyed ancient Europe."[21] It is true, of course, that the event which Pirenne calls "the invasion of Islam" took more time than it took Luther to nail his theses on the church door, but it is certainly an episode by contrast to the state of Europe to which Pirenne refers when he speaks of the world-order which "was not able to survive the invasion of Islam."[22] Pirenne's explanation was of course offered by a historian who was exceedingly conscious of the relevance of underlying causes, but he very properly avoided the view that the cause is always an underlying cause.

In fairness to Gottschalk, it must be pointed out that although in some places he seems to adopt the view that the cause is always a state and hence to conclude that a precipitating event can never be the cause of something, at others his view seems more complicated. He seems to recognize that some precipitants are different

[20] Ibid., p. 309.
[21] Pirenne, op. cit., pp. 23–24.
[22] Ibid., p. 23.

from others and hence *might* be regarded as causes. He says that "the immediate cause or occasion *often* [my italics] seems to partake of the nature of accident: if Henry VIII's daughter, Mary, had been a son, Henry might not have wished to divorce Catherine of Aragon and the English Reformation might not have come; if Louis XVI's message had been properly delivered, there might have been no Tennis Court Oath and hence no formal defiance of the Old Regime of the Bourbons and hence no French Revolution; or if Franz Ferdinand's chauffeur had not backed up to correct a wrong turn at Sarajevo, the crown prince might not have become a good target for assassination and the First World War might have been averted."[23] On the other hand, Gottschalk seems to think that the death of a great leader like Cromwell, Lincoln or Lenin—also precipitating events—might be regarded differently. He implies that whereas the birth of a daughter rather than a son to Henry VIII, the improper delivery of Louis XVI's message, and Franz Ferdinand's chauffeur's backing up were "trivial accidents"; the deaths of Cromwell, Lincoln, and Lenin were not trivial accidents. One infers that in spite of some of his remarks Gottschalk does seem to think that some statements of the cause of an event might refer to precipitating events like the deaths of Lincoln, Cromwell, and Lenin.[24] But if he does, he must surrender the view that all historical causes are "underlying," that is to say, the untenable view that whenever we say that A is the cause of C we imply that A is a state rather than an event.

Even Marx, of whose views Gottschalk's are so reminiscent, seems to leave open the possibility that on some occasions a historian may refer to a precipitant as *the* cause of an event. It is true that in his *Eighteenth Brumaire of Louis Bonaparte*, Marx presents a classical illustration of a historical explanation in which the cause of a historical event is thought of as underlying, for he says there that whereas Victor Hugo regarded the *coup d'état* of

[23] Gottschalk, op. cit., p. 210.
[24] Ibid., p. 211.

December 2, 1851, as the violent act of a single individual, he, Marx, showed "how the *class struggle* [Marx's italics] in France created circumstances and relationships that made it possible for a grotesque mediocrity to play a hero's part."[25] And no doubt, if asked why the *coup d'état* took place, Marx would have cited those circumstances and relationships. But nothing that he says in the *Eighteenth Brumaire* implies that *the* cause among several cooperating facts is always a conjunction of underlying social circumstances. Presumably some historical events are brought about by men who are not grotesque mediocrities, who masterfully exploit the circumstances of their times, and whose actions may therefore be singled out as the causes of those historical events.[26] Marx said in a much-quoted passage: "Men make their own history, but they do not make it just as they please; they do not make it under circumstances chosen by themselves, but under circumstances directly found, given and transmitted from the past."[27] He might also have said that men make their own fires but they do not make *them* as they please, but under circumstances and with materials directly found, given, and transmitted from the past, and hence have allowed us to identify an arsonist's action as *the* cause of a fire and a political leader's action as *the* cause of a revolution. Just as the statement about fires does not imply that we must always say that the man's lighting the match rather than the presence of the oxygen, or vice versa, is *the* cause of the fire, so Marx's statement does not imply that the causes of historical events are always circumstances rather than individual actions.

Whatever the limitations of Gottschalk's point of view, it is worth remarking that he does not say that the reason why so-called immediate causes are not real causes is that immediate causes are always *produced* by underlying causes, that the powder gives rise to the spark which then ignites it. As a rule, powder does not generate sparks, and Carlyle was surely right when he said:

[25] See Karl Marx, *Selected Works*, II, 311–12. Marx criticizes Hugo for regarding the work of Louis Bonaparte as "like a bolt from the blue."
[26] See Sidney Hook, *The Hero in History* (Boston, 1955), esp. ch. IX.
[27] Marx, op. cit., II, 315.

I am well aware that in these days Hero-worship, the thing I call Hero-worship, professes to have gone out, and finally ceased. This, for reasons which it will be worth while some time to inquire into, is an age that as it were denies the existence of great men; denies the desirableness of great men. Show our critics a great man, a Luther for example, they begin to what they call "account" for him; not to worship him, but take the dimensions of him,—and bring him out to be a little kind of man! He was the "creature of the Time," they say; the Time called him forth, the Time did everything, he nothing—but what we the little critic could have done too! This seems to me but melancholy work. The Time call forth? Alas, we have known Times *call* loudly enough for their great man; but not find him when they called! He was not there; Providence had not sent him; the Time, *calling* its loudest, had to go down to confusion and wreck because he would not come when called.[28]

But then Carlyle went to the opposite false extreme of the doctrine advanced by Gottschalk, for Carlyle may be construed as having argued that only the action of a man—a great man, to be sure, but that part of his thesis is irrelevant for the moment—can be regarded as the historical cause. Ironically, Carlyle uses virtually the same thermodynamic metaphor as does Gottschalk in order to make the exact opposite, but equally false, point. The times, said Carlyle—and we may here identify the times with underlying causes—are like "dry, dead fuel, waiting for the lightning out of Heaven that shall kindle it. The great man, with his free force direct out of God's own hand, is the lightning." Carlyle, after saying that dry sticks do not produce lightning and that the great man is the lightning that brings about the fire, almost implies that the wood had no causal role at all to play in the fire, and yet, when we say that A is *the* cause of C, A does not always refer to an event or to the act of a man. Let us now consider another absolutistic and metaphysical view of the distinguishing feature of the cause.

[28] Thomas Carlyle, *Heroes and Hero-Worship*, Lecture I. Compare the following from Shakespeare, *Henry IV, Part I, III*, 1:

> GLENDOWER: I can call spirits from the vasty deep.
> HOTSPUR: Why, so can I, or so can any man;
>   But will they come when you do call for them?

Actions

That the cause is not always the act of a man may be seen by turning to the question: how far back in time should a historian go in his search for causes? By limiting ourselves to an examination of Mill's view, we have confined ourselves to only one kind of multiplicity of causes from which a historian is supposed to pick *the* cause. In effect, Mill is concerned with one kind of multiplicity that is provided by Thesis I, what may be called the horizontal multiplicity of causes that is spread before us when we have to decide whether to say that the cause of the fire was the presence of the dry sticks or the lightning, or whether to say with Alexander H. Stephens that "the real cause" of the Civil War was the North's violation of the South's constitutional rights, whereas "slavery so-called" was merely the "occasion" or "main exciting proximate cause". But Thesis I also licenses reference to a multiplicity of contributory causes that are more or less removed from the effect in time. This second kind of multiplicity may be called vertical and is succinctly portrayed in the following statement by a student of the literature on the Civil War:

One writer finds in events of the immediately preceding years an adequate explanation of the War; another feels he must begin the story with 1831 or even 1820; still another goes back to the importation of the first slaves, to descriptions of geographic differences before white men appeared, or to differentiation in Europe between those who settled North and South. For instance, John W. Draper treated at length such subjects as geography, the Negro in Africa, colonization of America, the white man in Europe, the Saxon and Norman invasions of England, and the shift from Roman to Gothic architecture; out of 634 pages of his *American Civil War* devoted to the coming of war, 350 pages dealt with these comparatively remote influences.[29]

The difference between horizontal and vertical multiplicity may best be seen by reference to our familiar schematic representation of a deductive explanation of the fact that a is Q in the following argument:

---

[29] H. K. Beale, op. cit., pp. 55–56.

Whatever is P, R, S, and T is Q.

a is P.

a is R.

a is S.

a is T.

Therefore,

a is Q.

When we distinguish between, say, the statement "*a* is *T*" and all of the other statements of initial conditions, on the ground that "*a* is *T*" refers to *the* cause of *a*'s being Q, whereas all of the others express mere conditions, the contributory causes make up a horizontal multiplicity. We may assert, "Partly because *a* is P, *a* is Q," "Partly because *a* is R, *a* is Q," "Partly because *a* is S, *a* is Q," and "Partly because *a is T*, *a* is Q." However, although we know that "*a* is P," "*a* is R," "*a* is S," and "*a* is T" state contributory causes of *a*'s being Q, we may go on to ask for an explanation of any one of the facts referred to in these antecedents. Why was the powder dry? Why was the match thrown? In explaining each of these antecedent facts, we may be able to assert a quartet of statements. Thus we might assert, "Partly because *a* is S_1, *a* is S," "Partly because *a* is S_2, *a* is S," "Partly because *a* is S_3, *a* is S," and "Partly because *a* is S_4, *a* is S," in explanation of the fact that *a* is S; and there may be three analogous quartets in explanation of the fact that *a* is P, *a* is R, and *a* is T. Whatever is a contributory cause of a contributory cause of *a*'s being Q, is a contributory cause of *a*'s being Q, and this proliferation of contributory causes may go on indefinitely. We can move backward in time and gather an enormous number of contributory causes.

And this is not the end of such temporally produced proliferation. Not only can we go beyond *a* is P, *a* is R, *a* is S, and *a* is T in search of earlier causes of the fact that *a* is Q, but we can also try to extract causes that are temporally sandwiched in between them and the fact that *a* is Q. One can easily imagine someone moving to the very razor edge of the Civil War in his search for contributory causes and saying that the war occurred partly because a certain person fired a bullet at Fort Sumter, or that the bombing of Hiroshima took place partly because of the decision of the man who actually worked the instrument that released the bomb rather than by Truman's decision or anything before that. And yet even though Thesis I does not distinguish between one true "partly because" statement and another on the basis of the amount of time separating cause and effect, it may be said that certain rules of historical inquiry require the historian to pick one event as *the* cause on the basis of an absolute feature of that event, like the fact that it is the first human action in the causal chain preceding the event to be explained.

In order to make clear the sort of view I have in mind, I turn to the situation in law. There, "a voluntary human action intended to bring about what in fact happens, and in the manner in which it happens, has a special place in causal inquiries . . . because, when the question is how far back a cause shall be traced through a number of intervening causes, such a voluntary action very often is regarded both as a limit and also as still the cause even though other later abnormal occurrences are recognized as causes."[30] Thus, although the presence of arsenic in a dead man's body may be said to be the cause and explanation of his death, in law we often press further in order to find a "more satisfying explanation," like the fact that someone deliberately put poison in his food, because reference to the poisoner allows "a fuller explanation in terms of human agency." A legal search for the cause passes "through" the presence of arsenic in the body to the deliberate act of the poisoner, but stops there. A deliberate act, we are told, is often a goal and a barrier in tracing back causes in the law.

From the point of view of Thesis I, the statements (a) Jones died partly because a large amount of arsenic was in his body, (b) Jones died partly because he was poisoned by Smith, (c) Jones died partly because of the greed of his poisoner, Smith, are all on

[30] Hart and Honoré, op. cit., p. 39.

a logical par—equally true and hence indistinguishable. But do statements like (b) have a special status in historical inquiries? And if they do not, is there something corresponding to the idea of a deliberate human act that plays an analogous part in historical explanation?

It is extremely difficult to answer such questions with confidence, but I venture to say that although a deliberate human act is "very often"—to use the words of Hart and Honoré—a *goal* toward which a historian will drive when he is inquiring into causes, it is a *barrier* for him less often than it is for the lawyer. One historian tells us:

> The oath of the Tennis Court, sworn on 20 June 1789, when the king had decided against the Third Estate, and shut them out of their regular meeting place, the speeches and affirmations when their act of rebellion was denounced, may be taken as the essential and revolutionary act of the French Revolution; from this act proceeded the destruction of the *ancien régime*.[31]

This certainly illustrates a willingness to treat a deliberate act as a *goal* of a historical inquiry into causes, so that the author might even be willing to say that the cause of the French Revolution was the swearing of the Tennis Court Oath and that anybody who did not trace causes as far back as this would be derelict in his duty as a historian of the Revolution. But other historians, as we know, might wish to go beyond the oath of the tennis court, explain it as the effect of a larger social force playing on those who swore the oath, and then say that this force was *the* cause of the revolution. In doing so such historians do not merely say that the action cooperated with social circumstances to bring about a historical event but that certain circumstances brought about the act. They think, in other words, that when we try to explain the revolution and reach a deliberate human action, we do not reach a barrier in the search for the historical cause of the revolution. They "pass through" such deliberate acts on the way to social circumstances. Many a future historian will speak in this way about the psycho-

[31] E. L. Woodward, *French Revolutions* (Oxford, 1934), p. 28.

logical atmosphere in Dallas when President Kennedy was assassinated and hence "pass through" the deliberate action and even the motive of the assassin in an effort to get an explanation.

In agreeing that a deliberate human action is very often a *goal* in cause-seeking inquiries, I am agreeing that historians very often are not content to rest with the analogue—in a detective's inquest —of merely discovering that a dead man's body contained arsenic. Historians, like ordinary people, will often ask, "Who did it?" and feel that until they have answered such a question they have not achieved a satisfactory explanation of "it." But often historians will feel that such reference to a deliberate human act is not a satisfactory stopping place and hence will press on in their effort to explain something like a revolution or even an assassination.

This suggests that the notion of a voluntary human action does not play as central a role in historical explanation as it does in legal explanation. All of which is quite understandable, given the basic purpose of causal language in the law. After all, the fundamental notion in this part of law is that of an act being the cause of harm,[32] whereas the historian is not as preoccupied as the lawyer is with finding the cause of harm nor with attributing that harm to deliberate human acts. He casts a wider causal net, and therefore the basic form of statement in his causal language is not "Harm Y occurred because of deliberate human act X" but rather something more general. He may seek the cause of an event which is not harmful, and sometimes he may achieve satisfactory explanations only by pressing beyond deliberate human acts. In any case, we cannot say that *the* cause which a historian seeks and with which he rests is always a deliberate act and in this sense categorially identifiable.

If one were to ask, however, whether we may find in history some analogue to the idea of a voluntary human action, some other sort of categorially distinguishable cause that plays the role in historical explanation that the voluntary human act plays in law—that of goal and barrier—I should have to say that I cannot produce any. Different historians, for whatever reason, may seize

[32] Hart and Honoré, op. cit., p. 5.

upon certain kinds of antecedents and treat them as goals and barriers in causal inquiries; but it is, I think, difficult to single out anything in history the role of which is comparable to the role of voluntary action in law. The most we can say is that a historian will not normally rest with a physical explanation if he knows or thinks that beyond that lies a human act or a social condition. If a tidal wave strikes a city like Lisbon, historians who are not religious are not likely to press on to ask why the tidal wave rose, but the devastation of Hiroshima is another matter. There the historian will press on to ask why it was destroyed but will not treat the action of one man—whether he be an aviator or a president—as something through which the historian cannot pass in a search for explanations. Of course, an individual historian may think like a lawyer and automatically stop asking "why" when he reaches a deliberate act, but that merely marks him as one kind of historian, who may be pejoratively labeled "legalistic" by those historians who feel that he takes an excessively narrow view of his subject. But even if the historian should press on and seek an earlier fact, I do not think it will be possible to characterize that earlier fact as having a feature which will serve as *the* differentiating feature of *the* cause in all cases. The historian cannot present a general rule by saying that *the* cause is a state of being, an episode, or a voluntary action. No such metaphysical or categorial feature distinguishes *the* cause.

Thoughts

Nor will the historian be able to rest with Collingwood's "thoughts." Collingwood holds that all history is the history of human thought, and declares: "When an historian asks 'Why did Brutus stab Caesar?' he *means* 'What did Brutus think, which made him decide to stab Caesar?' "[33] It would appear, then, that if Collingwood is right, explanation by reference to human thoughts has priority in history, and that *the* cause which a histo-

[33] R. G. Collingwood, *The Idea of History* (Oxford, 1946), p. 214. The emphasis on the word "means" is mine.

rian seeks will be distinguished by virtue of its being a thought, i.e., by virtue of falling into a special metaphysical category that is absolutely definable. However, it must be pointed out once again that the cause of a historical action—and, we may add, a historical belief—may fall into a variety of classes. Just as there are circumstances in which we may explain an explosion by citing the dryness of the powder, so there are occasions on which a historian will explain an action by citing the agent's thought and others on which he will cite other items. On some occasions, the agent's thought that an action ought to be performed may be cited as the explanation of the action, on others the resoluteness and strength of the agent may be cited, and on still others social circumstances may be cited. The mere fact that each of so many factors other than thoughts may be cited as *the* cause of an action—even an action of an ordinary person—makes it absurd to say, as Collingwood does, that when a historian asks, "Why did Brutus do it?" he *means*, "What did Brutus *think* which made him decide to do it?" For to say that the question *means* this is to imply that the only singular explanatory statements that historians properly make in reply to "why" questions are those that refer to the "thought in the mind of the person by whose agency the event came about." We may see the absurdity of this as a general account of "*the* cause" sought by historians simply by observing that the major concern of the historian is with man as a social animal. Insofar as he deals with social behavior, with social events, with group action, the historian can hardly be described as someone who seeks the thoughts in the mind of *society*. The Collingwoodian scheme is too rationalistic as a model for the explanation of all individual behavior, and it leads to difficulties if we wish to analyze the distinctive task of the social historian.

It is necessary only to open the pages of historical works in the most casual way in order to see that many historical explanations do not fall into the Collingwoodian pattern. In his *Three Centuries of Harvard*, for example, Morison tells us that on October 28, 1636, The Great and General Court of Massachusetts voted some money toward a "schoale or colledge," but that over a year elapsed before anything was done to carry this vote into execution. He then says:

> The causes of the delay, one infers, were two-fold—the Hutchinsonian faction, which preferred inspired exhortation to learned exposition of the Bible, and the short but ferocious war with the Pequot Indians.[34]

Here neither of the so-called "causes of the delay" in forming Harvard College were *thoughts*: one was a war and the other a faction or a preference. There may be some argument as to whether a preference is a Collingwoodian thought, but surely a state of war is not. It involves thinking, to some extent, but it is hardly a thought in the sense in which Brutus' thought that Caesar was a tyrant or ambitious is a thought. Morison also presents us with the following passages:

> Any stranger who in 1936 is hurled out to Harvard Square by subway or taxicab may well wonder why the puritan fathers in their wisdom chose "Newetowne" (renamed Cambridge when the College was at the point of opening) as the site . . . Salem offered a tract of three hundred acres on the borders of Marblehead, with an ocean frontage of a good quarter-mile, which was rejected in favor of a house and lot measuring slightly over an acre among the cowyards of Cambridge. One reason, doubtless, was a desire to do something for the New Town which had already been once emptied of its inhabitants by the emigration to Connecticut, and abandoned by Massachusetts as the colonial capital. Another reason, explicitly stated by contemporaries, was the personality of Thomas Shepard, the young minister of the New Town, a Master of Arts of Cambridge who had a winning way with young men . . . and who had kept his parish clean of the Hutchinsonian heresy with which Boston was still tainted. And we should like to think that the winding Charles, reminiscent of Cam and Isis, and the plain smooth as "a bowling green" that sloped to it, had something to do with the choice, even though the College turned her back on the river for over two centuries.[35]

[34] Samuel Eliot Morison, *Three Centuries of Harvard* (Cambridge, 1937), p. 6.

[35] Ibid.

Here we see that the word "reasons" is ambiguous in a way that makes it difficult to take a straight Collingwoodian line on historical explanation. A desire, a personality, and *possibly* a river are all said to be "reasons" in this typical stretch of historical prose. And in another relevant passage, Morison explains a decision by citing the position or circumstance of the agent—not his thoughts:

> . . . John Harvard and Nathaniel Eaton had settled in Charlestown and decided to stay in Massachusetts; the first, because he was candidate for assistant minister of the church there, and the second, because he had been chosen master of the new College.[36]

On the basis of the foregoing considerations, we may conclude that so far as the actual language of historians is concerned, we cannot identify the item which is *the* cause by showing that it falls into one metaphysical category—whether the category be that of event, state, voluntary action, or thought. Moreover, I am inclined to think that if the distinguishing feature of the cause cannot be identified with such an absolute property, the whole effort to find an absolute property is wasted—although the doctrine of abnormalism may help us see why some thinkers may be prompted to move in this absolutistic direction. Such thinkers may overgeneralize on the basis of a limited observation of causal language. Either they themselves or the historians they read may be disposed always to regard the subject of their inquiry as abnormal in a manner that leads them to fix on a certain category of antecedent, and so, bound by such limited habits of thought and speech, they may be unable to see the more general character of *the* cause's distinguishing feature. They may, so to speak, always regard the subject whose behavior they wish to explain as the woman in our earlier example regards her husband, and never regard their subject as the physician regards the husband. And so they may become, as it were, advocates of actions, thoughts, episodes, or standing conditions rather than of relativistically conceived abnormality in their efforts to identify *the* cause. On the

[36] Ibid., p. 8.

other hand, they may very consciously maintain—in the face of what I have said earlier—that there *is* a hierarchy of manners in which the subject of inquiry may be regarded, and that we give the *real* cause only when we regard the subject in that manner which leads to the conclusion that *the* cause has a certain absolute property, whether it be that of being an episode, a state, a thought, or an action. This, I think, is indefensible. Such writers have a prior metaphysical prejudice about what real causes are, and they say, in effect, that the proper way of regarding the subject under inquiry is that which leads one to say that the cause is the cause as they conceive it. But, as we have seen, sometimes the metaphysician's favorite kind of antecedent will not be *the* abnormal antecedent from any point of view that could be adopted, and I see no reason under such circumstances why they should persist in calling it *the* cause except out of indefensible metaphysical prejudice.

4. THE CAUSE AS INDISPENSABLE OR NECESSARY CONDITION

Now that we have examined the view that *the* cause is chosen capriciously, the view that it is the abnormal contributory cause, and the view that it is a contributory cause that falls into a certain metaphysical category, we may turn to another unsuccessful but instructive effort to characterize the decisive cause. This time we shall consider the idea that we single out a's being P as the cause of a's being Q on the ground that it is not only one of the conditions that are jointly sufficient to bring about a's being Q, but also an indispensable or necessary condition. Once again we may consider the view under test as applicable in a case where a given explanatory deductive argument is available and we may ask whether the typical historian, when he singles out one of the statements of initial conditions as that which presents the cause, does so because that one—as distinct from the others—also states a necessary condition for the event to be explained. In order to answer our question, however, we must be clear about what is meant by the phrase "necessary condition," for unfortunately it has meant different things in the literature on explanation. Indeed, the value of examining this theory derives as much from the value of trying to discover whether it is true as it does from the worth of seeing how ambiguous the whole language of "necessary" and "sufficent" conditions can be.

Some preliminary remarks are in order. In what follows we are not concerned with what might be called the necessity of a given explanatory deductive argument, for that raises different questions. So different that it might be worth digressing for a moment to point out how the validity of an entire explanatory deductive argument might be thought to be necessary for the truth of a given singular causal statement, the better to see how this notion of necessity is distinct from the notion we are primarily concerned with. Suppose that a match has lit and we present our familiar explanatory deductive argument with "a lit" as its conclusion. Can we say that if the following conjunction of premises were false: "All matches which are dry and struck in the presence of oxygen light; a was a match; a was dry; a was in the presence of oxygen; a was struck," that the match would *not* have lit? Strictly speaking the answer to this question is "no," simply because it is not logically excluded that there is *another* explanatory deductive argument, containing "a is Q" ("The match lit") as its conclusion. This may be seen abstractly as follows. It may be the case that in addition to its being true that the following is an explanatory deductive argument:

> Whatever is P, R, S, and T is Q.
> a is P.
> a is R.
> a is S.
> a is T.
> Therefore,
> a is Q.

it is also true that the following is an explanatory deductive argument:

> Whatever is P', R', S', and T' is Q.
>
> a is P'.
>
> a is R'.
>
> a is S'.
>
> a is T'.
>
> Therefore,
>
> a is Q.

where P' is distinct from P, R' is distinct from R, S' is distinct from S, and T' is distinct from T. This particular match might, for all we know, have a set of properties other than P, R, S, and T which lead by laws to its lighting. Although we have used one explanation of a's lighting, it is logically possible that there is another.

Now most discussions of the problem we are now faced with disregard this possibility of what might be called "concurrent explanations." They proceed on the assumption that there exists exactly one explanatory deductive argument that facilitates logical passage to the effect, and then try to make distinctions within that one argument. They assume, in other words, that if this particular explanatory deductive argument were not to have been valid, a would not have been Q, and therefore that the validity of this explanatory argument is in some sense a necessary condition for its being the case that a is Q. I call attention to this assumption not so much to dispute it as to indicate that the sense in which an explanatory deductive argument is said to be necessary is only of secondary interest to me here. The doctrine that in general only one explanatory deductive argument can be mustered in behalf of its conclusion raises a question which goes well beyond our immediate concern.

I cannot leave it, however, without calling attention to a related puzzle that appears in the writings of John Stuart Mill on this subject. One gets the impression that Mill held that when one explains a particular event, one presents an explanatory deductive argument whose universal premise—if there is only one—need not do more than state the *sufficient* conditions for the sort of event to be explained, in other words, an argument of the kind we have been illustrating by the use of "Whatever is P, R, S, and T is Q; a is P; a is R; a is S; a is T; therefore, a is Q." But then Mill speaks of P, R, S, and T as "the set of antecedents which determined it [the event to be explained, in this case the fact that a is Q], and but for which it would not have happened." Now what worries one is the phrase "but for which it would not have happened" because it seems to suggest that a's being P, R, S, and T (the whole cause) is not only a sufficient condition for a's being Q but also a necessary condition. This is troubling because Mill believes in the plurality of causes, and therefore would acknowledge the possibility that, in addition to its being the case that "Whatever is P, R, S, and T is Q," it might also be true to say "Whatever is P', R', S', and T' is Q." What he seems to balk at, however, is the notion that there could be two valid explanatory *arguments* which have "a is Q" as their conclusion, two which contain these two universal statements and correspondingly different statements of initial conditions as their respective premises. Why else should he say of the set of antecedents which causally determine that a is Q, that but for them a would not be Q? My own view is that it is enough to characterize an explanatory deductive argument as one which has the form already outlined, leaving open the possibility that an event has two explanations, that is to say, is recorded in a statement which is the conclusion of two explanatory deductive arguments. Only when it can be established that there is only one such argument—and that will be a hard thing to establish—may we speak of it, or of the truth of its premises, as *necessary* for the truth of its conclusion, the fact to be explained. I repeat, however, that this sense of "necessary" is not our major concern in this section, so let us return to the problem of how to single out one statement of initial conditions in a *given* explanatory deductive argument as that which states *the* cause, and in particular to the view that that statement expresses a necessary condition for the truth of the statement referring to the fact to be explained. To put the problem concretely, when we say that *the* cause of the match's lighting was its having been struck, do we do so because the striking is indispensable to the lighting in a way in which, say, the dryness of the match is not?

Here, as I have already indicated, the phrase "necessary condition" is used in many different ways, but I wish to show that there is no clear sense of the phrase which permits us to say that *the* cause is always the contributory cause which is necessary. Let us examine a few of the senses that have been proffered.

(1) Oddly enough, sometimes what is meant by saying that a's being P is a necessary condition for a's being Q is that "a is P" is one of the statements of initial conditions in an explanatory deductive argument whose conclusion is "a is Q," in other words, that a's being P is one of the conditions that are jointly sufficient for a's being Q. But clearly this conception of necessary condition is not going to help us single out "a is P" from among the other statements of initial conditions.[37] They are all statements of necessary conditions in this (peculiar) sense. On this basis one can hardly distinguish the striking of the match from the presence of the oxygen or from the dryness, and so on.

(2) Let us turn, therefore, to an interpretation of the statement "The fact that a is P is the cause of a's being Q" according to which "a is P" stands in a special relationship to the law in the explanatory deductive argument (in cases where there is only one such law). So far we have put no restriction on the form of the laws that may figure in an explanatory deductive argument, but it might be maintained, on the basis of certain analyses made by Ernest Nagel,[38] that *the* cause of a's being Q is that contributory cause which is also what he calls a contingently necessary condition for a's being Q. A contingently necessary condition for a's being Q, relative to a given deductive argument, is one, for example, that occupies the position that "a is P" occupies in the following sort of argument:

[37] See Hook, in *Theory and Practice in Historical Study*, p. 114, for this use of "necessary condition." He does not think that the necessity of a condition singles it out but rightly thinks that other criteria must be used.

[38] Op. cit., pp. 559–60.

For every *x*, if *x* is R, S, and T, then *x* is Q if and only if *x* is P.
a is R.
a is S.
a is T.
a is P.
Therefore,
a is Q.

The statement "*a* is P" occupies a unique position in this argument, one that it would not occupy if the generalization were to read "For every *x*, if *x* is R, S, T, and P, then *x* is Q." So one might say that *the* cause of *a*'s being Q is a contributory cause which is, in addition, one of the contingently necessary conditions for *a*'s being Q.

What is to be said about this view? Simply that it does not analyze that relation of *being the cause* which is referred to in typical statements made by the historian. On the basis of such a view we would have to say that when the historian singles out the archduke's assassination as *the* cause of the First World War, the historian implies that there are conditions, like R, S, and T, which are such that they, *together with and only with* the assassination lead by law to the war. But this is much too stringent a requirement for the cause to satisfy if we are to keep in touch with actual historical usage. Notice, too, that the ordinary man says that the striking of the match is the cause of the lighting even though he cannot show that there is a law which has the form. "Whenever a match has characteristics P, R, and S, it will light if and only if it is struck." It is enough for him that there should be a law of the form "Whenever a match has characteristics P, R, and S, it will light if it is struck."[39] Requiring the insertion of "and only if" after the "if" in the second generalization is just too much, because it means that one must show not only that the striking cooperated with P, R, and S to bring about the lighting, but that

[39] "Whenever a match has characteristics P, R, and S, it will light if it is struck" is equivalent to "Whenever a match has characteristics P, R and S and it is struck, it will light."

nothing else would cooperate with *P, R,* and *S* to bring about the lighting. As I have said, it is doubtful whether a historian who said that the assassination of the archduke was *the* cause of the outbreak of the First World War would agree that he meant to imply that even given those circumstances described by Fay as underlying factors, nothing but the assassination would have led to war. I do not deny that one can, using something like Nagel's notion of contingently necessary condition, pick out one statement of initial conditions in a given explanatory deductive argument and call it by fiat the statement that refers to *the* cause. But if one is interested in analyzing the notion of the cause in a way that will fit in with the most typical use of historians or of ordinary people, I do not think this theory will work. It is too restrictive.

(3) We must also reject another view according to which the cause is a necessary condition in a sense which is best conveyed by reflecting on the role that oxygen plays in fires. Even if we assume that there is a plurality of causes of fire, one may say that oxygen plays a peculiar part in the laws that govern fires. For one thing we may say that the presence of oxygen—unlike other conditions —is always one of the sufficient conditions for a fire; for another that whenever fire is present, oxygen is present.[40] Thus, if we were to list all of the known laws governing the outbreak of fire, they would read as follows:

Whenever *R, S, T,* and oxygen are present, fire breaks out.
Whenever *U, V, W,* and oxygen are present, fire breaks out.
Whenever *X, Y, Z* and oxygen are present, fire breaks out.

and so on, using different letters in order to mirror the possibility that oxygen can combine with a variety of factors to bring about fire. However, as we have seen, we can also go further in describing the relationship of oxygen to fire. We know that the presence of oxygen is not only a contributory cause of every fire, but also that if there is no oxygen, there is no fire, i.e., that it is a law that whenever fire breaks out, oxygen is present. And yet even though

[40] See Hart and Honoré, op. cit., ch. V, for an illuminating discussion of the notion of necessary conditions.

no one seems to think that when asked, "Why did Rome burn that night?" we must answer: "The cause was the presence of oxygen that night," there is an unfortunate tendency to think that a historian, when *he* states *the* cause of an event, must fix on something that stands to the historical event as the presence of oxygen stood to the burning of Rome, i.e., to fix on that one of the jointly sufficient conditions which is also a necessary condition in this third sense for events of the kind to be explained.

In order to illustrate the point, I turn to an essay by Arthur Schlesinger, Jr., entitled "The Sources of the New Deal."[41] Its main concern is conveyed in the following question: "What were the preoccupations which urged the nation into a cascade of reform in the years between 1933 and 1938?" Although Schlesinger seems to be limiting himself to what he calls "preoccupations," and although he uses the word "urged," it is obvious from the context that he might just as well have framed his question in a more conventional manner by asking, "Why did the New Deal come about?" Having asked his question, he remarks: "One obvious answer to this, of course, is the collapse of the American economic system in 1929," but he thinks this is an inadequate answer. He goes on: "To sharpen the issue, consider the question: would there have been a New Deal if there had been no depression?" And then Schlesinger concludes: "One must answer that there would very likely have been some sort of New Deal in the Thirties even without the Depression."[42] From this, and other things he says, one gets the impression that Schlesinger is seeking, in answer to the question "Why did the New Deal take place?" something that corresponds to the presence of oxygen in the case of a particular fire. In other words, he is not satisfied with presenting *any one* of the conditions that were jointly sufficient to bring about the New Deal. He seeks one that was also a "necessary prelude" to the New Deal. He says, for example:

[41] *Paths of American Thought*, ed. Arthur M. Schlesinger, Jr. and Morton White, pp. 372–91.
[42] Ibid., pp. 372–73.

Contemporary thinking has come too unreflectively to assume depression as the necessary prelude to reform. Students of American history know better. The fight against depression was, to be sure, the heart of the New Deal, but it has not been the central issue of traditional American reform: it was not the heart of Jeffersonian democracy nor of Jacksonian democracy nor of the anti-slavery movement nor of the Progressive movement. What preceded these other epochs of reform was an accumulation of disquietudes and discontents in American society, often noneconomic in character, and producing a general susceptibility to appeals for change—this and the existence within society of able men or groups who felt themselves cramped by the status quo and who were capable of using the spreading dissatisfaction to advance policies and purposes of their own. This combination of outsiders striving for status and power and a people wearying of the existing leadership and the existing ideals has been the characteristic model of American reform.[43]

When Schlesinger says that the fight against the depression was the heart of the New Deal, he implies that the depression was a factor in bringing about the New Deal, but since his conception of explanation leads him to think that a factor which is not "the necessary prelude" of *every* reform movement is not the cause of *any* reform movement, he downgrades the depression and puts in its place a factor which resembles oxygen as a factor in the production of fires. In his mind, I suggest, the "combination of outsiders striving for status and power and a people wearying of the existing leadership and the existing ideals" plays a part is *all* American reform movements comparable to the part that oxygen plays in all fires and, for this reason, is *the* explanation of the New Deal. Of course, I do not wish to deny the historian the right to seek such factors, but I do not think that he must refer to them when he is presenting *the* cause of a historical event. On the basis of such a criterion of the cause, the number of statements of *the* cause would be much smaller than it is normally thought to be.

I conclude from my examination of this and the other senses of the phrase "necessary condition" that we cannot distinguish *the* cause by saying that it is that one among the jointly sufficient

[43] Ibid., p. 373.

conditions which is also a necessary or indispensable condition. The first criterion is too weak and the second two are too strong. And I know of no other way of defining "necessary" that will do the trick.

5. ENTER PSYCHOLOGY AND EPISTEMOLOGY

Some of the previously examined efforts to define the relation of *being the cause of* do not succeed because they proceed on the assumption that *the* cause has an intrinsic feature by virtue of which we distinguish it from every other cause licensed by existential regularism. By an intrinsic feature I mean one like being a state or being an event, one that the cause has independently of the context and independently of how the investigator views the situation. Because Mill in his most conspicuous statements on this subject thought of the task of singling out *the* cause as one in which we try to present such an intrinsic feature and could not find such a feature, he abandoned the search for an analysis of "the cause" as hopeless and with it the idea that there is a relation of *being the cause of* which is distinct from the relation of *being the whole cause of*. But, although Mill is usually and properly interpreted as holding this skeptical view by those who concentrate on the text of his *System of Logic*, tucked away in the footnotes of the section of the *Logic* in which this main view is advocated, there is, as Hart and Honoré have noted,[44] a view which seems to allow for a relation that resembles that of *being the cause of* as opposed to *being the whole cause of*. And Mill's analysis of this relation is such as to warrant our calling his theory in the footnotes psychological or epistemological because of its essential employment of the concepts of knowledge and ignorance in analyzing *the* cause.

In very fine print, Mill says that when it can be assumed that the person to whom we present an explanation *knows* that a certain condition is a contributory cause, we do not tell *him* that that

[44] Op. cit., p. 17. See Mill, op. cit., Bk. III, ch. V, sec. 3, note.

condition is *the* cause since we know then that he cannot be seeking information that he already possesses. Thus Mill says: "The possession of bodily organs is a known condition, and to give that as the answer, when asked the cause of a person's death, would not supply the information sought." Mill adds that whenever there is one and only one condition which—among the whole set that cooperates to bring about the event—is unknown to the hearer, there is "occasion for speaking of a single condition as if it were the cause," by which he means as if it were the whole cause. This is a retreat from the doctrine that selection of *the* cause is unregulated even though Mill continues to hold that the single condition is spoken of "as if it were the cause," and that such a way of speaking is appropriate only "when scientific accuracy is not aimed at." But we may easily drop Mill's idea that in such cases we are treating the single condition merely *as if it were* the entire cause and construct a Mill-like, if not a Millian, view according to which there is a genuine, nonfictitious relation called *being the cause of* which is identified as follows: A is the decisive cause of C if and only if A is a contributory cause of C and A is the only contributory cause of C that is not previously known to be a cause. However, when confronted with such a formula, we are immediately led to ask standard philosophical questions. Shall we identify the cause as the one and only contributory cause of which an average person would be ignorant, or as the one and only cause of which a rational person familiar with the subject can be expected to be ignorant, or as the one and only cause of which the particular person to whom we are addressing the explanation is ignorant?

It seems clear that the selection of *the* cause does not depend on what people do or should know in the sense employed by Mill. When the historian writes his statement of the cause, he usually does not focus on any particular person as his audience, and it is certain that he does not always have in mind some standard person whose knowledge and ignorance alone will determine what he should call the cause. When Pirenne stated that the Moslem invasion was the cause of the collapse of a Mediterranean Commonwealth in Europe, he was obviously not giving this as an answer to the question "Of which one of the contributory causes are my readers ignorant?" Nor was Bury thinking in this way when he presented the contingencies that in his view precipitated the collapse of the Roman empire. It is true that very often a historian will present as *the* cause a cause of which his audience may be ignorant, but this will still leave open the question as to whether he is right in calling this cause *the* cause. Moreover, the historian, like the lawyer, will often have before him a set of true statements licensed by existential regularism and ask himself, "Which among these presents *the* cause?" Obviously, under such circumstances his problem is not to present that cause which someone did not know was a contributory cause. Even when a man is ignorant of a cause, he may, when it is presented to him, come to the conclusion that it is not *the* cause of the event, but rather that some factor which he had known about is *the* cause. A man may at first deny that the contingencies which Bury identifies as constituting the cause of the collapse of the Roman empire do constitute the cause, but later be persuaded by Bury. For all these reasons we must reject this psychological or epistemological view of the cause.

Nevertheless it is an instructive theory because it pries us loose from the idea that the differentia is an intrinsic feature of the cause, and to this extent it is allied with abnormalism. It accords with our feeling that what one man regards as *the* cause may be what another would regard as a mere condition, even if it does not present a credible analysis of the general grounds on which this regarding, as it were, goes on. I should put special emphasis on the phrase "regards as the cause," for I think that when we speak in this way we come closer to understanding the problem of analyzing causal interpretation. As soon as one recognizes that a factor may be regarded as the cause in some contexts and not in others, the problem we are dealing with becomes easier to understand. It is not that of finding some feature that the cause possesses as it possesses the feature of being a state if it is a state, or the feature of being an episode if it is an episode, or even the feature of being the necessary condition. It is the problem of finding the circumstances in which the *expression* "is the cause" is applied to an item. On this point Mill's instincts were extraordinarily sound, for he speaks of singling out "one only of the antecedents under the *denomination* [my italics] of Cause, calling the others merely Conditions," and of giving "the name of cause," and even of a fact being "dignified with the name of cause," when he is being somewhat ironic about the process. Mill sees that being the cause is the result of men speaking in a certain way, of using language in a certain way, of *interpreting* in a certain way. With this in mind, we may view the epistemological theory as asserting that historians interpret A as the cause of C when and only when A is the cause of which their audience is ignorant. Unfortunately, in spite of the fact that it sends us in the right direction, this theory is not a correct general account of the conditions under which historians typically regard *a* cause as *the* cause. For another, more plausible, but also unsuccessful, attempt in this direction, I now turn to a pragmatic or technological approach to the problem.

6. TECHNOLOGY AND THE CAUSE

It might be thought that a historian regards an item as the cause when and only when it is the sort of thing that can be prevented or produced by a human being. In other words, it might be thought that when an event has been brought about by a conjunction of factors, then the one and only factor which can be prevented or produced by a human being—and no other factor in the situation —is regarded as the cause of the event. Interestingly enough, Collingwood, who tried to characterize certain uses of the expression "the cause" along these lines, denied that his view was relevant to history because he thought that history employed an altogether different concept of causation.[45] But in spite of Colling-

[45] R. G. Collingwood, "Causation in Practical Natural Science," *Metaphysics* (Oxford, 1940), ch. XXXI.

wood's own protest against the view that history employs such a technological or pragmatic concept of causation, that view is tempting enough to be worth our consideration even if we have to reject it.

Let us begin with some nonhistorical examples of statements which might be thought to be analyzable by reference to what is producible or preventable by a human being:

The cause of John's contracting malaria was his having been bitten by a mosquito.

The cause of the sinking of the S.S. *Steam* was its having been overloaded.

The cause of that book's going moldy was its being in a damp room.

The cause of John's sweating was the dose of aspirin he took.

The cause of the furnace's going out in the night was the fact that the draught door was insufficiently open.

The cause of those seedlings dying was the fact that they were not watered.[46]

Let us suppose that each one of these statements implies a statement of the kind licensed by existential regularism. Hence each implies the existence of a complex explanatory argument, and this circumstance allows us to acknowledge Collingwood's point that "a cause [in the technological or practical sense] is never able by itself to produce the corresponding effect."[47] The electric switch, which is a prime example of the sort of thing

---

[46] These illustrations are modeled on Collingwood's, Ibid., p. 299. I have merely transformed them so that they are obviously singular in form.
[47] Ibid., p. 301.

Collingwood has in mind, will work the light if there is current in the wire, and so on. The statement by the occupant of an apartment that the cause of his kitchen light's going on was his turning on the switch implies that there is an explanatory deductive argument which contains as a premise the statement "The switch was turned on." But it also implies, according to Collingwood, that the turning on of the switch has some distinctive feature. This becomes clear when we ask why the occupant of the house does not usually say, "The cause of the light's going on is the presence of current in the wire." For Collingwood the distinguishing feature of the cause is its manipulability: the occupant of the apartment can manipulate his wall switch, but he cannot manipulate the current in the line.

Once we introduce the idea of manipulability, we also introduce relativity, just as we do on the epistemological theory of the cause. Although the occupant does not say that the cause of the light's being on is the fact that there is current in the line, the engineer at the power station may say so—in which case the fact that the occupant's switch is on would be for the engineer a condition that he, the engineer, does *not* regard as the cause of the light's being on in the man's apartment. The engineer, as he looks at the man's apartment from the power station, can assert truly: "The cause of the light's being on in that man's apartment is the fact that the main switch is on"; whereas the occupant may say, also truly, "The cause of the light's being on in my apartment is the fact that my wall switch is on." And presumably only John Stuart Mill, speaking in "scientific discourse," would say something along these lines: "The cause of the light's being on in that man's apartment is the fact that the main switch and the wall switch are on and there is current in the line."

Our question is whether the technological way of defining the notion of being the cause is adequate in most cases in which historians say that A is the cause of C, and the answer is that it is not. Some historians call standing conditions of a kind that *they* are not able to manipulate the cause of an event; for example, the economic conflict between North and South. Other historians will refer to a great leader's death from old age or an incurable disease as the cause of the collapse of a nation or government, even if these are events of a sort that the historian cannot produce or prevent. It should be realized that the technological theory of *the* cause does not fail because the historian cannot go back to the past and arrange facts otherwise. Such an objection would miss the point of the theory by construing it as an absurd view of causal statements connecting two events in the past. But the theory does not assert that I must now be able to undo an event in the past in order to say, for example, that the cause of a particular light's going on in the past was my switching on of the light a little earlier. It merely asserts that switching on a light is the *sort* of thing that I, the person who asserts that A is the cause of C, can do.

The main difficulty with the technological theory is that it describes the conditions under which a historian regards something as the cause of an event too narrowly, and this may be seen when we realize that it makes even more demands than the view that the cause of an event is a contingently necessary condition. The technological theory not only says that the cause must be a contingently necessary condition but also that it must be the kind of event that is producible or preventable by the person who says that it is the cause. The theory, therefore, makes a greater demand than an already demanding theory of *the* cause. It would rule out as faulty or false many historical explanations in which a natural disaster like an earthquake is said to be the cause of a certain event. Yet an earthquake, a storm, a hurricane, a crop failure, or a flood is often cited as *the* cause of a historical event. And many such natural causes are events of a kind that are not producible or preventable by human will, even in the most liberal sense of these terms. Such events stand—along with unpreventable events—as counterexamples to the technological theory of what *the* cause of a historical event is. Collingwood says that if a medical man should assert that cancer is caused by something that could not be produced or prevented, he "would be ridiculed by his colleagues in the profession,"[48] the implication being that physicians will call something the cause of a disease if and only if it is producible or preventable at will. Unfortunately, however, the view also seems to imply that if a person says that the cause of a man's death was that he was struck by lightning, that person would also be ridiculed. I think this is false as an account of the linguistic habits of physicians, and I am sure that it is a faulty account of the linguistic habits of historians. I repeat, however, that Collingwood does not *say* that the technological theory is applicable to history, and that my argument is therefore directed against any one who might think that it was.[49]

We should not conclude our discussion of the technological theory without pointing out that the fact that it does not present an adequate general account of the conditions under which historians regard something as the cause of an event does not mean that a historian will never cite a manipulable item as the cause of an event. They often do, just as they often cite states, events, and voluntary actions as the causes of events. But like all of the other faulty theories, the technological theory does not present a correct *general* theory of the majority of statements of *the* cause. The only way for the technological theory to become correct is for the historian to *make* it true by stipulation, but once he starts doing this, he can make any theory true in the same way.

7. ETHICS AND THE CAUSE

So far I have rejected the idea that the cause is selected capriciously because that is too wide, and I have rejected the categorial theory, the theory of necessary conditions, and the technological theory because they are too narrow. I have, however, spoken up in defense of abnormalism when it is conceived in such a way as to allow for a kind of relativity that permits expression of the histo-

[48] Ibid., p. 300.
[49] See Hart and Honoré, op. cit., p. 33, for a criticism of Collingwood.

rian's values and interests in regarding the subject of his inquiry in a certain way. Nevertheless, many philosophers who wish to keep the similarity between history and the natural sciences to an absolute minimum find the doctrine of abnormalism insufficiently attentive to the role of value judgment in causal inquiries. It gets into the act only with a small part, they might say, and that part is out of proportion to its centrality. I have acknowledged that a historian's interests and values may play a part in determining which statement of the cause of a revolution he will make, but for some philosophers this is much too meager a concession to their moralistic view of causal interpretation. It will hardly comfort philosophers who look upon history as peculiarly evaluative or normative by comparison to the generalizing sciences, for they appear to hold that value judgments are more intimately connected with causal statements in history. They seem to think that a statement of the cause of a historical event contains a value judgment *as a logical ingredient,* as some of them say, whereas, according to abnormalism, there is no moral statement which is a logical ingredient in the doctor's statement that the cause of John's attack of indigestion was his ulcers; and there is no such ingredient in the wife's diagnosis of the cause. Analogously, the statement made by the historian who calls the archduke's assassination the cause of the First World War, does not contain a logical ingredient that is moral. Nor does the statement made by the historian who attributes the war to the system of secret alliances.

In order to assess the moralistic theory, we must first ask what is meant by saying that a value judgment is an "ingredient" in a causal finding.[50] Possibly, that an appropriate value statement stands to the statement "A is the cause of C" as the statement "A is male" stands to the statement "A is the father of C"; in other words, that a value statement appears as a conjunct in the analysis of the causal statement. According to the view in question, the value statement expresses part of the meaning of the causal state-

[50] William Dray, "Some Causal Accounts of the American Civil War," *Daedalus* J. of the Amer. Acad. of Arts and Sciences, Summer, 1962, p. 580.

ment, some philosophers might say, so that anyone who asserted the causal statement and denied the value statement would contradict himself, just as the man who asserted that James Mill was the father of John Stuart Mill, but that James Mill was not male, would also be contradicting himself. But such a concept of logical ingredient rests on philosophically obscure notions like analyticity and synonymy, and I therefore find it hard to evaluate the thesis which employs the concept. For this reason I shall construe the moralistic thesis as asserting something weaker, namely, that if a statement of the cause is true, then the factor which is said to be the cause has a value property by virtue of which it is singled out. In other words, I shall construe the moralistic theory as extensional in character and try to show that even then it will not work for the vast majority of contexts of the form "A is the cause of C". On all known theories of synonymy, if two expressions are synonymous they will, a fortiori, have the same extension, so that if the weaker, extensional version of the moralistic theory fails, the stronger, intensional version will, a fortiori, fail. I propose to refute the weaker version of the thesis and therefore by implication the stronger version.

The question now arises: *what* value judgment is thought by the moralistic theorist to be an ingredient of the statement "A is the cause of C"? Since the moralistic theorist is often in reaction against a version of abnormalism according to which "A is the cause of C" implies the statistical abnormality of A, the moralistic theorist may say that what is implied is rather the *moral* abnormality—i.e., the immorality—of A. And since to be morally abnormal is to be an act which violates a moral norm, the moralistic theorist may be interpreted as holding that when a historian says, "A is the cause of C," what he says is logically equivalent to "A is a cause of C and A is an act which violates a moral norm." Of course, there may be variants of this view which formulate the moral component of such statements differently, but this is one of the most commonly held views precisely because it may be dramatically contrasted with the statistical view.

Can it be successfully maintained as an analysis of the vast majority of historical statements of the form "A is *the* cause of *C*"? No elaborate argument is needed in order to show the weakness of this thesis. All we need to realize is that some historians do not have moral attitudes toward certain events that they are trying to explain and therefore do not seek an explanation of what they regard as a harmful outcome. Even when the historian feels that an event is sad and feels sorry for those who suffer as a consequence of it, as when a natural disaster strikes them, he need not think of the natural disaster—i.e., the cause—as a morally wrong act, since he need not regard it as an act at all unless he is theologically minded. A historian will often cite an unpredictable natural disaster as the cause of a state of social disorganization without thinking that the disaster was a reprehensible *action*.

One may also cite other statements of the form "A is the cause of *C*" which do not imply that A is a reprehensible action. Surely historians sometimes refer to an action which is *in accordance* with a moral duty as *the* cause of an event. And therefore, if the moralistic theorist asserts that *all* statements of the form "A is the cause of *C*" imply statements to the effect that A is a *violation* of a moral norm, he is obviously making a mistake. In his reaction to abnormalism he has been led to replace the idea of statistical abnormality by the idea of moral abnormality, and as a consequence has probably forgotten that there are many contexts of the phrase "is the cause of" which do not involve any violation of a moral norm. To its credit, abnormalism does not force us to say that the expression "is the cause of" is used differently in cases where we cite an immoral action as the cause of an event. Abnormalism allows us to say *in the same sense* of the expression "the cause of" that the Tokyo earthquake was the cause of great social disorganization, that the failure of the gardener to water the flowers was the cause of their dying, and that the little boy's putting his finger in the dyke was the cause of the town's *not* being destroyed. Hart and Honoré rightly call attention to the fact that although in many cases "what is selected as the cause from the total set of conditions will often be an omission which coincides with what is reprehensible by established standards of behavior and may be inhibited by punishment. . . . this does not justify the conclusion which some have drawn that it is so selected merely because it is reprehensible."[51] It should be added that in many cases what is selected as the cause from the total set of conditions will often be an action which coincides with what is laudable, supererogatory, even heroic by established standards of behavior, and that the cause may even be something that would not be called an action at all, as in the case of an earthquake or a tidal wave. The fact that the cause can have all of these different features is what makes a moralistic theory of the kind we have been examining so implausible and what makes abnormalism so plausible as a theory of the preponderant use of "is the cause of".

The advocate of the statistical theory need not be fazed by the fact that a historian might say, "The action of that *saint*, the boy who put his finger in the dyke, was the cause of the countryside's not being flooded," or "The action of that *sinner*, John Brown, was the cause of the Civil War." In other words, abnormalism is not refuted by calling attention to the fact that a historian will often use a "value-charged" word when referring to what he regards as the cause. The historian may regard the cause of a deplorable event as deplorable without thinking that whenever something is *the* cause of an event it is deplorable. This is particularly evident when one considers certain disputes about the cause of a conflict like the Civil War or the First World War. The so-called "conspiracy theories" of the origin of the Civil War, according to which the war was brought about by the intrigues of certain individuals or groups, have encouraged some philosophers to think that a value judgment is an ingredient in statements of *the* cause, especially since Northern and Southern historians have advanced theories in which they seize on different conspirators and hence on different causes. According to the moralistic analyst of historical causation, when the historian wishes to find *the* cause, he must

[51] Hart and Honoré, op. cit., p. 35.

find at least on some occasions who the aggressor was; and this, according to the moralistic theorist, is an ethical inquiry at the end of which historians with different values may come to different conclusions. It is pointed out that to Southerners the secession of the South was a justified response to a Northern threat and not the cause of the Civil War even though the secession may have initiated it; whereas Northerners, who denied the right of secession, regarded the actions of the South as constituting resistance to the rightful occupation of federal property by Northerners and hence as constituting the cause of the war. From this the following philosophical conclusion is drawn:

The concept of causation employed by such conspiracy theorists on either side is thus logically tied to the evaluation of those actions which are candidates for causal status. That the actions of either Black Republicans or the Slaveholders and their allies were causes of the war is a judgment which requires the prior judgment that these same actions were reprehensible.[52]

Everything hinges on the vague expression, "logically tied," but even if we construe it extensionally, the moralistic theorist cannot sustain his thesis. The contributory cause which is *the* cause is not always an aggressive act or a reprehensible act. The connection among the concepts "the cause," "reprehensibility," and "aggression" is different. Aggressive actions are abnormal in certain situations; and if one can show that an aggressive action is the abnormal factor when viewed in a certain way, one may argue that it is *the* cause. According to the doctrine of abnormalism and common sense, we can assert that an action which is neither aggressive nor reprehensible is the cause of some event, and we can assert that a nonaction is the cause of some event in the same sense of "is the cause" as we employ when we say that an aggressive, reprehensible action is the cause of some event. The Lisbon tidal wave, the saintly action of the boy who put his finger in the dyke, and the allegedly sinful action of John Brown may each be said to be *the* cause of something in the same sense.

[52] Dray, in *Daedalus*, Summer, 1962, p. 581.

For that reason we may reject the following argument by Dray against the view that the gardener's failure to water the flowers is called the cause of their dying because the failure was an abnormal event:

Is it really because we expected the gardener to perform his duties, simply in the predictive sense of "expect," that we regard his failure as the cause? If expectation comes into it, is it not in the prescriptive sense? We cite the omission as cause because flower-watering was to be expected of a gardener; it is what he ought to have done. In a similar way, the revisionist historian, Avery Craven, supports his causal conclusion with the judgment that it is the statesman's business to seek compromise. One might surely doubt, too, that the Northern conspiracy theorist's causal conclusion implies his belief that the institution of slavery was abnormal in the sense of not being customary. Is it not, rather, that he regards it as abnormal in a value-charged sense? It is true that historians themselves sometimes make use of the concept of "abnormality" in a way which might be thought to vindicate the contention of Hart and Honoré. Thus Stampp writes, " 'revisionist' historians apparently believe that pre-Civil War political leaders were unusually incompetent, that their acts and decisions were grotesque and abnormal. Their exaggeration of sectional differences, their invention of allegedly fictitious issues (such as slavery expansion) created a crisis that was highly artificial and eventually precipitated a 'needless' war." But as the coupling with "grotesque" and "incompetent" suggests, it is not at all clear that the term "abnormal" is used here in a purely descriptive sense. This is even clearer in Randall's own revisionist use of it. "Omit the element of abnormality, of *bogus* leadership or *inordinate* ambition for conquest," he says, "and diagnosis fails."[53]

This argument does not succeed in showing that the "coupling" of the words "incompetent" and "grotesque" with the word "abnormal" in the passage from Stampp tells against abnormalism. It is no more effective than the argument that when we say, "The action of that saint, the boy who put his finger in the dyke, was the cause of the countryside's not being flooded," we are offering a counterexample to abnormalism. Why can't we construe Stampp's statement as indicating that historians pass a moral obiter dictum upon the cause, which cause is nevertheless selected on the

[53] Ibid., p. 589.

grounds of its statistical abnormality? And why can't we do the same thing in the case of Randall's statement? In both cases the statistically abnormal item called the cause is viewed with moral feeling by the historians, but it does not follow that they justify its selection as the cause on the grounds of their moral feelings about it. Moreover, the very "coupling" that Dray points to tells against his view, for it shows that the historian does not think that "abnormal" implies "grotesque."

Although I have confined myself to arguing against the view that the historical statement "A is the cause of C" is equivalent to a conjunction of statements, one of which is that A is reprehensible or a departure from a moral norm, my argument applies equally well to the view that it is equivalent to a conjunction which has as one conjunct the statement that A is laudable. On the basis of the foregoing argument it is obvious that in its typical use, the statement "A is the cause of C" no more implies the statement "A is laudable" than it implies the statement "A is reprehensible." Furthermore, by implication I have already shown that the moralistic theorist will not fare any better if he should say that typically *the* cause is that contributory cause which is either reprehensible or laudable, or that it is the contributory cause which is susceptible to moral judgment. Such a view is refuted by the simple fact that *the* cause of a historical event may be an earthquake.

8. AN UNTYPICAL USE OF "THE CAUSE"

Even though it is obvious that a vast number of historical statements that purport to state *the* cause of events do not imply moral statements, it would be unwise to say dogmatically that historians *never* speak in a manner that might encourage something like the moralistic view. For it cannot be said that whenever a historian asserts something of the form "A is the cause of C," he always thinks of A as the statistically abnormal antecedent. The notion of *being the cause of* is sufficiently loose to allow a slide in the direction of language that is less empirical and more evaluative in nature, and some historians certainly take the opportunity to slide in that direction. For example, they sometimes say that a man's omission was the cause of an event even though that omission was not an unusual omission, as when they regard a failure to perform a heroic action as the cause of something they are trying to explain. When they say that the explanation of the town's being saved was the boy's putting his finger in the dyke, they speak in a manner that is easily analyzed by the advocate of abnormalism, but when they say that the destruction of the town is explained by the boy's *failure* to put his finger in the dyke, they speak in a way that is grist for the moralistic mill. Of course, the failure of a *hero* to act heroically on a given occasion might be called the cause by a historian who thought that the abnormal element in the situation was the hero's unexpected lapse from heroism. But it would seem that some historians are prepared to call the omission of a man the cause of an event on the ground that the man did *not* act heroically, even though the man was not habitually heroic in his behavior nor, so far as they know, a member of any class of individuals who usually do the sort of thing he failed to do. Some historians of the Civil War seem to have made this sort of statement about the failures of certain politicians to avert the war. I have in mind historians who have said that a political leader's failure to do something was the cause of an event on the ground that he did not extend himself, because he did not act in a supererogatory way, because he did not sacrifice himself, because he did not transcend the statistically normal. One certainly can find historians saying things like this, and one would be hard put to construe their statements in the manner described by the statistical theory.

What, then, is to be said about such statements? An overzealous advocate of abnormalism may insist that his theory works even in such cases, and argue as follows in defense of the statement that the little boy's failure to put his finger in the dyke was the cause of the flood: "It would be unusual for a rational boy who knew that failure to put his finger in the dyke would mean the flooding of the town, not to put his finger in the dyke." But surely this is false as an account of how rational boys behave. It sounds more like a description of how irrational boys behave. Of course, one might try to find some other class to which the boy belongs, a class whose members usually perform the heroic action in question, but not every historian who called the boy's failure the cause of the flooding of the countryside would feel obliged to seek out such a class and show the boy to be a member of it in order to substantiate his causal statement. For this reason one hesitates to say that in all cases "the cause of" is equivalent to "the abnormal condition among the jointly sufficient conditions for." It seems wiser to sum up the actual linguistic situation by saying that in some contexts—but a relatively small number—"the cause of" is used moralistically. Sometimes historians regard a man's failure to do something as the cause of an event even though his failure is not like that of a gardener to water the flowers, and when they do they may have in mind what they take to be the man's moral duty to perform certain actions even though these actions are not expected of him in the predictive sense. Having said this, a philosopher may consistently add that it is unwise for historians to use the same expression—"is the cause of"—in both cases. The philosopher may argue that a historian who says that a failure of an ordinary man to perform a heroic action is *the* cause says something that would be better expressed by the use of the words "ought to be held responsible for" instead of by the use of the words "is the cause of"; that when a historian goes so far as to say that a man's failure to do something heroic was the cause of the Civil War, the historian has deviated from the standard or more customary use of the expression "is the cause of"; and that he should use different language to express his thought. A good deal of the protest against revisionism in historical writing about the Civil War may be viewed in this light. To some it seems that the so-called blundering generation has been called the cause of the war in superficially objective language, when really certain historians with standards of moral responsibility about which there might well be disagreement have been asserting that the blundering generation should be held responsible for the war. In short, some historians protest that a statement of the cause, which is typically supported by empirical knowledge, is here being atypically supported in part by reference to moral conviction.

Now the philosopher may *record* the historian's tendency to use one linguistic expression under such widely different circumstances, but he need not condone it, and may recommend its abandonment. In other words, he may doubt whether the practice of using the expression "is the cause of" moralistically as well as in accordance with the doctrine of abnormalism is a wise, fruitful, prudent policy. In doing so the philosopher need not argue that historians should avoid saying that certain people ought to be held responsible for certain outcomes, but he may justifiably recommend that the reader be given full opportunity to see when the historian is using the expression "is the cause of" so as to reflect what might be the historian's, but not the reader's, standards of morality. In effect this might lead to a recommendation that the historian use two distinct linguistic expressions, one that signalizes that his selection of *the* cause has been made on wholly empirical grounds and another that signalizes that the selection has been made on moral grounds.

In assessing this recommendation, we may compare the situation here with that involved in the generalization of the concept of number in mathematics. In the case of mathematics, rationals and reals are both called numbers in spite of their difference from natural numbers. Should the historian imitate the mathematician and call the morally selected antecedent and the factually selected antecedent "*the* cause" in spite of their differences, or should he use another expression for one of them? We know that mathematicians employ *one* term for their different kinds of numbers for good reasons, but it must be acknowledged that when we put under one rubric statements that are supported in a wholly empirical way and those that are partly supported by value considerations, we are "generalizing" the relation of *being the cause of* in a way that rightly unsettles some thinkers. In other words, they may feel that it is all right to use the word "number" so as to cover things as widely different as naturals, rationals, and reals; but they feel, by contrast, that when you use the same expression, "is the cause of," to cover statements of *the* cause which are supported in a wholly empirical way and statements which are supported in part by moral arguments, you are courting confusion. Everything depends on what the gain is in assimilating the two, and since I cannot see anything like the advantages that may be cited by the mathematician who generalizes the concept number, I am inclined to think that it would be well in writing history to use the expression "is the cause of" when one is thinking in wholly empirical terms and another expression when one's conclusions rest in part on a moral judgment that one's colleagues and readers might not share. This is particularly advisable when one is trying to discover historical causes in an effort to punish, when the cause is in the recent past. For here so much rests on the causal conclusion that one wants more than ever to know whether the conclusion is arrived at in a wholly factual way, or whether a moral judgment that some men might reject on moral grounds has entered into the conclusion. On balance then, I think that historians should use "is the cause of" in only one of the two situations I have considered, although I do not—and this is extremely important—rest my conclusion on any view as to the "true" meaning of this expression. Since it seems to me that in the majority of cases in which "is the cause of" is employed, the historian in fact tries to support his statement wholly on objective grounds, I should recommend that the expression be reserved for those cases and that another expression be used in the cases where a judgment that someone ought to be held responsible underlies the selection of *the* cause. It is worth observing that such a recommendation is likely to be more acceptable in a culture which does not tend to moral consensus than it is likely to be in a culture which does. For at the heart of the idea that we should clearly distinguish statements based on wholly factual grounds and those which are partly supported by moral convictions is the idea that the wholly factual statement is more likely to win consensus than the moral statement. If men were given to arriving at the same judgments of moral responsibility, there would be less reason than there is for adopting the linguistic recommendation I have made.

I also wish to repeat that although I have argued in this chapter against one view of the role of value judgment in historical investigation, I have in my formulation of abnormalism given free scope to the idea that different interests and hence values may lead one historian to make one statement of *the* cause rather than another, where there is a choice. There are, in short, cases where the decision to make one statement of the cause rather than another may be grounded on an inarbitrable difference. This should be enough value for the most value-conscious philosophers of history. The value judgment is not a "logical ingredient" of the causal judgment but sometimes a value judgment will determine which causal statement will be made and in this sense play a part in causal interpretation. We shall see a similar situation in the theory of historical narration—as opposed to explanation—when we come to it.

9. A CONCLUDING REMARK ON PHILOSOPHICAL METHOD

After having read the foregoing argument the reader may wonder whether some of the rejected theories of causal interpretation have been treated too harshly and also whether they can not instead be treated as so many different analyses of "the decisive cause," as used in different contexts. Thus, it might be said that in certain contexts "the decisive cause" is equivalent to "the standing condition," sometimes to "the action," sometimes to "the thought," sometimes to "the episode," sometimes to "the reprehensible action," sometimes to "the producible or preventable factor," sometimes to "the unknown factor" among the contributory causes. This irenical approach might make every theorist happy by giving him a crumb, so why is it not acceptable? I think that the simple answer is that there is no context of "A is the cause of C" for which any one of the rejected theories provides a necessary and sufficient condition. It should be noticed, of course, that the doctrine of abnormalism does not preclude the possibility that the cause is a standing condition, an action, a producible or preventable factor, and so on. On some occasions the cause may be one or the other of these sorts of contributory causes, just as it may be a reprehensible action. The virtue of abnormalism is that it allows us to say that a standing condition, an episode, or an action, and so on, is the cause in just those cases in which our philosophically guided reflection on causation leads us to such a conclusion. Abnormalism as presented in Thesis II provides us with a unified theory of *the* cause just as existential regularism as presented in Thesis I provides us with a unified theory of *a* cause.

It may now be argued that we should think of the various rejected theories as presenting different *reasons* for asserting something of the form "A is the cause of C" rather than as different equivalents for different contexts in which those words are used. But this view of the matter also seems inadequate to me. I don't think that it is ever sufficient to say, for example, that A is the cause of C *because* A is a contributory cause of C and A is a state, even where A is a state. Nor do I think that it is ever sufficient to say that A is an episode. We say that being α is a sufficient condition for being β if and only if it is true that every α is β. So clearly being the *state* among several contributory causes is not sufficient for being the decisive cause among them. Some states are not decisive causes, some actions are not decisive causes, some episodes are not decisive causes, and so on for all the sorts of entities put forward by the rejected theories. And conversely, as we have seen, some decisive causes are not states, some are not episodes, some are not actions, and so on. Therefore we cannot say that any of our rejected theories states a sufficient condition, and we cannot say that any one of them states a necessary condition for being *the* cause. A fortiori, no one of them presents a necessary and sufficient condition. Only in one case have I admitted that *the cause* might be used in accordance with a view that departs from abnormalism, but there I have exercised the philosophical analyst's right to propose that such usage be abandoned in the interests of clear thinking and effective communication.

Finally, it should be clear that the various theories that have been considered in this chapter—notably abnormalism—must be distinguished from the various speculative philosophies of history that are sometimes called "historical determinisms." For example, the advocate of such a determinism may fix on geography, climate, race, religion, philosophy, or the material conditions of life and may argue that one such variable is fundamental, that all the other variables of history are functions of it, as in some versions of Marxism. By contrast, the analytic philosopher who tries to identify *the* cause in general terms is trying to state the necessary and sufficient conditions under which historians apply a certain expression. The analytic enterprise is metahistorical in so far as it is an effort to describe the language of ordinary historians, whereas the speculative enterprise is metahistorical in so far as it goes beyond the ordinary historian's concern to make true singular statements—both causal and noncausal—and on to the formulation of laws of history. Even the analytic doctrine that the historical cause is always an underlying cause is not to be identified with any of the classical theories of geographical determinism, economic determinism, racial determinism, and so on. For advocates of these theories fix on one *sort* of underlying cause and do not content themselves with analyzing *the* cause as the underlying cause. Therefore they must speculate and try to defend their views by methods that are fundamentally different from those employed in the analytic philosophy of history.

CHAPTER V

Reasons and Causes

     The moralistic view of historical explanation which was examined in the last chapter is not incompatible with existential regularism, for moralism as there construed is a theory of how we select *the* cause from among contributory causes that are connected with the event to be explained in accordance with Thesis I. But there is another variety of moralism which goes further and challenges existential regularism itself by denying that empirical laws play any part in historical explanation. According to this second variety of moralism, when the historian asserts that Brutus assassinated Caesar because he thought that Caesar was a tyrant, the historian's statement does not imply the existence of empirical laws but rather that of moral laws. Such an attack on the wholly empirical view of singular explanatory statements shifts attention away from the problem of whether the decisive cause is chosen on empirical or on moral grounds, and to the connection between a contributory cause and the effect.

  The second variety of moralism rests first of all on the belief that when we ask why a person performed an action we are asking a question which should be answered by presenting the *reason* that the agent had for performing the action, and secondly on the belief that presenting reasons is very different from presenting causes. It would be granted, of course, that a historian often uses the word "because" in his explanations and that the natural scientist may use the word "reason" in his, but nevertheless, it is said, when the historian says that Brutus stabbed Caesar because Brutus thought that Caesar was a tyrant or about to become one, the historian's use of the word "because" is very different from the chemist's use of it when the chemist says that a particular piece of litmus turned red because it was immersed in an acid. Presenting a reason is thought to be radically different from what a chemist does when he presents a contributory cause, since a historian's statement of the form "His reason for doing C was his thinking that A" is held to imply, presuppose, or involve—and as usual in such discussions the verb that is thought to be appropriate at this juncture of the argument varies—a statement about what is reasonable for a person to do under certain circumstances.

According to the variety of moralism now under consideration, a statement about what is reasonable for a person to do under certain circumstances is not an empirical law. It is more like a moral law, a statement of what ought to be done or what it is right to do under certain circumstances. And according to the view we are now considering, this sort of law figures in the historian's explanation rather than the empirical laws of which the regularist speaks. According to this variety of moralism, a historian can understand an action if and only if he regards it as a reasonable action, and he can regard it as reasonable if and only if it falls under some principle or normative rule which he, the historian himself, accepts. Therefore, on this view, the process of explanation, if it is one of subsumption at all, is a process in which the historian subsumes the acts he explains under moral principles rather than under descriptive laws.

Advocates of this variety of moralism not only reject all forms of regularism but also offer a positive view of explanation which is intended to show why regularism is false as a theory of historical explanation. They maintain that the reason why one cannot find empirical laws underlying historical explanations is that there *could not be* any laws which underlie historical explanation when that is properly understood. Instead of relying on descriptive empirical laws, they say, the historian relies on normative principles of action, judgments of the reasonableness of certain sorts of action. Instead of relying on explanatory deductive arguments of the kind analyzed by the regularist, they claim, the historian relies on practical arguments, arguments offered in support of the conclusion that something *ought to be done*. And so, if the historian looks to other disciplines for logical support and cooperation in his effort to explain historical actions, he is advised to consult, not the social scientist and the psychologist, but that ancient stalwart, the moralist. Another way of looking at the methodological implications of this doctrine is to say that it lends support to the view that the historian is self-sufficient when it comes to explaining human actions, that he need not rely on what the social sciences have discovered, since he, as an intelligent human being, is able to tell when an action is reasonable without the advice of scientific specialists who seek to discover general empirical propositions about human behavior.

This same view is sometimes supported by an appeal to the traditional doctrine that events which we explain causally are determined and hence cannot be voluntary actions, whereas voluntary actions are just those which are performed for reasons which the historian aims to discern. Therefore, it is held, the actions which the historian wishes to explain must be radically distinguished from the events explained by the natural scientist with the help of his laws and his explanatory deductive arguments: there is one logic of explanation for the sciences of nature and another for the discipline of history.

What is to be said of this view? First of all, it is essential to point out that it cannot be taken seriously as an account of *all* historical explanations, and certainly not of all the explanations that the regularist tries to analyze. As we have noted earlier, historians do not try to explain only individual human actions and individual human beliefs. They try to explain wars, revolutions, collapses of empires, intellectual movements, political reforms, economic changes, and other sorts of things that can hardly be thought of as the rational actions of single individuals. We may assume, therefore, that those philosophers who oppose the regularity theory of explanation because they believe that there is such a thing as rational explanation, do not really mean to say that *every* explanation of the kind offered by historians may be regarded as a rational explanation. We may therefore construe them as asserting rather that *some* are, and that those are not amenable to the covering law analysis.

Diminishing the claim of this view, however, does not make it any more plausible. It is true, of course, that historians often report the reasoning of a historical agent in their effort to explain his action, and that *the agent's* reasoning will often be moral in character—though obviously not always—and to that extent contain premises that are not empirical laws. But it does not follow from this that the historian's account of the agent's moral reasoning will itself be moral or evaluative in character, or that the historian, when he cites the reasoning in his explanation of the agent's action, must approve of the moral reasoning of the agent. In other words, when the historian asserts that the agent performed his action because the agent had certain moral views, the historian's singular explanatory statement will often be empirical in character: he will use the word "because" as the natural scientist uses it when the natural scientist makes a singular explanatory statement, and hence in a manner that is analyzable in accordance with Thesis I.

EXPLANATION AND EVALUATION

Let us suppose that the historian is trying to explain Brutus' assassination of Caesar and that, for the sake of simplicity, Brutus' ethical argument in defense of his action is deductive in form. Let us also suppose that the historian has, on the basis of his research, assured himself that Brutus would have accepted the following as a formulation of the structure of his argument (it may be called BA for brief future reference):

> BA: (1) I am in a situation characterized by
>   X, Y, and Z.
>   (2) When in a situation characterized by X,
>   Y, and Z, one ought to act in manner W.
>   Therefore,
>   (3) I ought to act in manner W.

It is obvious, of course, that *Brutus* engages in evaluation in the broadest sense, since he voices acceptance of a moral principle. But in order to see the limitations of the view that the *historian* must engage in evaluation when he explains Brutus' action, we must first make a number of important distinctions. First of all, each of the above three statements must be distinguished from the belief in or the acceptance of the statement. The moral principle (2) must be distinguished from Brutus' acceptance of it, so must Brutus' acceptance of factual statement (1) be distinguished from (1), and so must Brutus' acceptance of moral conclusion (3) be distinguished from that conclusion. In addition to these three statements and three beliefs, there are two other important elements in the situation: the agent's effort to carry out the action prescribed in (3), and if he is successful, the action itself. Having made these distinctions, we can now see how the argument used by the historian who tries to explain the action performed by the agent is different from that of the agent. The historian's reasoning may be causal even though the agent's is not. I shall call the historian's argument *HA*. It may be broken down into several steps, each of them a singular explanatory statement:[1]

> HA: (4) Partly because Brutus believed (1) and (2),
>   Brutus believed (3).

[1] It will be recalled that "Partly because A, C" is equivalent to "A is a contributory cause of C."

(5) Partly because Brutus believed (3), he tried to act in manner W.

(6) Partly because Brutus tried to act in manner W, he acted in manner W.

And if the historian wishes to do so, he may conclude from these three statements:

(7) Partly because Brutus believed (1) and (2), Brutus acted in manner W.

One can see from this that the historian need not engage in evaluation when he explains an action. No one of his singular explanatory statements (4), (5), (6), and (7) is evaluative, and all may be analyzed in accordance with Thesis I. For example, when he asserts (4), he implies that there are true singular statements about the agent—such as "Brutus is logical-minded"—and that there are psychological laws which, together with the antecedent of (4), imply that Brutus believes that he ought to do W. When the historian asserts (5), there is an analogous implication that there are singular statements—for example, the statement that Brutus is resolute—and that there are laws which, together with the statement that Brutus believed that he ought to do W, imply that Brutus tried to do W. And when the historian asserts (6), he implies that there are singular statements about the circumstances in which Brutus made his effort and that there are laws which, together with the antecedent of (6), logically imply that Brutus did W. It is clear from this that the agent's own argument, *BA*, differs markedly from *HA*, the historical explanation of how one belief in that argument causally *leads* to another. To reason morally is not to make causal statements about one's self, and the historian's "partly because" is not the "therefore" of the agent himself.

How can one establish that because a man believed one proposition he believed another? One cannot deduce the statement "Brutus believes *q*" from "Brutus believes *p*" even if *q* is itself deducible from *p*, simply because Brutus may not believe certain propositions that are deducible from those he does believe. It is clear, therefore, that the connection between the two believings is empirical and that underlying it there are psychological laws, just as there are physical laws underlying the statement "Partly because the match was struck, it lit" or the statement "Partly because the match was dry, it lit." And just as the singular explanatory statement "Partly because the match was struck, it lit" implies that there are certain other features of the match which cooperate with the striking to bring about the lighting, so there are other features of Brutus which cooperate with his believing the premises to bring about his believing the conclusion, for example, his logical acuity. The reasoning which we attribute to Brutus here is comparatively simple, and therefore the singular explanatory statement we assert about him will imply the existence of other true statements about him which refer to a rather low degree of logical acuity. But if we were making a causal statement about the connection between two beliefs of, say, Leibniz, the situation might be quite different, for we might be able to say, "Partly because Leibniz believed *r*, he believed *s*," where the logical connection between *r* and *s* is much more complex than the connection in the case of Brutus' premises and conclusion. However, if we made such a statement about Leibniz, we would also imply that there are true singular statements about him and laws that together implied "Lebniz believed *s*."

Although we have considered a case in which the historian explains one belief by reference to another where there is a logical implication between the propositions believed, this is not the only sort of case in which we can explain one belief by reference to another. The statement which explains why Brutus believes that the sun will rise tomorrow morning may also cite Brutus' belief in other propositions which *inductively* support the proposition that the sun will rise tomorrow. But the pattern of *causal* explanation is the same whether the inference is deductive, inductive, valid, or invalid. The savage's belief that a person is a witch may be causally explained by reference to another belief of the savage which, as *we* might say, does not logically support it. There are explanatory deductive arguments that connect one mad, false, or superstitious belief with others. And the point is that the historian is engaged in causal explanation *in the same sense* whether he is explaining the beliefs of a sane or insane man, a civilized man or a primitive man, a genius or a fool.

Let us return to statement (5) and observe that the connection between a man's believing that he ought to perform an action and his trying to perform an action, is similar in important respects to the connection between his believing one proposition and his believing another. Once again the singular explanatory statement implies the existence of a statement asserting that the man had certain properties, and once again the singular explanatory statement implies the existence of laws. How else can we analyze the causal connection between believing and trying? The historian is not asked to give reasons for the agent's action in the sense in which the agent is asked to give reasons, i.e., to justify the action. The historian is merely required to tell what caused the agent to do something.

Having argued in this way, I want to make perfectly clear that I do not hold that belief in the premises of an argument constitutes one *event* which brings about another *event*, belief in the conclusion, which brings about a third *event*, the effort. Saying that a man believes a proposition is more like saying that he is in a state, or has a disposition, although his efforts and actions are certainly events in the normal sense of that word, as is his *coming* to believe a proposition. In earlier discussions we concentrated on singular explanatory statements in which events are causally explained, but states may be explained and explain too. A man may be in the state of believing something—have a certain disposition—because he is in the state of believing something else, and the causal connection between these two dispositions may be analyzed in accordance with Thesis I. Moreover, the connection between a disposition, like believing that an act of kind W ought to be performed, and an event, like trying to perform an act of kind W, can also be analyzed in accordance with Thesis I. The singular statement "Because Brutus believed (1) and (2), he believed (3)" is analogous to "Because this is sugar, it is soluble in water," whereas the statement "Because Brutus believed that he ought to act in manner W, he tried to act in manner W" is analogous to "Because that was soluble in water, it dissolved."

All of this supports the conclusion that when the historian tries to explain Brutus' action by citing Brutus' reasoning, the historian is not implicitly asserting or defending a *moral* or *evaluative* principle. The historian who explains Brutus' assassination of Caesar by citing Brutus' use of argument BA is not obliged to *accept* either one of the premises in Brutus' argument—the factual or the moral—in order to accept the explanation given in (7). Analogously the historian of the Russian Revolution need not accept the political morality of a Communist who announces that the end justifies the means as he liquidates his political enemies, even though the historian cites the acceptance of such a principle on the part of the Communist in an explanation of why the Communist did liquidate his enemies. It may happen that the historian approves of the argument that the historical agent used, but the point is that he need not approve of it in order to understand the agent's action.

It is true, of course, that there is a usage in accordance with which one says, "I cannot understand why he did that," when one means, not that one does not know the person's motives, but rather that one does not approve of his motives or his behavior. But this usage should not stand in the way of our seeing that one need not accept an argument in order to see that its acceptance *led* to a certain action. This is true even when the historian who tries to understand Caesar's actions goes through a process, as Collingwood describes it, of "envisaging for himself the situation in which Caesar stood, and thinking for himself what Caesar thought about the situation and the possible ways of dealing with it." When the historian asks himself, "What would a man in Caesar's situation, having Caesar's thoughts, ambitions, feelings, and desires, try to do?" and comes to the conclusion that such a man would try to cross the Rubicon, the explanation that the historian may then offer will imply the existence of generalizations containing the descriptive word "would" and not the moral word "should." It is true that *sometimes* the historian's conclusion that a certain action ought to be done will lend support to his belief that a historical agent did it, especially if the historian happens to believe that the agent is an admirable person who generally does the right thing. And sometimes a historian can say of a man that he did something because he thought that it was the right thing to do. But neither of these considerations militate against the view that the historian can explain an action without passing judgment on the action or on the process whereby the agent arrived at the conclusion that he ought to perform the action.

This may be even more obvious when the historian is trying to explain an action which is performed by an agent for nonmoral reasons. We have confined ourselves to cases in which the historian tries to explain an action by citing a situation in which the agent used a moral argument in the sense of one containing a moral principle as a premise, but clearly Kant was right in pointing out that some actions are performed by agents who operate with what he called imperatives of skill in mind. They perform an action of a certain kind in order to accomplish a certain kind of end which they think can be accomplished by the performance of that kind of action, and they need not *in that context* evaluate the end. The historian who explains the action of such an agent by pointing out that he *wanted* to achieve a certain kind of end and that he *thought* that kind of end could be achieved in that way, need not pass judgment on the end and, as we have seen, need not even pass judgment on the agent's belief that his goal can be reached in a certain way. The historian can explain the actions of a prince by pointing out that he accepted certain maxims of Machiavelli, even though the historian disapproves of monarchy and thinks that Machiavelli gives bad advice about how to keep a populace subjugated. The logical moral is once again clear. The historian may cite beliefs and arguments in explanation of actions without passing judgment on those beliefs and arguments, and he need not evaluate the actions he explains.

Nor need he evaluate the beliefs he explains when he is an intellectual historian. Not only the singular explanatory statement (4) illustrates this point, but also singular explanatory statements which are offered in intellectual history in the usual sense. This may be seen if we turn to cases where a historian concludes that a person held one philosophical or scientific belief because he held another. It is important to bear in mind that when we make a statement of the form "B believed q partly because he believed p, r, s, and t," where the propositions are of any kind, we are making an empirical statement about the person B, a statement the truth of which does not depend on whether B was right in believing the conjunction of premises or the proposition that he derived from them. For this reason I think that the following statement by Collingwood is not acceptable as an account of what intellectual historians must do:

The historian not only re-enacts past thought, he re-enacts it in the context of his own knowledge and therefore, in re-enacting it, criticizes it, forms his own judgement of its value, corrects whatever errors he can discern in it. This criticism of the thought whose history he traces is not something secondary to tracing the history of it. It is an indispensable condition of the historical knowledge itself. Nothing could be a completer error concerning the history of thought than to suppose that the historian as such merely ascertains "what so-and-so thought," leaving it to someone else to decide "whether it was true." All thinking is critical thinking; the thought which re-enacts past thoughts, therefore, criticizes them in re-enacting them.[2]

I do not reject this statement because of what it says about the division of intellectual labor, since I do not wish to dispute here whether some students of Plato should confine themselves to saying *merely* what he thought, whereas others should decide whether what he thought was true. For a variety of reasons I think it might be practically impossible for a student of Plato to avoid passing

[2] R. G. Collingwood, *The Idea of History* (Oxford, 1946), pp. 215–16.

some judgment on what Plato said. But it seems to me false to say that in order to explain why Plato held certain beliefs a historian *must* pass judgment on the content of those beliefs or on the modes of argument Plato used in arriving at them.

Of course, I agree that typical historical explanations differ from typical scientific explanations of individual events, because obviously the natural scientist does not usually cite *beliefs* in order to explain the behavior of his algae, rocks, stars, galaxies, and electrons. And I do not deny that historians sometimes explain human actions by citing the moral principles to which the agent is known to have subscribed. But these principles need not be evaluated by the historian in the course of his explanation, and his reference to the agent's acceptance of them does not eliminate the implication that there are empirical laws which stand to his explanation in the manner described in Thesis I.

The basic error of those who do not see the situation in this way may derive from their failure to see the difference between the role of a moral principle in the deliberation of a moral agent who becomes the subject of historical investigation, and the role of reference to it in some historical explanations. The difference may be described roughly with the help of the analogous logical distinction between using an expression, in this case a principle, and merely mentioning it. When Brutus comes to the conclusion that he ought to assassinate Caesar, he may *use* the moral principle "When in a situation characterized by features X, Y and Z, one ought to act in manner W." But in the historian's explanation of Brutus' action, which may read "Partly because Brutus believed the principle 'When in a situation characterized by features X, Y and Z, one ought to act in manner W,' and believed the statement 'Brutus is in a situation characterized by X, Y and Z,' Brutus acted in manner W," the moral principle is merely mentioned by the historian. When Brutus asks himself, "Why *should* I act in manner W?" he may answer his own question completely by presenting what was earlier called argument BA. But it does not follow from this that when the historian asks why Brutus *did* act in manner W, the historian will answer the question in the same way and hence have to believe in the correctness or "rationality" of the moral principle. The historian is engaged in a different sort of inquiry when he asks, "Why did Brutus assassinate Caesar?" Indeed, as we have seen, even if the historian were to confine himself to asking, "Why did Brutus come to the *conclusion* that he ought to assassinate Caesar?" he would be asking a question different from that asked by Brutus of himself. For Brutus tried to find grounds in *defense* of his moral conclusion whereas the historian wants to explain why Brutus came to that conclusion. That is why the historian may avoid the question whether Brutus' reasoning was valid, i.e., may avoid asking whether his premises are true and whether his moral conclusion followed from those premises. The historian may assert empirical singular explanatory statements like (4), (5), (6), and (7), each of which implies the existence of empirical laws. These laws help one predict what moral conclusions a certain kind of man will come to if he holds certain beliefs, what efforts a certain kind of man will make if he comes to certain moral conclusions, and what actions he will perform if he makes certain efforts. That is why the historian, when he comes to support his singular explanatory statements, may appeal to general knowledge of what men will believe and do when they hold certain beliefs. The historian is not primarily a moral judge. With Spinoza he may say after much of his work, "I have laboured carefully, not to mock, lament, or execrate, but to understand human actions."[3]

CAUSAL AND NONCAUSAL RATIONAL EXPLANATION

The foregoing account of the explanation of belief and action is compatible with the idea that sometimes when a historian of ideas tries to explain why a thinker believed a certain proposition, or a

---

[3] *Tractatus Politicus*, I, § 4. The main theme of the preceding section is stated in the slightly revised version of my "Historical Explanation" (*Mind*, 1943), repr. *Theories of History*, ed. Patrick Gardiner, (New York, 1959), pp. 357–58. See also J. Passmore, "Review Article: Law and Explanation in History," *Australian Journal of Politics and History*, IV (1958), 275; and Carl G. Hempel, "Reasons and Covering Laws in Historical Explanation," in *Philosophy and History*, ed. Sidney Hook (New York, 1963), pp. 152 ff.

biographer tries to explain why a historical personage performed a certain action, the historian and the biographer may confine themselves to presenting the rational arguments used by their subjects. But we may use the word "explanation" in two different ways when we characterize such presentations as explanations.

(1) In one case we think of them as explanations in the same sense as we think of the dropping of the spark as the explanation of the explosion, i.e., we think that the spark was the abnormal factor, the factor that made the difference. One can imagine a case, for example, in which the thinker whose thought or action we are trying to explain has just learned something new and where his new belief causes him to change or adopt some other belief. A classic case of this sort occurred when Newton realized that a certain calculation of the size of the earth that he had previously accepted was wrong. When Newton came to accept the correct calculation, he came to believe as a consequence that his theory of gravitation was not defective, as he had originally thought. The reader will be able to supply many dramatic illustrations of this sort of thing in biography, cases in which a man acts in a certain way, or has a certain belief because of a belief that made the difference. In such cases Thesis II is clearly applicable because the question "Why?" may be construed as a request for the decisive cause and the answer to this question may be given in a singular explanatory statement whose antecedent refers to a psychological fact which may be singled out on the same grounds as we single out the spark as the explanation of the explosion, or the fact that the water comes from the sea as the explanation of its saltiness. We may call this causal rational explanation, since a belief is cited as the cause of another belief or action.

(2) By contrast to such cases, there are cases in which the historian presents a historical figure's thoughts or arguments, not because the historian thinks that a belief or an argument was the contributory cause that "made the difference," but because he understands the question "Why?" in an entirely different way. The historian may be working in an area of intellectual history or biography where the interest is simply in the recounting of rational

arguments used by intellectuals or by men of action and where there is no interest in causal explanation. In such cases he presents what may be called a noncausal rational explanation. Let us consider intellectual history first.

Often when historians of science and philosophy ask questions of the form "Why did Newton accept proposition *p*?" and "Why did Descartes believe *q*?" they mean simply to ask, "What reasons did Newton offer—or might he have offered—in behalf of *p*?" and "What reasons did Descartes offer—or might he have offered—in behalf of *q*?" It is an accepted convention of much work in intellectual history to construe the question "Why?" in this way, and no student of the language of history can fail to record the fact that such a convention exists. Those scholars who use the word "why" in this way may be perfectly aware of the fact that if they were to undertake a causal study of the thinking of Newton and Descartes, they would be obliged to consider other factors and might give different answers to their question. Nevertheless, they think that there is a useful and important job to be performed by finding and presenting the reasons that are stated by the thinkers or half-stated by them, or the reasons they would have stated if they had been asked certain questions. We all know, however, that sometimes a man believes a proposition because he *wants* to believe it or because there are great sanctions against disbelieving it. And when such a man also offers rational arguments for his belief, it is common for some historians of thought to point out that whereas he *said* that he believed *p* because it followed from certain other propositions which he thought were true, the *real* cause of his believing *p* was the fact that he wanted to believe it or was scared into believing it or was in the grip of some neurosis. When such a contention is made by a historian of this persuasion to the historian who concentrates on rational argumentation, the latter may dig his heels in and insist, "No, the *real* cause of Descartes's belief in God was Descartes's conviction that God's existence followed from the definition of 'God,' his acceptance of the ontological argument." In such a case the second historian demonstrates his interest in *causal* rational explanation. On the other hand, the historian who is interested in noncausal rational explanation may say that he is interested *only* in revealing the logical defense that Descartes offered for his belief in God, and not in causally explaining Descartes's belief.

It is pointless to deny that a study of the rational arguments of past thinkers can be useful and interesting and that it may be conducted in order to answer the question "Why?" as that word is sometimes used. Such a study lies behind the standard way of teaching the history of philosophy to those who are primarily interested in becoming philosophers themselves and who are interested in rationally arriving at philosophical truth. It proceeds on the eminently sensible theory that one can learn much about how to arrive at and to defend his own philosophical beliefs by examining the intellectual argumentation of his forerunners in the subject. Moreover, the historian's presentation of the defense that a philosopher once offered in behalf of a belief can be objective and need not presuppose either agreement with that belief or approval of the mode of defense used in its behalf. It is true that those who study the history of thought in this way will often be tempted to intersperse critical comments on the beliefs and arguments advanced by those whom they are studying, but there is a difference between showing that Descartes defended his belief in the existence of God by reference to the ontological argument, and agreeing with the belief or accepting that argument as valid. In short, even if the question "Why did Descartes believe that God exists?" is asked in a sense which is noncausal, its answer may be purely factual.

By the same token, the question "Why did Caesar come to the conclusion that he ought to cross the Rubicon?" may also be asked in a sense which is not causal, if what the questioner seeks is an account of Caesar's defense of this conclusion, and this question too may be answered in an objective manner. Students of the history of military strategy, political action, and a variety of other subjects may be interested in this sort of question without being interested in a causal question about the agent. In effect such a historian asks, "By what rational process did the agent take himself to have established his conclusion?" And I can see no reason for denying that such investigations go on or that they should go on. Sometimes when a historian asks why a certain philosopher held a certain belief or why a certain politician performed a certain action, he means simply to ask, "What were his arguments for his conclusions?" I know that there is a special way of pronouncing the word "explain" by means of which we can express our conviction that such a historian is not explaining the belief or the action, as when we ask, "But do such historians really *explain* beliefs and actions when all they do is to recount the agent's reasons?" Yet it cannot be denied that there is a way of using the word "why" in order to find out merely what the subject's arguments were. On such a view we do not have to defend our singling out the argument as *the* cause of the explained belief by saying it was the abnormal item that made the difference. Therefore, I am prepared to admit that the word "explain" is used in a noncausal sense, and I see no reason for saying that only the causal sense of "explain" is the "true" sense of that word.

FURTHER ILLUSTRATIONS

As we have seen, then, there are noncausal rational explanations of beliefs, causal nonrational explanations, and causal rational explanations. In what follows I shall illustrate these concepts in further detail by reference to certain problems in American intellectual history.

Noncausal Rational Explanation of Belief

We may begin by selecting an example of the most common form of explanation in the history of ideas, noncausal rational explanation, in which the intent of the historian is simply to recount how a thinker tried to support a certain belief. It is worth noting that the belief in such a case need not be an unusual one, either in the career of the thinker or in the history of the subject in which he worked, although the historian may focus on it for this reason. Moreover, it may be true or it may be false, and the historian may either share or reject the belief. The historian focuses on the method whereby the thinker in question tried to justify the belief, whether successfully or not is another question. On some occasions the historian may present a noncausal rational explanation of a belief simply by quoting the thinker in question, but on others the thinker's language may demand simplification or amplification. If the historian takes upon himself the task of simplifying or amplifying, he must understand what the thinker in question says, and no amount of presentation of cultural background will do instead. That is why research in the history of technical subjects, for example, in philosophy, if it is directed at noncausal rational explanation, is usually best conducted by those who specialize in that subject. Sometimes, of course, as in the history of science, specialists in the subject will be so preoccupied with its problems as not to be interested in its history; and sometimes, as when the past phase of the subject—for example, medieval or ancient physics and philosophy—is linguistically or intellectually remote from its contemporary phase, the contemporary physicist or philosopher may not be fitted for the task of presenting the arguments of past thinkers. In such cases a new specialty, like the history of science or the history of philosophy grows up, one whose practitioners need not be professional physicists or professional philosophers. For a variety of reasons which we need not discuss here, the class of historians of ancient physics and the class of physicists overlap less and less as time goes on. But the situation is quite different in the field of American philosophy, where there is no linguistic problem and where the subject is not so remote in time as to require that sort of interest in the distant past which is so often the hallmark of the historian. For this reason, it is likely that noncausal rational explanation in the history of American philosophy will be carried on by professional philosophers themselves. The past they study is so near to them that when they explicate the texts of their forerunners, they do not feel as though they are expounding the doctrines of thinkers with interests altogether different from their own.

With this preface behind us, we may now turn to a simple illustration of noncausal rational explanation in American intellectual history. We may explain why John Dewey subscribed to the belief that ethical statements are scientific in character, in particular, to the belief that statements of the form "X is desirable" are scientific in character, by presenting the following noncausal rational explanation. We may point out that Dewey's argument begins with the observation that scientists do not assign objective properties to things without being sure that certain conditions are satisfied. Before a scientist asserts that something is objectively red, as distinct from asserting that it merely appears red now, he makes sure, for example, that the light is normal. He selects certain standard conditions of vision and asserts that the object is really red just in case it appears red to him under those conditions. But if the object looks red to him when the light under which he is viewing it is not white, he will not assert that it *is* red. Now Dewey argues similarly about a statement to the effect that something is desirable. Dewey seems to hold that a thing is desirable if and only if it is desired under normal conditions. He thinks that statements of desirability are statements that something is desired under conditions like those employed by scientists as test-conditions when they are attributing objective colors.[4]

Causal Nonrational Explanation of Belief

While the foregoing exposition of Dewey's argument may be construed as presenting an answer to the question "Why did John Dewey believe that statements of desirability are empirically scientific?" it does not present a causal explanation of that belief. It states in indirect discourse what might be communicated by a

[4] Here I summarize an explanation offered in my *Social Thought in America: The Revolt Against Formalism* (New York, 1949; Boston, 1957), pp. 213–14.

simple quotation of an appropriate statement by Dewey himself, just as one might present in indirect discourse Brutus' argument for assassinating Caesar. Therefore, a historian who addressed himself to the question "What *caused* Dewey to believe that statements of desirability are empirically scientific?" might well construct another explanation which would be in no sense incompatible with that in the quoted passage. For example, the fact that Dewey was a political liberal who wanted to reform the society of his time and who felt that such a reform movement should be based on arguments that could command general, objectively based assent was a factor in his coming to the conclusion that ethical statements are scientific. We might say that the decisive cause of Dewey's believing that ethical statements are scientific was the fact that he wanted to believe that they were objectively grounded, and therefore reference to this want and its own causal roots provide a *causal* explanation of why Dewey came to his ethical naturalism. Some social thinkers might be willing to rest their critique of society on the supernatural ethics of Christianity, others on the antinaturalistic ethics of, say, G. E. Moore, and still others might be willing to rest it on a mere preference for another kind of society. But such defenses were psychologically impossible for Dewey, and therefore he needed, more than most men, to rest his liberalism on a scientifically oriented ethical naturalism. In these last few sentences I have sketched an explanation of why Dewey was an ethical naturalist which is quite different from the explanation offered in the previous section. In this section I have presented a causal explanation that is not rational because it cites feelings and wants in explanation of a belief. It may be analyzed, unlike the previous explanation, in accordance with Thesis I.

Causal Rational Explanation of Belief

I now want to illustrate the idea of a causal *rational* explanation of another belief of John Dewey's. As we have just seen, Dewey held that ethical beliefs are empirical, and indeed the whole of his philosophy was dominated by a conviction that there are no nonempirical self-evident truths of the kind celebrated by those who believe in the doctrine of natural law. In general, he vehemently opposed Continental rationalism in the theory of knowledge, whether it be applied to ethical, physical, or even to mathematical knowledge: he fought for more than a half-century against the idea that merely by reflecting on essences, concepts, or meanings one could arrive at validly held beliefs. And yet I think he lapsed into a form of rationalism at one point in his writings.[5] This is puzzling, for Dewey's lapse is in important respects like the incident which puzzled the woman whose husband came down with an attack of indigestion, and like the fact that puzzled Pirenne in his study of the collapse of the Mediterranean Commonwealth. Just as the woman wondered why her husband, who had gotten along without an attack for a long time, came down with an attack, so one might wonder why Dewey, who had viewed the history of philosophy as a fruitless quest for certainty, as a misguided effort to discover a class of stable and self-evident truths, would have come to the conclusion in his *Logic* that certain laws of *physics* are what he calls "ideational" as opposed to "existential." By an existential proposition Dewey means one which refers "directly to actual conditions as determined by experimental observation," and for him ideational propositions are "conceptual, consisting of interrelated meanings, which are non-existential in content in *direct* reference but which are applicable to existence through the operations they represent as possibilities."[6] Because Dewey's ideational propositions are not very different from what Kant called analytic propositions, which are established merely by examining the relationship between the meanings of terms, one may well be surprised by Dewey's saying that certain laws of natural science are, in effect, analytic, established merely by examining interrelated meanings. Were one reading Descartes, one

---

[5] For an expanded treatment of this problem, see my "Experiment and Necessity in Dewey's Philosophy," *The Antioch Review*, XIX (Fall, 1959), 329–44. The lapse, I believe, occurs in the second half of Dewey's *Logic: The Theory of Inquiry* (New York, 1938).

[6] Dewey, op. cit., pp. 283–84.

might not be surprised, but if one thinks of Dewey's total philosophy, one is. Therefore, we may set the stage for an explanation by asking the question "Why did Dewey adopt a rationalistic view of the laws of science when for most of his life he had opposed such a view?"

One begins to see the glimmerings of a causal rational explanation of Dewey's lapse when one reads further and discovers that Dewey was struck, as well he might have been, by a difference between two kinds of statements which begin with the word "all" —the very difference that we have had occasion to consider in our earlier discussion of the concept of scientific law. Dewey speaks of "the ambiguity of 'all' as sometimes having existential reference, in which case it represents an inference having at best a high order of probability, and sometimes having non-existential reference, when it stands for a necessary relation which follows, by definition, from analysis of a conception,"[7] and he also implies that the proposition "All men are mortal" is ideational, whereas the propostition "All men have died or will die" is existential.[8] This pair of illustrations helps one see *why* Dewey fell into rationalism, into thinking that the laws of natural science are "ideational." He failed to see that there is a kind of statement in between that which is illustrated by "All men have died or will die" and that which is illustrated by "All bachelors are unmarried," that is to say, an intermediate kind of statement which is neither a mere summation of fact nor easily called analytic. For example, the statement "All men are mortal." Clearly we do not verify the law that all men are mortal by examining "interrelated meanings"; we verify it by examining men. It is true that there is a problem about how to characterize laws of natural science, but the solution we expect from Dewey is certainly *not* to call them ideational or analytic. Dewey is troubled by a difficult problem, but in the place we are concerned with, he can see no solution other than the rationalistic solution of identifying the notion of a law with the

[7] Ibid., p. 296.
[8] Ibid., p. 256.

notion of an ideational proposition. "In science," he says, "there are many propositions in which the clause introduced by '*if*' is known to be contrary to conditions set by existential circumstances; that is, to be such that they cannot be existentially satisfied, as 'If a particle at rest is acted upon by a single moving particle, then,' etc. In such propositions *if* and *when* designate a connection of conceptual subject-matters, not of existential or temporo-spatial matters. If the word 'conditions' is used, it now refers to a logical relation, not to existential circumstances."[9] Because Dewey made statements like this in his *Logic*, we may explain Dewey's lapse into a rationalistic theory of scientific laws by saying that since the only kind of necessity he thought such laws could have was logical necessity, he attributed that kind of necessity to scientific laws, and then concluded that they were analytic or ideational.

I think this is a very good example of a causal rational explanation of a belief. For here we explain an abnormality in Dewey's views—his lapse into rationalism—by a failure on his part to see that there are truths which express causal necessities as opposed to logical necessities. One lapse led causally to another. Dewey accepted a premise which was not typical of his thinking, and this led causally to a conclusion which was abnormal. Some readers who hold a view analogous to the ethical theory of causal interpretation may think that we are seizing upon Dewey's failure to distinguish causal necessity from logical necessity because we regard it as a *mistake* and therefore pick it out as the cause on evaluative grounds; but I do not think that this is a correct account of the process of selection. I said earlier that we would not be surprised if, say, Descartes had come to Dewey's conclusion. In other words, we do not pick it out because it was a mistake—even though we may think it is—but because it was an *un-Deweyan* belief that led causally to another *un-Deweyan* belief. One might represent Dewey's reasoning as having the form:

[9] *Ibid.*, p. 255.

(1) All necessary truths are ideational.
(2) The laws of physics are necessary.
Therefore,
(3) The laws of physics are ideational.

It was because Dewey believed (1) and (2) that he believed (3), just as Brutus believed that he should assassinate Caesar because he believed two other statements. And if we seize upon Dewey's belief in (1) as the cause of Dewey's belief in (3), it is because we think that (1) was the unusual belief for Dewey. For it was Dewey who had once said, "Mathematics is often cited as an example of purely normative thinking dependent on *a priori* canons and supra-empirical material. But it is hard to see how the student who approaches the matter historically can avoid the conclusion that the status of mathematics is as empirical as that of metallurgy"; and it was Dewey who once said, "Logic is a matter of profound human importance precisely because it is empirically founded and experimentally applied."[10] And since logical truths and mathematical truths were regarded by Dewey as necessary, it is clear from these passages that at one time—and indeed I think for most of his philosophical life prior to what I have called his lapse—he did not accept premise (1), namely, "All necessary truths are ideational," since to be ideational, on his view, *is* to be a priori and dependent on supra-empirical material.

A word should be added about the difference between this last explanation and the noncausal rational explanation that I presented in the previous section when I said why Dewey believed that statements about desirability are empirical. If one were to ask merely, "Why did Dewey believe that the laws of physics are ideational?" one might simply present the above syllogism in quotation marks, preceded by the words "Dewey argued as follows." But if one poses the problem as I posed it, namely, "Why did Dewey *lapse* into rationalism?" then one is asking a question

---

[10] See Dewey, *Reconstruction in Philosophy* (orig. ed., New York, 1920; quotations from Mentor Ed.), pp. 116–17.

that calls for a causal answer. One is not merely asking for an account of Dewey's defense, one is asking for an explanation of a bit of abnormal intellectual behavior on his part.

THREE DIFFERENT ATTACKS ON RATIONALISM IN HISTORICAL EXPLANATION

Once we distinguish between causal rational explanation and noncausal rational explanation, and hence between two ways in which a historian may cite the thoughts of historical agents, we are able to distinguish three different attacks on what is sometimes called rationalism in historical explanation. We are also able to see that some of these attacks on rationalism are unjustified, whereas others are justified. Some things that are called the mistakes of the rationalist historian are not mistakes at all, whereas others are.

(1) If to be a rationalist in history is to recognize the possibility of noncausal rational explanation, then there is no objection to rationalism. Once its critics recognize that this kind of explanation is not intended as causal, their objections to it dissolve.

(2) If to be a rationalist in history is to argue that *causal* rational explanation is impossible, then rationalism deserves to be attacked. Once we see that beliefs are empirical phenomena, we are not only liberated from the idea that explanation in the history of ideas is limited to the recitation of the arguments offered by past thinkers, but are also liberated from the idea that the *only* way in which we can causally explain a man's believing something is by pointing out that he *believes* something else. Once we come to see that the item to be explained by the intellectual historian is a piece of human behavior, we realize that beliefs—believings— may be causally related to the attitudes, fears, feelings, and experiences of the individual intellectual whose beliefs we are trying to explain and also to the circumstances in which he lived, whether of his family, his village, his city, or his society. And therefore if we ask why a man held a certain belief and mean to ask a causal question, it is logically possible to cite any one of these sorts of

things in explanation, just as we may if the thing to be explained is an attitude, an effort, or an action.

(3) Unfortunately, a third sort of attack has been leveled against what is also called rationalism. Some so-called antirationalists are not content to argue that *sometimes* we can explain a belief, effort, action, or attitude by reference to nonbeliefs. They go on to assert that *the* cause in such cases will *never* be a belief. Such thinkers may espouse an extremely crude version of the doctrines advanced by Freud and Marx, and maintain that whenever we want to explain a particular belief, action, effort, or attitude, the only true singular explanatory statement we can make is one which refers either to the kind of nonrational motivation studied by psychoanalysts or one which refers to the sort of considerations adduced by Marxists. In this way such thinkers go far beyond the truth and end up defending a monistic dogmatism which is as narrow-minded as the rationalism they oppose. Their view may be analyzed in many different ways, no one of which yields a defensible position. They may, for example, take the view that all laws which are capable of explaining human behavior make reference in their subject-terms to nonbeliefs. But this is obviously false, and so someone who is still inclined to underplay the importance of other beliefs in explaining a given belief might weaken the claim as follows. He might say that although there are some laws in which a kind of belief is one of the jointly sufficient conditions for certain kinds of behavior, an example of that kind of belief is never cited as *the* cause of a particular instance of such behavior in a singular causal statement. This would be like saying that although there are some laws which assert that the presence of oxygen is one of the jointly sufficient conditions for bringing about fires, the presence of oxygen is never cited as *the* cause of a particular fire. Thus it might be said that having a certain kind of belief is never to be cited as the decisive factor in explaining a man's behavior. But can such a view be supported? I do not think so, and therefore I think that the attack on rationalism, when that attack goes to the extreme of holding that beliefs have *no* causal efficacy in history, is indefensible.

THE LIMITATIONS OF MONISM IN THE
EXPLANATION OF BEHAVIOR

The moral, therefore, of our earlier discussion of causal interpretation is as relevant in intellectual history as it is in social
history, as relevant when we are trying to explain why a man
believed, felt, or did something on a given occasion as it is when
we are trying to explain why a society was in a certain state at a
certain time. Neither psychoanalysts nor Marxists provide us with
a criterion that we must always use in selecting one from among
many jointly sufficient conditions when we are trying to state the
cause of a particular man's belief. The abnormal factor—the factor that made the difference and hence the one to be singled out
when we are trying to explain human behavior—is not *always* an
instance of repression, identification, or projection, and so on. Nor
will it *always* be a matter of the intellectual in question having
sold out to the ruling class or having been a child of the economy
in which he lives.

This is not to deny that *sometimes* a Freudian or a Marxian
factor may be the cause, but rather to assert that sometimes it may
be another belief that should be cited as the cause of an intellectual figure's coming to the belief he holds. And to the extent to
which the historian is interested in causally explaining a given
phenomenon—this man's believing this particular proposition—
he must investigate the phenomenon as carefully as a legal judge
should investigate the cause of a harm. To adopt a monistic theory
of *the* explanation in intellectual history, or in any branch of
history, is as indefensible as it would be to adopt one in the law. It
is much like saying that automobile accidents are always to be
explained by reference to the icy condition of the road, or always
to be explained by reference to the drunkenness of the driver, or
always to be explained by reference to faulty brakes. An advocate
of Marxism or psychoanalysis may, of course, collect statistics
which are comparable to those collected by insurance companies
when they report that in so many accidents the cause is drunken-

ness, in so many the icy condition of the road, and in so many faulty brakes; and on the basis of these statistics the Marxist or psychoanalyst may assert that an economic or psychosexual factor is the most frequent cause of intellectuals coming to the beliefs they hold. But such statistics would not eliminate the need for studying each case individually if one is interested in determining the cause of a particular man's holding a certain belief. Clearly the knowledge that the cause of most automobile accidents is drunkenness does not settle the question as to whether the cause of a given accident is drunkenness. For the same reason, even if it were shown that most philosophers have come to a certain conclusion because they are gripped by a neurosis, or by what Marx called "the illusion of the epoch," one could not validly infer from this that a particular philosopher has come to that conclusion because *he* was neurotic or deluded. The idea that we can cite only nonrational considerations in causally explaining the particular thoughts, attitudes, and actions of particular human beings is as one-sided and misguided as the idea that we can cite only rational considerations. It is in conflict with the plurality of causes and the complexity of causes. We know that we may consistently explain Jones's death by citing the fact that he took poison and Smith's death by citing the fact that he was shot—this rests on the plurality of causes of death. We also know that we may explain one man's attack of indigestion by citing either his ulcers or the fact that he ate parsnips—and this option rests on the complexity of a single whole cause in Mill's sense. Because psychological causes may be plural, we may consistently explain one man's belief, attitude, action, or effort in one way and also explain the same belief, attitude, action, or effort in another way. And one man's behavior may be explained in different ways because of the complexity of psychological causes. This perfectly obvious feature of ordinary and historical language is often overlooked by students of causation who, even if they are not affected by Marxian or Freudian monism, may be under the influence of the false methodological maxim that like effects must have like causes.

The idea that different men may believe or do the same thing for different reasons is so obvious that it would not be necessary to illustrate it if it were not commonly defended by a confused use of the idea that generality is necessary in historical explanation. But there is such a thing as misplaced generality. Let me be concrete. It is, I believe, a fact of American history that its most influential and most distinguished writers have felt an unusual amount of antipathy toward the American city.[11] One may find it expressed in the writings of Jefferson, Emerson, Thoreau, Hawthorne, Poe, Melville, Henry Adams, William Dean Howells, Theodore Dreiser, Frank Norris, Josiah Royce, George Santayana, John Dewey, Jane Addams, Robert Park, Louis Sullivan, and Frank Lloyd Wright. They have in common a fear of the American city as it was, or a fear of what the American city might become. This is puzzling for a variety of reasons, and so the question arises, "Why have all these intellectuals felt antipathy to our cities?" The phenomenon may certainly be regarded as abnormal from a certain point of view.

When one asks for an explanation, one often hears in reply that something called "romanticism" is responsible for the phenomenon, and this can be just as monistic an explanation of a particular kind of behavior as the explanation that it all derives from sexual disappointment. The citation of romanticism may be made under the misapprehension that when we give an explanation of why many individuals behaved in the same way, we must state something they all have in common. But the notion that the antipathy of each of these intellectuals was caused by one thing—in particular, by subscription to one philosophy—is as absurd as the idea that it was caused by one neurosis, or as the idea that all automobile accidents are caused by drunken driving. If by romanticism we understand at least an attachment to the wilderness, a love of spontaneity as against reason, of the heart as against the head, of poetry as against calculation, then it is simply not true to

[11] See Morton and Lucia White, *The Intellectual Versus the City: From Thomas Jefferson to Frank Lloyd Wright* (Cambridge, 1962), esp. ch. XV.

say that all American writers who have chosen to attack the American city have done so because they view it as inferior to the wilderness, as the scene of calculation rather than as the home of poetry, as a place in which the values of the head take precedence over the values of the heart. "The American city has been so vast, so varied and so much in flux that it has provided men either in fact or in their imagination with a variety of things to dislike. The American city has been thought to be: too big, too noisy, too dusky, too smelly, too commercial, too crowded, too full of immigrants, too full of Jews, too full of Irishmen, Italians, Poles, too industrial, too pushing, too fast, too artificial, destructive of conversation, destructive of communication, too greedy, too capitalistic, too full of automobiles, too full of smog, too full of dust, too heartless, too intellectual, too scientific, insufficiently poetic, too lacking in manners, too mechanical, destructive of family, tribal and patriotic feeling."[12] Given any complaint on the above list, one could probably find an intellectual who would offer it as the reason for his dislike.

One need not deny that some simplification might be made. It is true that some of the complaints do cluster into a unit of the kind that we associate with romanticism, so that it is possible to link, let us say, our explanation of Emerson's distaste for the American city with Thoreau's by saying that they both exhibited a typically romantic dislike of the city, and hence possible to cut down on the number of causes of anti-urbanism in our explanations. But on the other hand, some intellectuals, like Henry James and John Dewey, have disliked the city for very antiromantic reasons.[13] Henry James's dislike of New York was not rooted in any preference for the soil but rather in the fact that he missed in New York the society, the civilization, and the brilliance he admired so much. He found that it lacked a history, what he called "organic social relations," and most of all, refined and interesting conversation. And certainly John Dewey's criticism of the American city of the

[12] Ibid., p. 222.
[13] Ibid., ch. VI and ch. X; also p. 223.

twentieth century was not that of a Thoreauvian. His criticism was that of a man who valued what the sociologists of his time called "the primary group" and who measured cities by their capacity to live the good life in accordance with a scientific ethic. In other words, even when we try to boil down the welter of causes that explain the reactions of different American intellectuals to the American city, we come upon two more general causes that are in a sense *opposite* to each other. "The American city has been criticized by writers who doubted or despised the values of civilization as well as by writers who were intensely dedicated to civilized life. In short, the American city has been caught in the crossfire of two powerful antagonists—primitivists and sophisticates; and no mechanical recitation of the misleading aphorism that like effects are produced by like causes can gainsay this fact."[14]

The moral of this excursion into American history is that while it is proper and fitting for the historian to explain individual behavior causally, sometimes by citing beliefs, it is simply false to say that *the* cause of all human actions, beliefs, efforts, and attitudes is the same. Our discussion of causal interpretation showed that if we construe *the* cause of an event as the factor that made the difference, *the cause* can, as it were, vary just as the cause of automobile accidents can. The root error in these matters is monism, and antirationalistic monism is as far from the truth as its rationalistic contrary. Neither of them is implied by the regularity theory of explanation in any of its forms.

EXPLANATION, VAST IMPERSONAL FORCES,
AND PHYSICALISM

Causal explanation in history not only does not entail monism, but it does not entail two other views which are sometimes associated with it. To say that the historian explains some events in the same sense as that in which some natural scientists explain events is not to say that the historian appeals to what T. S. Eliot calls

[14] Ibid., p. 225.

"vast impersonal forces," or that he thinks that history may be reduced to physics. The effort to explain historical events by the use of singular explanatory statements as analyzed in Thesis I or Thesis II, so far from involving a belief in such entities as the Hegelian "world spirit," is often accompanied by an explicit disavowal and condemnation of the Hegelian mode of explanation. And the idea that causal explanation is physical explanation is simply a misunderstanding.[15]

No doubt some self-appointed spokesmen for scientific history, like Toynbee and certain Marxists, have appealed to obscure entities in an effort to explain the course of history, but it would be a mistake to think that they are *the* scientific historians of our time and hence a mistake to think that one may reject the view that historians can give causal explanations of human action by rejecting the view that there are vast, mysterious, impersonal forces which dominate men. What an irony it would be if those philosophers who strive so hard to eliminate any appeal to a mysterious causal *connection* that has nothing to do with regularities should at the same time appeal to mysterious causes. Usually those thinkers who hold that we can apply scientific method in history are those who adamantly refuse to countenance mystical, transcendental forces, whether vast or small, whether personal or impersonal. And from the fact that they maintain that a historian should use the same *method* as an engineer or a physician in establishing a singular explanatory statement, it hardly follows that they hold that history may be reduced to or deduced from physics, i.e., that they are "physicalists." The view that singular explanatory statements in history may be analyzed in accordance with Theses I and II does not entail the view that all of Pirenne's explanations, or Bury's, or Beard's may be deduced from physics. It is sometimes said that underlying such a view of explanation is the belief that "men are objects in nature," and from this it is but

---

[15] See Isaiah Berlin, *Historical Inevitability* (London, 1954), passim; also the review article on the same in my *Religion, Politics and the Higher Learning* (Cambridge, 1959), pp. 75–84.

one short, erroneous step to the conclusion that its advocates think that history is reducible to physics. The fact is that men *are* objects in nature, whose behavior we study when we explain historical events, but it does not follow from this that the historian is a physicist.

The question whether history "is reducible to" physics should be separated from the question whether there is one method for establishing singular explanatory statements, whether they be made about men or about rocks or beavers. History may use the same method without being reducible to physics. Biology, which uses the scientific method, is not obviously "reducible to" physics. For the same reason it is misleading to identify the view that men are objects in nature with the view that everything we can say about men can be said in the science of physics. If men are not objects in nature, where are they? Are they any less in nature than bees and beavers? Of course men have characteristics which bees do not have and some which beavers do not have. Men write philosophy and make intercontinental ballistic missiles. But this of itself does not imply that *the way* in which we detect the characteristics which distinguish man from the bee and the beaver is radically different from *the way* in which we detect the characteristics which man shares with the bee and the beaver. Both are detected by what is commonly called scientific method, the method of advancing hypotheses, deducing their consequences, and checking these consequences by experiment or observation.

It is not only misleading to imply that men are not objects in nature but also misleading to imply that the historian never treats them as objects in nature. When they explain certain social or psychological phenomena, historians will often make reference to the fact that men have certain purely biological features, that they will die from want of food or drink. It is not as if the historian were not concerned with what Marx called the less celestial characteristics of human existence. Moreover, even where the historian makes a psychological, as opposed to a purely biological, statement about an individual man, it is false to say that the subject of his investigation is different from the subject of the biologist's investigation. It is not as if the biologist were talking about a machine and the historian about what Gilbert Ryle calls a ghost in that machine. J. Holland Rose in his *Life of Napoleon I* asserts the following two propositions about his subject: (1) "At Valence, while shrinking from his brother officers, he sought society more congenial to his simple tastes and restrained demeanor"; (2) that Napoleon and his first love, Caroline de Columbier, had once "eaten cherries together." And although eating is a purely natural phenomenon, something which beavers also do, the same Napoleon, the same thing, entity, or object in nature, is referred to in both of these statements even though one statement is psychological and the other biological. Moreover, both statements are true in the same sense of the word "true," and biographers use the same method in supporting both of these statements.

In sum, the following may be said: (a) that there is a sense of "using the same method" in which historians use the same method in establishing singular judgments of a psychological-historical kind *about human beings* as they do in establishing singular judgments of a more biological, physical, physiological, chemical kind; (b) that no attempt to distinguish persons from natural objects is defensible if it implies that there are different realms of entities— some natural, some nonnatural; (c) that the main problem concerns the nature of the predicates used in these different sentences about natural objects, for even where the psychological predicates applied to human beings, like "seeking society congenial to his tastes," are not reducible to, or definable in terms of, or analyzable in terms of physical predicates, we are not justified in denying that one method is used in validating singular psychological-historical judgments about human beings and bio-chemico-physical statements about human beings; (d) that this "one method" involves using hypotheses, deducing their consequences, and checking these consequences against experience.

One may grant that certain data that are used in testing a

judgment which is biological, chemical, or physical will be different from data that are used in testing a psychological judgment. One may also grant that a historian may test some of his explanations by trying to re-live the experiences of a man like Napoleon, or by trying to imagine the kind of experiences a man like Napoleon would have under certain specified circumstances. But it does not follow that he is abandoning what is commonly called the method of experience when he tries to imagine what Napoleon felt. Moreover, even though some biographers have more flair and more insight into human behavior than others, so that they can size up a man's motives more quickly and more brilliantly, when they come to support their statements of motivation, they must present evidence of the kind that their less brilliant colleagues must present. In the end they must both appear before the court of experience.

CONCLUSIONS

The argument in this chapter leads to the following main conclusions. First: there are at least two uses of the question "Why?" when it is asked about beliefs, attempts at action, actions, and attitudes. We may use it in order to ask in a noncausal way for the arguments used by the agent in defense of, or in justification of, an item of any one of these kinds, and we may use it in order to ask for a causal explanation of any one of them. Second: whichever sort of question the historian asks by using the word "why," his answer need not depend on a favorable evaluation of the agent's beliefs, efforts, actions or attitudes, or modes of argument as reasonable. Third: when the historian answers the causal form of the question, his answer may be analyzed in accordance with Theses I and II. It will be a singular explanatory statement which implies the existence of explanatory deductive arguments and hence of laws even if the historian cannot present those arguments and laws in full.

Those laws, as we have seen in earlier chapters, need not be laws about how all men—without qualifications—behave. In order to make singular explanatory statements, the historian need not be in possession of principles of human nature which transcend all cultural differences. I believe, therefore, that Hume was right when he siad: "The most irregular and unexpected resolutions of men may frequently be accounted for by those who know every particular circumstance of their character and situation. A person of an obliging disposition gives a peevish answer; but he has the toothache, or has not dined. A stupid fellow discovers an uncommon alacrity in his carriage; but he has met with a sudden piece of good fortune."[16] On the other hand, this conclusion need not lead us to another view of Hume's. "Would you know the sentiments, inclinations, and course of life of the Greeks and Romans?" he asks. And he answers: "Study well the temper and actions of the French and English: you cannot be much mistaken in transferring to the former *most* of the observations which you have made with regard to the latter. Mankind are so much the same, in all times and places, that history informs us of nothing new or strange in this particular. Its chief use is only to discover the constant and universal principles of human nature by showing men in all varieties of circumstances and situations, and furnishing us with materials from which we may form our observations and become acquainted with the regular springs of human action and behavior."[17] As we saw earlier, both Hume and Mill defended two distinct doctrines: philosophical regularism and the doctrine that there are general principles of human nature from which, or with whose help, one can infer the more modest laws whose existence is implied by singular explanatory statements according to regularism. It was the second doctrine against which Collingwood inveighed, but his argument against it does not touch the fundamental thesis of regularism, which stands even if the search for transcultural principles of human nature fails. And, ironically, while Marxists think of Hume's principles of human nature as

[16] *An Inquiry Concerning Human Understanding*, Sec. VIII, pt. I.
[17] Ibid.

much too general, they, in their system, replace these principles by the even broader generalities of dialectical materialism. It must be repeated that the theory of singular explanatory statements presented earlier is a logical theory of the causal use of "why" and not a speculative theory of history. It purports to state the conditions under which the historical counterpart of the following sort of statement is true: "The volume of that gas went down partly because the pressure went up," and it asserts that such a statement will be true if and only if there are laws and true statements about the volume of gas of the kind described in Thesis I. It does not purport to state a physical theory from which the gas laws may be derived, nor does it even assert that there is such a theory. In the same way it purports to analyze singular explanatory statements about individual human behavior without purporting to have discovered the principles of human nature. So long as the regularity theory of historical explanation is properly understood, it may be seen to be consistent with the doctrine that thought is causally efficacious and causally explicable, and distinguishable from certain indefensible doctrines which have been historically associated with it. It is not dependent upon nor does it encourage a monistic theory of explanation; it is not dependent upon nor does it encourage an appeal to vast impersonal forces; it does not assert that history is a branch of physics. What it does assert is that historians can explain some events and states in just the sense in which natural scientists explain some events, and that their explanations of such events and states must and can be defended by an appeal to experience.

VI

Historical Narration

So far we have examined explanatory arguments and the generalizations they contain, singular statements in which something is said to be *a* cause, singular statements in which something is said to be *the* decisive cause, and the difference between a statement of *a* or *the* cause and a statement of *a* or *the* reason. Now we may turn to the narrative, a form of discourse in which all of these kinds of statements may figure, either explicitly or by implication, but which nevertheless raises philosophical questions that cannot be solved merely by analyzing or distinguishing the previously considered types of statements.[1]

The narrative is linguistically complex and sprawling by contrast to the statement that Caesar crossed the Rubicon, to the isolated singular explanatory statement, and even to the generalizations of the speculative philosopher of history. It is for this reason,

[1] The present chapter is a considerably revised version of my "The Logic of Historical Narration," in *Philosophy and History*, ed. Sidney Hook, (New York, 1963), pp. 3–31. Some of the revisions have been stimulated by comments on my paper by other contributors to the volume, and I wish to thank them for their helpful remarks.

perhaps, that analytic philosophers of history have concentrated on relatively simple statements that may be analyzed without departing too far from the actual language of historians, though even here a departure is necessary for purposes of clarification. For example, when we treated every explanatory statement as if it contained either the expression "is a cause of" or the expression "is the cause of" as its main connective, we simplified in an effort to describe the logic of explanation. Obviously not every explanatory statement contains these expressions: the explanatory expressions "as," "on account of," "due to," and many others immediately come to mind. In the same spirit, when a logician discusses universal statements, he may treat every one of them as if they had the form "All *S* is *P*," without thereby implying that people do not assert universal statements beginning with other words like "every," "whatever," and "whenever." But the historical narrative, the extended story, is so large and rambling by contrast to the single sentence treated by the logician that any effort to treat it as a repeatable and identifiable pattern of language may give an impression of remoteness and distortion well beyond what might be felt by the historian who finds his causal statements cast in a single syntactical mold. On the other hand, the very qualities of narrative which might lead a historian to think that logical analysis distorts it are those that might inhibit a logician from trying to discern its structure. The complexity and variety of narrative, the fact that one story seems so different in structure from another, may give both the romantically minded historian and the classically minded logician pause. Yet the vast differences that human beings exhibit do not prevent us from X-raying them in an effort to discern the skeletal structure that each of them possesses. Naturally, if upon discovering this structure a roentgenologist were to come to the absurd conclusion that men are nothing but skeletons, we should regard him as mad. And in the same way, if a logician of narrative, upon discovering its structure, were to conclude that narratives are nothing but logical conjunctions of certain kinds of statements, we should regard him as mad too. History is a literary art as well as a discipline aimed at discovering and ordering truth, and if we neglect some of the narrative's literary qualities in order to clarify certain epistemological problems connected with it, our procedure is like that of the sane roentgenologist, who searches for the skull without denying that the skin exists and without denying that the skin may vary enormously in color, texture, and beauty.

Having prepared the reader for simplification in the interest of clarification, I shall now take a step in that direction. I shall concentrate on one kind of narrative, not because I think it is the only kind but because I think that focusing on it will bring to the fore certain important philosophical issues. I shall concentrate on those narratives or histories which are histories *of* something like a nation, a society, or even a person insofar as biography may be considered a form of history. And in the course of my analysis I shall be primarily concerned to delineate the network of causal statements, noncausal factual statements, and value judgments involved in the construction of such a narrative.

THE STRUCTURE OF A NARRATIVE

The most typical narrative is one whose central subject has existed, or once did exist, for a reasonably long period of time, and the task of the typical narrator is to give a connected account of the development of that central subject. If we assume that each history has a central subject, we are led to focus on historical works which resemble novels like Defoe's *Moll Flanders* in being primarily concerned with one entity, but which differ from novels, of course, in not being fictional. E. M. Forster remarks that Moll Flanders "fills the book that bears her name, or rather stands alone in it, like a tree in a park, so that we can see her from every aspect and are not bothered by rival growths."[2] Limiting our reflections to this species of history will not make our problems overly simple, because in spite of this narrowing of our task we shall have to answer a number of thorny questions.

[2] E. M. Forster, *Aspects of the Novel* (New York, 1927), p. 88.

Chronicles

In order to explain what I mean when I say that a work is a history of something like the United States of America, I must first define the concept of a chronicle of such a central subject. The word "chronicle" is applied to historical writing in many different ways, and therefore I shall not pretend that I am about to analyze or explain *the* meaning of the word. A chronicle of a subject, I shall say, is a conjunction of noncausal singular statements which expressly mention that subject and which report things that have been true of it at different times. By a noncausal statement, I mean a statement that does not connect two statements of fact with a word like "because," a statement which is not employed by a historian in order to state a cause or effect of something— explicitly. It should be noticed that the condition that these statements expressly mention the subject severely limits the notion of a chronicle, and that the notion of a history will be correspondingly limited when we explain it. According to our definition, every statement in a chronicle of the United States of America, and in a history of it, will expressly mention the United States of America, although this is obviously not true of actual historical works on this subject. Accepting this condition will allow us to formulate certain philosophical issues without begging any serious questions or departing too far from the intent of the historian. It should also be observed that whereas all of the statements that compose a chronicle will be logically singular, some of them will be quite different in character from others. Chronicles do not contain only statements that record historical events in the narrowest sense of the word "event." A chronicle of England might begin with statements to the effect that the ancient British residents of England lived in small tribes under chiefs or kings; that they could not read; that they kept cattle, hunted, and fished; that they made baskets and pottery; that they grew barley in some places; that they mined for tin in Cornwall; that they were partially clothed in skins. These statements report what might be called the conditions of life of the ancient British inhabitants of England, and in that sense might be distinguished from a statement that Julius Caesar's army came to England in 55 B.C., the latter being a statement that refers to an event in a narrow sense of that term. Of course, statements about conditions and statements about events or episodes are different in interesting and important ways, but they may both be components of chronicles. Statements about conditions tell us what was true of England at certain times just as much as the statement that Caesar came to it in 55 B.C. does, only the times they refer to are more like generations than years.

If one conceives of a chronicle of England in this way, one may say that a chronicle of England is true just in case its component statements are all true, since a chronicle has been defined as a conjunction of statements. The truth of the chronicle is a function of the truth of its components alone.

Histories

I turn now to the idea of a history of a subject. A history will in the familiar way be distinguished from a chronicle by the fact that a history contains causal statements. As E. M. Forster has remarked in another connection, a chronicler leads his reader to ask merely, "And then what?" whereas a historian may lead him to ask, "So what?" The chronicler is likely to tell us: "The king of England died, and then the queen of England died, and then the prince of England died, and then the princess of England died. And there endeth our chronicle." But a corresponding history may read: "The king of England died, so the queen of England grieved. Her grief led to her death. Her death led the prince to worry, and he worried to the point of suicide. His death made the princess lonely, and she died of that loneliness. And so endeth our lugubrious history."

Since a history asserts causal connections, we may conceive of a history as a logical conjunction of statements most of which are singular causal assertions. In the simplest case, when each event but the first and last is causally linked with a temporal predecessor as well as a temporal successor, it asserts: "Because s was A at time t_1, s was B at time t_2. And because s was B at time t_2, s was C at time t_3. And because s was C at time t_3, s was D at time t_4." In more complicated cases, which are more typical, such a sequence of causal statements may be interrupted by an event or state of affairs which is not explained by anything earlier in the history, in other words, one which is introduced as the cause of a succeeding event even though it is not explained by anything in the preceding causal chain. A history may even contain some statements about s which are not known to record either causes or effects of other items: such statements may record facts which are deemed so important or interesting in themselves as to demand inclusion in the history even though they cannot be causally linked with others. This shows that the difference between a mere chronicle and a history is a matter of degree. A history is predominantly, though it need not be completely, integrated from a causal point of view. And it should be noted that its causal statements may state *a* cause or *the* cause as previously analyzed.

It will be evident that a history so conceived is true just in case its singular causal statements are true. Furthermore, according to Thesis I and II each one of the singular causal statements implies *its* components—its antecedent and consequent—and therefore a history will logically imply its associated chronicle, the conjunction of all the components of the history's causal statements plus any disconnected noncausal statements.[2a] If we say in a history of Germany that England declared war on Germany because Germany had invaded Poland, we imply that England declared war on Germany and that Germany had invaded Poland, and these last two statements form part of the associated or implied chronicle. Of course, an associated chronicle will not logically imply a history, since the true components of a causal statement do not imply the causal statement of which they are

[2a] In our model of a history no contrary-to-fact conditional statements appear.

components. Neither "England declared war on Germany" nor "Germany had invaded Poland" nor their conjunction implies "England declared war on Germany because Germany had invaded Poland."

THE FUNDAMENTAL PROBLEM OF THE PHILOSOPHY OF NARRATION

Even though the truth of a history is determined by the truth of its components alone, historians evaluate each other's works in ways that take them beyond the question of the truth or falsity of the statements composing those works. One historian who examines another's history of the same subject may agree that each singular causal statement made by the other is true and yet feel that the history as a whole is inferior. And so the question arises as to whether the considerations that are adduced in such assessments of inferiority (and superiority) are different in kind from the assessments of the truth or falsity of the component explanatory statements. Suppose that a historian or historical critic is presented with several distinct true histories of the United States of America, and suppose he is asked to choose the best general history among them. Having gotten beyond asking whether the histories are true, must he now make an evaluation of a fundamentally different sort, in which his interests and values play a part? In other words, we have been led to consider the question "Under what conditions do historians say that one history of a given subject is better than any other when all of the competing histories are true in the sense of being composed exclusively of true statements?"

It should be evident that this question amounts to a question about the implied chronicles of each of the rival histories, for when we compare two true histories of *s* which assert different causal propositions about *s*, the relevant difference between the two histories will appear primarily in the components of the causal assertions. Where the chronicles are completely different, we may compare a true history of the form "Because s was A at t_1, s was B at t_2; and because s was B at t_2, s was C at t_3; and because s was C at t_3, s was D at t_4" with a true history which replaces the predicates "A", "B", "C", and "D" by completely different predicates. In this way we shall be led to say that the best history of s is that history whose true chronicle of s is best. But then how shall we decide that one true chronicle—i.e., one conjunction of true singular noncausal statements about a given thing—is superior to another? This is what is sometimes called the problem of selecting the facts one incorporates in a narrative, the problem of defending one selection as against others that are possible. It is the problem of stating grounds on which one answer to the question "What happened in the career of s?" is preferred to another. It is a problem which we have not yet dealt with.

In stating the problem in this way, I do not mean to say that the effort to arrive at a history is a mechanical composite of two processes—selecting the facts and finding the causal cement that will stick them to each other. Nor am I subscribing to the slogan of Taine: "*Après la collection des faits, la recherche des causes.*"[3] Whatever the psychological order in which explanatory hypotheses and factual hypotheses appear in the mind of an historian, historians who present chronicles of one and the same thing often include different true statements about that thing. In other words, they record different conjunctions of singular noncausal truths about the same subject—different chronicles—and their works are often compared by comparing those different chronicles. Therefore, without any implication that the facts were chosen first and the causal links established later, we may ask, "On what grounds does the historian justify his choice of one true chronicle?"

It is conceivable, of course, that only one set of true statements about the central subject could—as a matter of fact—be constructed into a history as we have defined it, in which case there would be no rival true accounts of what happened. But generally

[3] For an interesting discussion of Taine's view, see Patrick Gardiner, *The Nature of Historical Explanation* (Oxford, 1952), pp. 70–80.

speaking, for any given subject there are many true histories and hence many true chronicles that may be distinguished in terms of merit. Such chronicles need not be mutually exclusive: they may overlap. No doubt the occurrence of the Revolutionary War, the Civil War, the First World War, the Great Depression, the New Deal and the Second World War will be recorded in any recently written chronicle of the United States. We know that a tradition within the discipline itself often will lead every historian of a nation to include certain facts, but no historian would or should be content with answering the question "Why include those facts?" by saying, "All present-day historians of the United States do." He should have better reasons than that. It will be noticed that the question is not what reasons the historian has for *believing* certain statements, but what reasons he has for including in a chronicle some statements that he believes rather than others that he believes.

THE FUNDAMENTAL PROBLEM CONTRASTED WITH OTHERS

In identifying the fundamental problem of narration in this way, I have done so with full awareness that there are other problems about statements in a narrative which also concern the degree to which evaluation, as opposed to factual investigation, plays a part in the writing of history. For example, it might be argued that an assessment of a history as *true* involves an appeal to values insofar as explanatory statements themselves rest on principles that are moral or evaluative in character. I think I have already shown the inadequacy of this view in Chapter V, but I wish to add that if a philosopher should persist in thinking that historical explanations are guided by moral principles rather than by empirical laws, he will still be faced with the problem of which truths should be incorporated in his chronicle. Even if it be thought that a philosophical analysis of the statement "Booth shot Lincoln because Booth thought that Lincoln was a tyrant" rests on some judgment of "reasonableness," that would still leave open the question of the nature of the decision to include Booth's assassination of Lincoln in a chronicle of the United States. This question will be of fundamental concern to us in this chapter, and we may ask it whether we think singular explanatory statements are factual or evaluative.

Another question which is peripheral to our main concern is whether chronicles—as opposed to histories—contain noncausal singular value-statements. It has been argued, for example, that the statement "Germany invaded Poland" is a value-statement, and perhaps it is. But our main concern is not with the fact that some components of chronicles are evaluative in character; for clearly, where this is the case, the truth of the chronicle will have to be settled, in part at least, by establishing the truth of a value-judgment. Our main concern in this chapter is over the fact that when a historian elects to tell a story about a given subject, he may be presented with a choice of true empirical or factual statements that he may assert about the subject of his history, and that the choice he makes from among these statements may rest on a value-judgment. We are not primarily interested in the historical value-judgment that may be included *in* the chronicle. One might say that in this chapter we are primarily interested in finding out whether the historian's choice of chronicle is defended, at least in part, by reference to a *metahistorical* value-judgment with which one must concur if one is to approve of his history.

It should also be pointed out that we are not concerned with whether historians might be led by their passions to a false factual conclusion. Everyone knows that this is possible, but it does not present us with a basic philosophical problem. Charles Beard once argued that President Franklin D. Roosevelt had planned to bring the United States into World War II soon after its beginning, had deceived the people into electing him for a third time by promising that he would keep us out of war, and had "maneuvered" Japan into attacking us at Pearl Harbor.[4] Other historians have tried to

---

[4] Charles A. Beard, *President Roosevelt and the Coming of War* (New Haven, 1948), passim.

refute these assertions by citing fresh evidence, by trying to discredit Beard's evidence, and by suggesting that he deliberately neglected available evidence which did not fit in with his isolationism. Here the issue was simply whether Roosevelt did plan, deceive, and maneuver in the manner alleged, and in principle this can be settled in an objective way. We should not excuse anyone who would distort the facts. And no reference to the differing political values of historians should lead us to say that two contradictory views of Roosevelt's behavior are logically admissible, that because Beard and his critics operated with different value-schemes their contradictory views were equally valid from their different points of view. Either Roosevelt did or did not do the things attributed to him, and double talk should be ruthlessly excluded.[5]

The situation changes dramatically, however, when we are asked to choose between two true general histories of the United States and ask why we should present one of them rather than the other. When Samuel Eliot Morison suggests that his shift from a Federalist to a Jeffersonian point of view in writing the history of the United States was determined by his conclusion that "the 'wise and good and rich' whom Fisher Ames thought should rule the nation were stupid, narrow-minded and local in their outlook,"[6] one is entitled to wonder whether Morison's shift from one sort of general history of the United States to another was dictated by a value-judgment which must be assessed in the course of assessing his history.

Before I turn to a detailed consideration of the issues involved in this question, I must try to prevent one other possible misunderstanding. It is necessary to bear in mind that the problem I shall discuss is inextricably bound up with the fact that the sort of history which I am considering is *a history of a given entity*. It concerns the work of historians who purport to depict, as they say,

---

[5] Most of the foregoing paragraph is taken from my "New Horizons in Philosophy," *Adventures of the Mind* (Second Series), ed. Richard Thruelsen and John Kobler (New York, 1961), p. 599.

[6] Samuel Eliot Morison, *By Land and By Sea* (New York, 1953), p. 357.

the career of such an entity, and not the work of those who may present a narrative composed of many singular explanatory statements without aiming to do for a nation what a biographer wishes to do for a man. It is obviously possible for a historian to explain why something is true of a given country at a certain time without producing a so-called historical picture of that country. He may ask why the serfs were emancipated in Russia without being especially interested in the history of nineteenth-century Russia as a whole, that is to say, he may be interested in what Lord Acton[7] calls *problems* as opposed to *periods*. And even though he may produce a conjunction of explanatory statements if he continues to seek causes that extend backward in time, his interest will be quite different from that of the narrative historian as here conceived. Unlike the narrative historian, he will not be fazed by the fact that he has not presented a full-blown picture of the career of the subject he is studying. By contrast, the narrative historian of a country *is* interested in presenting what he may call a picture of this kind, in stating true singular causal statements which together stand in a special relationship to the whole career of the subject of which his history purports to be a history. This is most obviously true in the case of the biographer who aims to do more than present a string of causally linked statements about his subject.

THE FUNDAMENTAL PROBLEM DIVIDED:
THE CHRONICLE'S DERIVED STATEMENTS

If we say that one true history of a given subject implies a chronicle which is superior to that implied by its equally true rivals, on what grounds do we make such a judgment? To answer this question it will be useful to bear in mind that every chronicle consists of at least three kinds of statements. First there are what may be called basic statements or charter members, as it were, of the chronicle. Even if it is not evident when one looks at his

[7] Lord Acton, *Essays on Freedom and Power*, ed. G. Himmelfarb (New York, 1955), p. 48.

finished product, every historian constructs his chronicle around a number of facts about his central subject which he treats as central in its career. In the case of American history such statements may record, for example, the occurrence of the Revolution, the Civil War, the First World War, the Depression, and the Second World War. But these basic events are not obviously linked with each other or with other events in American history; and because the historian is interested in forming a coherent history of the United States, he will try to weave these basic facts into a story. One of his efforts to bring about such integration may lead him to ask for the causes of such basic facts, and this will bring into his chronicle a second class of statements which may be called derivative statements of causes. He may also try to state the causes of these causes, and so on. Another of his efforts at integration may lead him to ask for the effects of basic facts; and this will bring into the chronicle a third class of statements that may be called derivative statements of effects. By the time he is finished with this insertion and interpolation of derivative statements, his originally porous conjunction of basic statements may become less porous and may be surrounded—at top and bottom, as it were—by other statements in the final chronicle. In an effort to simplify, one can imagine, for example, that the final chronicle amounts to a series of attributions to the central subject that consists of 26 statements:

$$s \text{ was } A \text{ at time } t_1$$
$$s \text{ was } B \text{ at time } t_2$$
$$s \text{ was } C \text{ at time } t_3$$

. . . .

. . . .

$$s \text{ was } Z \text{ at time } t_{26}$$

Of these, let us suppose that the fourth, ninth, twelfth, fifteenth, and nineteenth statements, which respectively attribute the features D, I, L, O, and S, form the class of basic statements in the chronicle: they will, for example, record the occurrence of the

Revolution, the Civil War, and so on. In that case, most of the other twenty-one statements will have entered as derivative statements of cause or effect. For this reason we may divide our question about the grounds on which statements are included in the chronicle into three questions: (1) On what grounds are the basic statements themselves included? (2) On what grounds are the derivative statements of causes included? (3) On what grounds are derivative statements of effects included? Let us begin with the second and third questions because they are more closely related to matters we have already discussed at length.

Derivative Statements of Causes

In answer to question (2) it must be repeated that *one* of the grounds on which we introduce a statement of, say, the cause of the American Revolution into the chronicle is the fact that the statement referring to the cause is true. This simply means that if the basic statement that the American Revolution took place is represented by "s is D at t_4," then when we say that the cause of the revolution was Britain's shortsighted colonial policy toward America, we imply first of all that Britain did have a shortsighted colonial policy; and if it did not, the statement that it did should not be in our chronicle. Moreover, our statement "The cause of s's being D at t_4 was the fact that s was C at t_3" must also be true if we are to be able to admit "s is C at t_3" into our chronicle as a derivative statement. But, as we saw in our earlier discussion of the notion of *the* cause, different historians may fix on different antecedents of the American Revolution as *the* cause of the Revolution, depending on the way in which they look at the Revolution. In an earlier chapter we saw that where a fact to be explained is unusual, it may be regarded as unusual in different ways. We argued that the way in which the event to be explained may be regarded as unusual may vary from historian to historian depending on his interest. Therefore, even if two historians seek to explain the same event, their explanations of it may differ. If one historian views the American Revolution as unusual in one respect and another regards it as unusual in another, each may fix on a different cause and therefore include different derivative statements in his history and chronicle of the United States. Even if they agree about the basic facts that are to be included (the Revolution, the Civil War, the First World War, the Depression, and the Second World War), they may trace each of these back to different causes because of the different ways in which they regard them as unusual or abnormal, and therefore present chronicles which are different at certain corresponding points. One history may imply the chronicle we outlined earlier, whereas another may imply one in which the statement "s was C at time t_3" is replaced by "s was C^1 at time t_3."

This difference between the two chronicles, and hence between the two corresponding histories, is independent of the truth of the statements in the chronicles and of the truth of the causal statements linking them, so that if one were inclined to choose between the two rival chronicles, and therefore between the two rival histories, one would be obliged to go beyond historical fact in the usual sense. It follows that if a historian were to try to justify his assertion of "s was C^1 at time t_3" instead of "s was C at time t_3," his argument might resemble that which might have been offered by the celebrated woman of an earlier chapter who explained her husband's indigestion by saying that he ate parsnips instead of explaining it, as the physician did, by saying that he had ulcers. If there were a debate between the woman and the physician about *the* cause of the attack, it might quickly reduce to a debate about which why-question would be the better to ask, for we know that the woman and the physician state different causes because they ask different why-questions. Although we have rejected the technological or pragmatic theory of *the* cause, it should be clear that we did not rule out the possibility that the wife may justify her interest in asking a certain kind of why-question by referring to her practical concerns. These practical concerns may in turn be governed by her values. If she can find an explanation of her husband's last attack which refers to something that *he* did or suffered, maybe she can help him avoid the next attack without his undergoing an operation. Analogously, when a historian concentrates his attention on a country in such a way as to unearth a brief episode as the cause of, say, a war, he may justify his way of looking at the country, and therefore his conclusion about the cause of the war, by pointing to his practical interest in finding out how to avoid future wars without trying to change the country radically. On the other hand, a historian who has an interest like the physician's—one which leads the physician to explain the man's attack in terms of the man's deviation from a standard condition of health—might well take the view that he is interested in the unusual standing features of the country that played a part in the onset of war, features that might take revolutionary surgery to change. In short, the grounds for introducing a derivative statement of cause into a chronicle may transcend the question of whether the statement is true, may transcend the question of whether it is connected by law with the statement to be explained, and may rest on values that are not shared by all historians. The question "In what way should I regard the country as unusual?" will not be answered in the same way by all historians, and a true explanatory statement may be viewed as defective by a historian who, for one reason or another, does not share his colleague's way of looking at the central subject's behavior at a certain time. Therefore, one ground for approving of a history—in addition to one's conviction that it is true—may be one's conviction that the historian has, in the course of an explanation, looked at the central subject in a way with which one sympathizes.

Derivative Statements of Effects

Because philosophers of history have been preoccupied with the problem of explanation, they do not always observe that causal statements—i.e., statements of the form "Because ――――,
. . . .—are not always made in answer to the question

"Why?" or "What is the cause?"[8] Sometimes the historian will make a causal statement because he is interested in tracing the *effects* of some event or state of affairs. This calls for a discussion of the difference between the question "What is *the* cause of *s*'s being *Q*?" and the question "What is *the* effect of *s*'s being *Q*?" When we ask the former question, we may select the fact that *s* is *P* as the cause because that is the abnormal antecedent in the immediate past of the central subject. But when we begin with, say, the American Revolution as a fact already included in our history and then ask for its effect, we face a different problem of choice. In our discussion of singular causal statements which are explanatory, we challenged Mill's doctrine that *the* cause is always selected capriciously. But it is not as easy to challenge a counterpart of Mill's doctrine which says that *the* effect is not selected in accordance with a factually based rule. What I have in mind is the absence of any defensible counterpart to the abnormalist's theory of *the* cause when we are trying to pick out *the* effect. If an explosion occurs in a city, many windows in the city may break immediately after the explosion. Therefore, if one asks, "What was the effect of the explosion on the city?" it would appear that if one says simply that the mayor's windows broke as a consequence, one will not be able to appeal to something like the doctrine of abnormalism in justification of this selection of one particular effect. Obviously we may say something similar about *the* consequence or consequences of the American Revolution. We cannot argue that the historian always selects as *the* effect of a given event one that might be called the *unusual* effect. When we conclude that the cause of the derailment of the train was not the speed of the train because trains going at that speed are sometimes derailed and sometimes not derailed, we thereby show that we think of *the* cause—the bent rail, for example—as something that made the difference between a normal trip and a derailment. But similar reasoning is not available to us when we try to pick out the

<hr>

[8] This point is stressed by H. L. A. Hart and A. M. Honoré, *Causation in the Law* (Oxford, 1959), pp. 59 ff.

effect to be recorded in a chronicle and history. It is not possible to identify the effect of the event with which we begin as the unusual difference made by the event. Therefore the labeling of one effect as *the* effect does not rest on a criterion which is as descriptive as that presented by the doctrine of abnormalism.

This may not be evident if one does not reflect on the difference between asserting that A is *the* cause of C and asserting that C is *the* effect of A. Not only are they not equivalent, but it is not possible to present an analysis of the latter along the lines of Thesis II. That thesis, it will be recalled, requires us first of all to expand the *analysandum* into "A is the cause of C from point of view *m*," so suppose we expand "C is the effect of A" analogously into "C is the effect of A from point of view *m*." Whereas one conjunct of the equivalent of "A is the cause of C from point of view *m*" is "A is the abnormal cause of C when the subject is regarded from point of view *m*," it is impossible to produce the analogous conjunct in the analysis of "C is the effect of A from point of view *m*." It is true that "C is the effect of A from point of view *m*" implies that C is *an* effect of A, and that this implied statement may be analyzed along lines suggested by Thesis I. But when we come to ask what feature D' of an effect, or what relation between it and something else, distinguishes it as *the* effect, we can produce no counterpart to the criterion of abnormality as conceived in Thesis II. Moreover, when we try to produce some different but equally "descriptive" distinguishing feature of *the* effect, we also have no luck. The reason for this is best understood by reminding ourselves that we were able to pick out *the* cause by asking ourselves a question like "Why does *a* have the property Q when *a* is P and most P's are not Q," thereby making it possible to answer our "why" question by saying, "Because *a* is R and all things which are both P and R are Q." But no analogous question may be asked when we reverse the order of our inquiry by *beginning* with an event and seek not only its effects in the plural but also one particular effect that may be called *the* effect. Indeed, it makes no sense to talk of the decisive effect of an event or state of affairs and define that decisiveness in any way that relates the effect to its cause. Therefore we seem to be in a situation in which a counterpart of Mill's view of *the* cause is quite plausible. We call an effect *the* effect of a given cause without being guided by a rule that is comparable to that provided in Thesis II.

The conclusion to which we are led is that derivative statements of causes of basic facts and derivative statements of effects of basic facts are introduced into the chronicle on grounds that may reflect the different interests and values of the historian though they reflect them in different ways. Let us now examine the basic facts themselves with similar questions in mind.

THE FUNDAMENTAL PROBLEM DIVIDED: THE CHRONICLE'S BASIC STATEMENTS

If the historian is asked to defend his choice of the five statements attributing features D, I, L, O, and S to the central subject, that is to say, to defend his view that the basic statements in the chronicle of the United States record the Revolution, the Civil War, the Great Depression, and the two World Wars, what answer should he give? Just as some philosophers have supposed that they could present a criterion for picking out *the* cause of a given event from among several jointly sufficient conditions, so some thinkers hold, or appear to hold, that they can present a criterion for picking out the set of statements which answer the question "What basically happened in or to *s*?" Moreover, there is a remarkable parallelism between the sorts of criteria that are offered in each case. There are moralistic and pragmatic views of what should be recorded as a basic fact, and there is a metaphysical view: there are views that might be called objectivistic in tendency and others that are plainly subjectivistic in tendency. But there is one notable difference between the concept of *the* cause of an event and the concept of what happened in the career of an entity, and that is that no single philosophical theory of what happened occupies the same favored position as the abnormalist's theory of the cause.

In other words, ordinary and historical usage allows us a greater variety in answering the question "What happened in America in 1929?" than it allows us in answering the question "What was the cause of the stock market crash?" In answering the first question historians are permitted to say a greater variety of things than they are in answering the second question, for, to the extent that they are guided by abnormalism, there is more constraint upon them when they answer the second question. For this reason if we were to try to present a recipe for answering the question "What were the basic facts in the history of the United States?" we could not do so by presenting a necessary and sufficient condition for being a basic fact even though we can do so when we try to present a recipe for answering the question "What is the cause of the Depression?" *The cause of what happened* is a more definite notion than the notion of *what happened*.

In order to show the looseness of the concept of what happened, I shall examine a number of monistic views of what we *must* say in answer to the question "What happened?" I shall argue that they are the results of misguided efforts to provide a definition or a criterion for being a basic statement in a chronicle. The first monistic view to be considered may be called "estheticism."

7 kinds)
important

Estheticism

On the basis of what some authors say, one gets the impression that they think, even when they do not confront our problem explicitly, that the historian's answer to the question "What happened, basically, in the career of *s*?" is given in a set of statements which report the most exciting, intriguing, or stimulating set of facts in the career of the central subject. On this view, the facts recorded as basic need not be those of which the historian approves, for they may simply move him, titillate him, aggravate him or amuse him. But sometimes it is implied that they must focus on what the American novelist William Dean Howells called the "smiling aspects of life." Surprisingly enough, even Henry James, that great student of life's darker aspects, encourages such a view of history in his essay on London, although he was not there engaged in writing narrative history. He observed that because London was immense,

one has not the alternative of speaking of London as a whole, for the simple reason that there is no such thing as the whole of it. . . . Rather it is a collection of many wholes, and of which of them is it more important to speak? Inevitably there must be a choice, and I know of none more scientific than simply to leave out what we may have to apologize for. The uglinesses, the "rookeries," the brutalities, the night-aspect of many of the streets, the gin-shops and the hour when they are cleared out before closing—there are many elements of this kind which have to be counted out before a genial summary can be made.[9]

There is, of course, no objection to constructing what James so felicitously calls a genial summary; but it is obvious that when a historian of the United States decides to take as his basic events the Revolution, the Civil War, the First World War, the Depression, and the Second World War, he is not concentrating exclusively on the genial features of the country's history. Moreover, even if a historian were to insist that his basic facts be genial, he could hardly maintain a genial attitude toward all the other facts that he would be likely to admit as derivative facts. It is, of course, easy to make a *mere* chronicle of genial facts, one that is not causally integrable, but it should be obvious that, beginning with such a set of facts as a basis, it is practically impossible to construct a chronicle which is causally integrable to the degree required of histories as we have defined them. The fundamental point is that interesting facts, like interesting people, may have boring antecedents and boring offspring. And an analogous thing may be said of beautiful facts, since the rose grows in manure.

Moralism

For similar reasons, it is difficult to construct a connected narrative that implies a conjunction of basic statements which supply admonitory or encouraging moral information to statesmen. When

[9] Henry James, *Essays in London and Elsewhere* (New York, 1893), p. 27.

in his famous Inaugural Lecture, J. B. Bury dissociated himself from Cicero's view that history was *magistra vitae* and from the view of Dionysius that history was "philosophy by examples,"[10] he might well have pointed out the difficulty of constructing a history composed exclusively of statements reporting facts useful to the politician. In the abstract it is possible to select such a set of facts and to connect them by causal links, but such facts are not easily forged into a causally coherent narrative. Moreover, it is simply not true that historians, as we know them today, construct their lists of charter facts on this moralistic principle.

To assert that neither a causally integrable chronicle nor its basic statements can be composed exclusively on esthetic or moral grounds is not to deny that one can examine the past with an eye on moments of pleasure and profit. Santayana defines the philosophy of history itself as an effort on the part of a philosopher to scrutinize the past in order to abstract from it "whatever tended to illustrate his own ideals, as he might look over a crowd to find his friends." "The events themselves," he says, "would be left for scientific inference to discover, where credible reports did not testify to them directly; and the causes of events would be left to some theory of natural evolution." But when Santayana says that "an estimate of events in reference to the moral ideal which they embodied or betrayed, might supervene upon history,"[11] he has in mind a work like his own *Life of Reason*, and neither a narrative nor a chronicle as we understand them here. A good chronicle may include all sorts of facts which have no bearing on the needs of a moral philosopher in search of friends.

Aristotelian Essentialism: A Metaphysical View of Narrative

A good chronicle need not contain "essential" facts either. According to a tradition which goes back to Aristotle, history is incapable of discovering universal truths or of discerning the es-

---

[10] J. B. Bury, "The Science of History," *Selected Essays of J. B. Bury*, ed. Harold Temperley (Cambridge, England, 1930), pp. 3–22.

[11] George Santayana, *Reason in Science* (New York, 1906), p. 58.

sence of an individual, but some historians and philosophers argue in the face of the Aristotelian tradition that one task of the historian *is* to discern the essence or spirit of the individual.[12] We may think of them as holding that each of the basic statements in a chronicle should present the essence of a nation, a civilization, a person, or a city as it is at a certain time. According to advocates of what may be called "essentialism," a doctrine which resembles the metaphysical view of the cause discussed in an earlier chapter, the basic facts in a chronicle of the United States of America may and must be selected in ways that are not determined merely by the esthetic taste, the moral preference, or the practical problems of the historian himself. Like the theorist of *the* cause who insists that it can be distinguished on metaphysical grounds from mere conditions or occasions, the essentialist does not think that enough has been granted to the demands of objectivity when it is merely said that the basic statements in the chronicle are true and causally connectible with others. The essentialist insists that each of the statements in the basis of the chronicle expresses a truth which is *deeper* than others about the central subject. Such a view is touchingly conveyed in the following passage from Dostoyevsky's novel *The Possessed*:

> Her literary scheme was as follows. Numbers of papers and journals are published in the capitals and the provinces of Russia, and every day a number of events are reported in them. The year passes, the newspapers are everywhere folded up and put away in cupboards, or

[12] Such a view is expressed in the following remark by H. R. Trevor-Roper in a review of the Earl of Birkenhead's *The Professor and the Prime Minster: The Official Life of Professor F. A. Lindemann, Viscount Cherwell*: "Facts are facts. But there are other facts too. When all is set down, the real character —that elusive, burning character whose flame formed the thick crust around it—becomes clear. Behind the anti-Semitic utterances we see tireless, successful efforts to rescue Jewish scientists from Germany. Behind the sneers at the 'humanities' we see the positive desire to widen both scientific and humane education. Behind the withdrawn, personal austerity we see the real belief that others should have a full life, and a proper material basis for it, even in war. We also see what his real wartime services were. In essence, the Professor was convinced . . ." (*New York Times Book Review*, Feb. 25, 1962, p. 3). In recent times Karl R. Popper has been one of the most active and most trenchant critics of essentialism. See his *The Poverty of Historicism* (Boston, 1957), pp. 33–34, and *The Open Society and its Enemies*, passim.

are torn up and become litter, or are used for making parcels or wrapping things. Numbers of these facts make an impression and are remembered by the public, but in the course of years they are forgotten. Many people would like to look them up, but it is a labour for them to embark upon this sea of paper, often knowing nothing of the day or place or even year in which the incident occurred. Yet if all the facts for a whole year were brought together into one book, on a definite plan, and with a definite object, under headings with references, arranged according to months and days, such a compilation might reflect the characteristics of Russian life for the whole year even though the facts published are only a small fraction of the events that take place.

"Instead of a number of newspapers there would be a few fat books, that's all," observed Shatov.

But Lizaveta Nikolaevna clung to her idea, in spite of the difficulty of carrying it out and her inability to describe it. "It ought to be one book, and not even a very thick one," she maintained. But even if it were thick it would be clear, for the great point would be the plan and the character of the presentation of facts. Of course, not all would be collected and reprinted. The decrees and acts of government, local regulations, laws—all such facts, however important, might be altogether omitted from the proposed publications. They could leave out a great deal and confine themselves to a selection of events more or less characteristic of the moral life of the people, of the personal character of the Russian people at the present moment. Of course, everything might be put in: strange incidents, fires, public subscriptions, anything good or bad, every speech or word, perhaps even floodings of the rivers, perhaps even some government decrees, but only such things to be selected as are characteristic of the period: everything would be put in with a certain view, a special significance and intention, with an idea which would illuminate the facts looked at in the aggregate, as a whole. And finally the book ought to be interesting even for light reading, apart from its value as a work of reference. It would be, so to say, a presentation of the spiritual, moral, inner life of Russia for a whole year.

"We want everyone to buy it, we want it to be a book that will be found on every table," Liza declared. "I understand that all lies in the plan, and that's why I apply to you," she concluded. She grew very warm over it, and although her explanation was obscure and incomplete, Shatov began to understand.

"So it would amount to something with a political tendency, a selection of facts with a special tendency," he muttered, still not raising his head.

"Not at all, we must not select with a particular bias, and we ought not to have any political tendency in it. Nothing but impartiality—that will be the only tendency."[13]

We may express Lizaveta's view in terms of our model as follows: Let us suppose that two historians divide their subjects into the same temporal periods, say twenty-six of them as indicated earlier. At any given time there are many predicates that may be truly applied to s: at time t_1 s is A, A', A'', and so on; at time t_2 is B, B', B'', and so on; and analogously all the way to t_{26}. But even though one historian of s may produce a causally integrated history whose list of basic true statements differs at certain points from that of another, on the view of the essentialist that list of basic statements is superior if and only if its conjuncts present *the* character of the individual s, say Russia, at t_4, t_9, t_{12}, t_{15}, t_{19}, whereas the inferior list contains statements that express, not essential, but "accidental" features of s. By hypothesis both histories are causally integrated, so we cannot choose between them on that account; moreover, both imply true chronicles, so we cannot choose between them on that account either. But since the chronicle of the first history radiates causally from a conjunction of basic statements each of which expresses the essence of s as it is at a given time in its career, whereas the other chronicle radiates from a conjunction of statements about its accidents, Lizaveta's idea is that the first history is superior to the second. The first history expresses *the* personal character of the Russian people at each time for which a basic attribution is made.

We have here an analogue of the ancient doctrine that individuals have essences, a view which is quite similar to Aristotle's view that we can present the essence of Socrates only by saying that he is a man. Certain historians who say that Europe was essentially characterized by a Renaissance at one time, and at

[13] Fyodor Dostoevsky, *The Possessed* (Everyman edn., New York, 1931), I, 114–16.

another by an Enlightenment, may think along similar lines. Both of these features of Europe are seen by such historians as analogous to Socrates' manhood in the scheme of Aristotle, whereas they view alternative true propositions about Europe in the same period as Aristotle would have viewed the propositions that Socrates was bald, white, and married to Xanthippe. On such a view, the best history of *s* would be that causally integrated account which—other things being equal—is based on an account of *essentially* what happened. Even the most cautious and unmetaphysical of historians are prepared to speak in some such vein of the "line" that the main stream of American "actuality" has followed.[14] And this image of *the* line of narrative, objectively determinable, the one that must be chosen from among all the other lines or paths through the jungle of historical fact, is paralleled in our model by the chronicle which radiates from the basic facts that allegedly express the essential truth about the historian's central subject.

Pragmatic Essentialism

Such an analogue of Aristotelian essentialism is subject to philosophical difficulties that are not unlike those to which Aristotle's doctrine of essence is subject, difficulties that I shall not rehearse. Aristotle's notion of an individual's essence is not philosophically defensible, and therefore the basic statements in a chronicle cannot be analyzed with its help. But there have been efforts at treating the notion of essence without Aristotelian tears, and in this connection the views of William James suggest themselves almost automatically. In his *Principles of Psychology* James followed what he took to be Locke's lead in an effort to undermine the Aristotelian view and to replace it by what James called a teleological conception of essence. James argued in terms that are familiar that "all ways of conceiving a concrete fact, if they are true ways at all, are equally true ways. *There is no property*

[14] See, for example, Morison, op. cit., p. 357.

ABSOLUTELY essential to any one thing."[15] Therefore, James said, the question "What is that?" as the questioner points to a concrete thing, may be answered in many true ways, depending on the practical concerns of the questioner or his respondent. The thing upon which he was writing, said James, might be regarded as a surface for inscription, or as a combustible material, or as a thin thing, or as a hydrocarbonaceous thing, or as a thing eight inches by ten inches in size, an American thing, and so on, ad infinitum. *What* one regards it as, depends, according to James, upon one's practical concerns, upon what one wants to do with it. And since one can only do one thing with it at a time, James continued, one can regard it in only one of these ways at a time.

It is easy to see the implications of this view of essence for a view of history. In a similar way one might argue that the historian should employ as the basis of his chronicle that conjunction of statements about his central subject which stands to *his* practical aims as James's regarding his piece of paper as a combustible was related to James's need to light a fire. And here we have the ground for what might be called a teleological view of a superior basis for a chronicle of *s*. On such a view, when we say that a certain basis is superior to another, we are speaking elliptically, for what we mean would be more properly expressed by saying that this basis for a chronicle is superior to another relative to a certain desire to do something to *s* or with *s*, i.e., that this way of regarding *s* is *the* way to regard *s* in the light of our practical interest in *s*.

However tempting such a view may be, we are immediately struck by one difficulty in it. James's view may be plausible as an analysis of essence when the object is present to us now, as his piece of paper was to him when he was penning his words. But what about the typical subject of the historian, the dead and

---

[15] William James, *The Principles of Psychology* (New York, 1890), II, 333; James's italics and capitals. For an earlier expression of a related point of view, see Mill, *A System of Logic*, Bk. I, ch. VI, sec. 3; for a more recent one, see Nelson Goodman, "The Way the World Is," *Review of Metaphysics*, XIV (1960), 48–56.

buried individual or the extinct civilization? Surely we have no immediate practical interest in such entities, that is to say, no interest in doing something overt *to* them or *with* them in the sense in which James had a practical interest in writing on or burning his piece of paper. For this reason a simple transfer of James's pragmatically teleological view of the essence of a thing to the history of a thing cannot be made. Even if James be right in suggesting that categorizing a contemporaneous concrete thing "is first and last and always for the sake of . . . doing" which is overt, we cannot hold the corresponding view about a piece of paper in the distant past or about ancient Greece. So a teleological view which is narrowly pragmatic seems incapable of sustaining an analysis of the superior basis for a chronicle of a thing which is in the distant past.

We might be tempted to revise the pragmatic view so that it no longer says that the superior true history of s is superior because it entails a chronicle whose basis facilitates action on or with s, the thing whose history is being written, but rather that it is superior relative to our desire to do something which is not necessarily *to* or *with* the central subject of our history. But this is simply a return to what was earlier called "moralism," and so long as this action is conceived as practical in the narrowest sense, even if it is not performed on or with the central subject, I cannot see how we can defend this view. Some basic statements are included in chronicles without any intention to facilitate practical action of any kind. Naturally, a reader of a history of ancient Greece *might* learn something of use to him in his efforts to do something about contemporary America, but not all historians write histories of ancient Greece with an intention that would make it proper to judge the merit of their chronicles by assessing the chronicles' capacities to guide overt action in the present. In other words, it is not true that each basic statement in a chronicle of s refers to the essence of s at that time even if we view its essence pragmatically rather than in an Aristotelian manner. One may try to construct a chronicle which is based exclusively on this pragmatic principle of selection, just as one may try to construct one based on the principle proposed by those who adopt the esthetic approach to this problem. But such principles of selection are not used in all of the histories that historians write, and it is unlikely that they will permit them to construct causally coherent narratives.

Abnormalism as a Doctrine About What Happened

I turn to a view which I label "abnormalism" and which may be thought of as the counterpart of the abnormalist theory of the cause. This view asserts that when a historian is trying to decide what feature the central subject has at a given time as he forms the basis of its chronicle, he selects the abnormal feature of *s* at that time. In other words, this view asserts that if a historian is required to say what happened at a given time, *t*, in the career of the central subject, he is bound to ask himself, "What was unusual about the central subject as it was at *t*?" About this view at least two things may be said. First of all, that historians do not limit themselves to including events that are unusual in their chronicles; and second, that when one does report an unusual event, it is unusual or abnormal only with respect to the way in which the central subject is regarded by the historian. In illustration of the first point: a city may be bombed over and over again during a war, and yet its historians may regard each of these bombings as worthy of recording in a history; and a country may have a tradition of pragmatism in its philosophy, to the point where most of its philosophers are pragmatists, and yet if all of them are sufficiently *good* as philosophers, the historian may feel obliged to report the views of each of them in his chronicle of the country's philosophy. In connection with the second point, we saw in our discussion of explanation that whether a historian regards an event as unusual depends on how he classifies the event. A war may be regarded as unusual if the historian is thinking of the country as it was just before the war, but it may not be unusual when one views it as an event in the career of a warlike nation.

It may be that when a historian tries to *explain* a fact about his central subject, he does so because the fact is unusual in some respect; but, as we have seen, not all causal statements are answers to the request for an explanation, "Why does the central subject, s, have feature P?" A causal statement may also be presented in answer to the question "What is the effect of the fact that s is P?" and therefore lead us to include in the chronicle statements of effects which are not unusual.

While we are considering abnormalism in this context, we should remark on the falsity of one of its extreme forms, namely, the view that the historian is interested in recording only the unique features of his central subject. If this means that each of his entries in a chronicle records something true of the central subject and only of the central subject at that time, this doctrine is obviously false. When it is said by the historian that the central subject was at war at time t_1, it is surely not implied that no other nation was at war at that time. It may turn out, after the entire chronicle has been presented, that it attributes a conjunction of features to the central subject and identifies it uniquely, in the sense that no other subject in fact had all these characteristics— being A at one time, B at another, C at a third, and so on. But it does not follow that each of the component predicates is applicable to and only to the central subject at the time in question. Being an abnormal feature, or being the abnormal feature, or being the unique feature is not what characterizes all of the features recorded in a chronicle, any more than being the essential feature does. We cannot say that every entry in a chronicle records a feature which is peculiar to the central subject at that time, just as we cannot say that every chronicle records a feature which is essential to the central subject at that time.

Encyclopedism

We may, upon abandoning estheticism and moralism, turn neither to essentialism nor to abnormalism, but to the view that the basis of a chronicle expresses a *fuller* truth about the central subject, rather than a more genial, a more helpful, or a deeper truth. The historian, it might be said, wishes to approximate the *whole* truth about his central subject, and therefore one basis for a chronicle will be adjudged superior to another if it characterizes the central subject in a fuller way than the other does. This doctrine resembles Mill's theory that the cause is the *whole* cause, and may be called "encyclopedism."

The encyclopedist has a goal which must be distinguished from that of the essentialist, especially if we associate essentialism with Aristotle's doctrine on this subject. For Aristotle does not think of statements of essence as conveying *more* than any other statement about the individual, but rather as conveying something which is deeper, as I have said—such that if the individual were not to have it, the individual would not be numerically the same individual as it now is. Hence the Aristotelian difference between saying of Socrates that he is a man and saying that he is white. Now it is true that there is a passage in the *Categories* in which Aristotle speaks of an essential statement about an individual as rendering a "more instructive account" of him. But this is where Aristotle is invidiously comparing a statement of Socrates' species, *man*, with one of his genus, *animal*, both of which are what Aristotle calls "secondary substances."[16] It is true that one of these statements expresses more about Socrates than the other, insofar as one of them implies the other and not conversely. On the other hand, when Aristotle invidiously compares *all* secondary substances with an accident like whiteness, he does not say that a person who would render a more instructive account of Socrates should say of him that he is a man rather than that he is white. The superiority of the attribution of any secondary substance to Socrates, whether it be *man* or *animal*, over the attribution of an accident like whiteness to Socrates, is not measured by the capacity of the former to say *more* about Socrates in the sense of coming closer to the whole truth about it. For this reason an Aristotelian essence is not what a historical encyclopedist would seek. The encyclopedist, as I have said, aims at the whole truth rather than the essential truth.

[16] *Categories*, 2ᵇ.

Macaulay defended some such view as this, but in the very passage in which he explains and defends it, he provides the strongest argument against it:

No picture . . . and no history can present us with the whole truth; but those are the best pictures and the best histories which exhibit such parts of the truth as most nearly produce the effect of the whole. He who is deficient in the art of selection may, by showing nothing but the truth, produce all the effect of the grossest falsehood. It perpetually happens that one writer tells less truth than another, merely because he tells more truths. In the imitative arts we constantly see this. There are lines in the human face . . . which stand in such relations to each other that they ought either to be all introduced into a painting together or all omitted together. A sketch into which none of them enters may be excellent; but, if some are given and others left out, though there are more points of likeness, there is less likeness. An outline scrawled with a pen, which seizes the marked features of a countenance, will give a much stronger idea of it than a bad painting in oils. Yet the worst painting in oils that ever hung at Somerset House resembles the original in many more particulars. A bust of white marble may give an excellent idea of a blooming face. Color the lips and cheeks of the bust, leaving the hair and eyes unaltered, and the similarity, instead of being more striking, will be less so.[17]

It is clear from this that the idea of approximating the whole truth about the central subject, even as it is at a given time, is not thought by its advocates to be simply a matter of telling more and more about it. For if it were, the least bit of additional information about a period that it gave would make one statement in a chronicle superior to another. And yet if a historian were to say that today is the age of analysis in American philosophy, and then add that today there are more than a hundred analytically oriented professors of philosophy in America who are bald, he would not be adding something by the assertion of the second statement which would bring him closer to the whole truth about philosophy in America today, as "the whole truth" is understood by those

[17] Thomas Babington Macaulay, *Critical and Historical Essays* (Boston and New York, 1900), I, 244–45.

who adopt the view that the historian should try to approximate it. Adding the fact about the number of bald professors would play the same ludicrous role as painting a black moustache on a statue because one has evidence that the original subject had a black moustache and because one wants to get as close as one can to the whole truth about him. This shows that even those who speak of approximating the whole truth think of approximating that part of the whole truth which is *significant*. After all, Macaulay speaks of the "*marked* features of countenance" when he tells us what a superior outline scrawled with a pen accomplishes by comparison to a bad painting of the same countenance in oils.

Even if the task of the historian were to record all the *marked* features of an age, he does not have the original before him so that he or we can tell by inspection whether he has come closer than a rival to recording all those marked features. We are unable to watch over his shoulder as he paints his subject, unable to turn from canvas to original in order to test his fidelity. We are not able to resuscitate the late Middle Ages in order to see whether its "most striking feature . . . was an exceptionally strong sense of guilt and a truly dreadful fear of retribution, seeking expression in a passionate longing for effective intercession and in a craving for direct, personal experience of the Deity, as well as in a corresponding dissatisfaction with the Church and with the mechanization of the means of salvation. . . ."[18] And even if we could, there would always be the possibility that what one historian regards as the most striking feature, hence to be emphasized, might be different from what another regards as the most striking feature.

Modified Encyclopedism

For this reason, the notion of approximating the whole truth as a standard for basic statements may be replaced by the notion of organizing all of the evidence available. The encyclopedist would

[18] William L. Langer, "The Next Assignment," *The American Historical Review*, LXIII (1958), 298.

thereby diminish the size of his goal, following the advice of William James, who once wrote: "Mr. Warner, in his Adirondack story, shot a bear by aiming, not at his eye or heart, but 'at him generally.' But we cannot aim 'generally' at the universe; or if we do, we miss our game."[19] The encyclopedist may continue to disapprove of the subjectivity of the method of Henry James's genial summary, but will now no longer insist that the historian seeks to say as much as possible about his subject. Instead he may say of each of the basic statements in his chronicle that they successfully organize all of the known data about his subject at a given time. This would be comparable to saying that the attribution of manhood to Socrates has priority over attributing whiteness to him, not because one is an essential attribute and the other accidental, but rather because one more successfully organizes or colligates everything that is known about Socrates. One may construe the advocate of modified encyclopedism as holding that the historian's question "What happened in or to *s* at time *t*?" should be replaced by the question "Which is the scientifically superior colligatory statement to be made about the central subject as it is at *t*?" This is part of an effort to show that just as *the cause* of the Enlightenment may be detected in a descriptive or factual manner, so the preferability of the statement that Europe was characterized by an Enlightenment at a certain period may be established descriptively because it is the statement or hypothesis which best ties together all the data about Europe at the time.

To this view there are two serious objections.

(1) It is a mistake to assume that for every period about which the historian asserts a basic statement, *the known data* are always fixed and agreed upon by all colligators, so that the issue is simply whether one colligation is superior to another as the colligation of these agreed-upon data. Suppose we assume that when two historians debate as to which of two colligating statements best colligates a given set of historical data, their debate can be resolved by analogy to the way in which we decide that the Coper-

---

[19] James, op. cit., pp. 333–34.

nican theory is superior to the Ptolemaic theory. Such an assumption still leaves open the question whether the historian who uses one set of data is using a set of data which is superior to a different set used by a fellow-historian of the same central subject in the same period. Of course, historians working on very remote periods for which there are few remains and documents, may try to colligate what all parties agree are *the only data* available, and then the issue between them, if they disagree, may simply be an objective one in inductive logic. When two archaeologists working with the same remains reconstruct an ancient building differently, or when two paleontologists working with the same bones reconstruct the skeleton of a prehistoric animal differently, we may believe that in each debate one of the investigators has more successfully organized the data agreed upon by both parties in the dispute. But this happy embarrassment of poverty is not the fate of all historians. Many historians try to colligate data which they select *from among* known data as the data *to be colligated* on the basis of a value-judgment which is not shared by their fellow historians. Therefore, even if the relationship between colligating feature and colligated data is like that between a scientific theory and its confirming data, we may hold that the choice of data often rests on a value-judgment. Such a value-judgment may be made by the historian of the United States during 1963 when he decides to record a certain day as that on which tensions in the cold war between the United States and the Soviet Union began to ease. In doing so he disregards an enormous amount of data that a Chinese historian who is writing a history of the United States might well include as data to be colligated. It is impossible to eliminate this element of interest, and hence of value, in the selection of the data to be colligated, whether one is writing a newspaper or a history. This element of interest also enters into the assessment of a chronicle's basic statements. One historian does not assess his rival's basic chronicle simply by asking whether those basic statements successfully colligate the data used by the rival, making no estimate of the significance of the data. It is not as if he were only interested in evaluating his competitor's powers in inductive logic, paying no attention to the data the competitor uses. His judgment of the rival's colligation is double-barreled, for he is prepared to reject as inadequate even a brilliantly logical colligation if it is based on data which he deems uninteresting or not salient.

It may be said, of course, that this is completely parallel to what goes on in natural science. We assess a physicist's theory not only on the basis of its powers to organize his data but also on the basis of certain features of the data. If his measurements are faulty, we may count that against the physicist, and if he fails to take into account certain data with which we are familiar, we may also criticize him. But—and this is a fundamental difference between the situation in physics and the situation in history—a historian may protest against the inclusion of data in the material to be colligated on grounds of interest or value in a way that is foreign to the method of physicists when they criticize each other. A historian may say that a certain datum does not merit his concern simply because it is uninteresting or unattractive by esthetic, moral, or political standards, but a physicist—who also selects his data, of course—does not usually exclude data on such grounds. The beauty or ugliness of the red-shift in the spectrum plays no part in the decision to regard it as a datum that a theory must deal with and link to other data. On the other hand, the data which a historian tries to colligate may be *deemed to be data* on evaluative grounds that another historian may not accept.

(2) Let us turn now to the second objection to the modified version of encyclopedism, which is that some basic statements are chosen without any regard to whether they present superior colligations by comparison to other true statements that could be made about the central subject. The decision to record Kant's epistemology in a chronicle need not be motivated by the conviction that his philosophy "sums up" the thinking of an age or that it had great impact on the life of the age. In this respect the historian of philosophy is motivated by considerations which differ from

those that operate when a social historian characterizes a certain period as feudal or capitalistic. A statement about Kant's epistemological views gets into the historical act, so to speak, because Kant's views are thought to be philosophically profound and not because it is thought that a summary of them would serve to colligate features of Europe in his time. It is absurd, therefore, to maintain that all of the basic statements in one's chronicle are colligatory in nature. Some of them are made not in order to organize a set of data about a period in history but because they describe events, thoughts, or conditions that we admire or detest. That is why we sometimes criticize a historian of ideas for treating the wrong figures or excluding the wrong figures.

Implicit in every history of philosophy there is a basic chronicle which takes the form of saying that one leading philosopher thought in a certain manner at a certain time, that another thought in another manner at a later time, and so on. The basic statements in the associated chronicle consist of statements about the views of these central figures. In selecting these figures a historian may bear in mind the originality of the philosopher, his insight, and his influence; but when the historian chooses these philosophers on the basis of their insight, he inevitably estimates their philosophical powers. He does not give them intelligence tests, or measure the degree to which they arrive at "philosophical truth" in a way that would command the consensus of all other historians of philosophy. Although many philosophers try to arrive at truth, the historian's conclusion that they have succeeded is often merely a measure of the degree to which the historian agrees with the philosophers' views or of the degree to which they adopt values that the historian shares. Even when the historian tries to rise above this sort of consideration and tries to decide whether a man is a first-rate philosopher in a way that might transcend doctrinal agreement, he must face the possibility of a fundamental sort of disagreement. Some of his readers will complain that he has chosen the *wrong* philosophers, and to the extent to which these readers disapprove of the historian's choice of leading philosophers, they will disapprove of the chronicle and of the history as a whole. Such disapproval, it should be noted, has nothing to do with whether the historian correctly traces out the causal links among the beliefs of the so-called leading philosophers, and nothing to do with whether the historian does or does not expound their views correctly. This disapproval is disapproval of the chronicle no matter how true.

It may be said that the history of ideas—and particularly the history of philosophical ideas—is an atypical sort of history in that the selection of its chronicle rests, more than any other kind of history, on judgments as to the worth of the items included. But surely one cannot deny that the history of social institutions and human action is often constructed with an eye to what is worth recording. When we call a scholar an antiquarian and not a historian, we express a judgment as to the value of the actions he records. We say that he is recording dreary things. And sometimes we disapprove of a history because it traces a "line" that depends on judgments which we do not share. Such values seem to have operated in Samuel Eliot Morison's reassessment of his own earlier Federalist approach to American history. And surely a moral judgment of certain men dictated the appearance of their names in the chronicle of Herodotus, to judge from the famous opening of the *History*: "These are the researches of Herodotus of Halicarnassus, which he publishes in the hope of thereby preserving from decay the remembrance of what men have done, and of preserving the great and wonderful actions of the Greeks and the barbarians from losing their due meed of glory; and withal to put on record what were the grounds of their feud." There in the first statement by the Father of History we find a clear indication that a historian may choose some of his basic statements for reasons connected with the value of what is recorded, i.e., because they describe *great* actions of Greeks and barbarians. It is true that some of the derivative statements in Herodotus' chronicle might have entered on "scientific" grounds—if "putting on record what were the grounds of their feud" be regarded as a scientific operation. And it is also true that some basic statements in his chronicle might have colligated universally accepted data about a given period, but neither statements of cause nor colligatory statements exhaust the class of statements in which Herodotus reported what happened, precisely because some of them could have recorded actions deemed to be great in statements that are not colligatory in nature.

A PLURALISTIC VIEW OF THE BASIS OF A CHRONICLE: COLLIGATION AND EVALUATION

In arguing that sometimes a basic statement will be included in a chronicle because it reflects the historian's evaluation of what he records and that sometimes it is included because of its colligatory power, I have been mainly concerned to show that there is no one simple criterion on the basis of which we select the main facts in a chronicle. I grant that some basic statements may be chosen over other statements in the way that we choose one scientific theory rather than another, but I insist that some are not chosen in this way. If one were to examine history books with an eye to finding reasons for the inclusion of statements in their basic chronicles, one would find that some are included for reasons of curiosity, some for the beauty of what they report, some for the moral grandeur of what they report, some for the bizarreness of what they report, some for the practical lessons they teach, some for their capacity to organize a set of data associated with their central subject. My argument, therefore, has been directed against a monistic theory of what happened, against the idea that we can present a recipe for giving answers to the question "What should be recorded as basic in a chronicle of *s*?" which will, in effect, be a definition of what it is to be a basic element in a chronicle of *s*. In its place we must adopt a pluralistic view of admissibility to the set of basic statements about what happened in the career of the central subject, and to the chronicle as a whole. There are many different reasons that may be given for recording one true statement rather than another in the basic chronicle of the central subject and some rest on value-preferences even if others do not.

Such a pluralistic view of what happened may make it easier to see why different true general histories are written of the same central subject and why they are judged differently by different people and different historians. Such a view does not deny the importance of fact and causal connection in the construction of a narrative, but according to it, as we have seen, a historian is less limited in the formation of his basic chronicle than he is in the answers he can give to the question "What is the cause?" In answering the second question he may be bound to refer to the unusual antecedent of the event to be explained, whereas in answering the question "What happened?" he may behave much as Mill supposed he could behave when asked, "What is the cause?" He may choose what is conspicuous, interesting, useful, fascinating, frightening, instructive, or beautiful, so long as he constructs a coherent narrative, even though no one of these standards is *the* standard appealed to by the selecting historian. Therefore a historian of the United States of America may follow any of a number of "lines" so long as he presents a true history in the sense defined earlier. The number of "essential" histories he may tell will be greater than even a Jamesian historian would permit, for his lines of narration may be dictated by goals that are not crudely practical. Provided that he can construct a history in the sense defined, a historian may concentrate primarily or exclusively on the interesting, the genial, or the unattractive features of his subject. And of course he may, if he can, construct a narrative out of them, fill his book with statements that he thinks will guide or influence action in the present. He may even follow the advice of E. H. Carr and write what has been called "Big Battalion" history: he may select his facts with an eye on the ruling classes of the past, the present, or the future. Such approaches do not usually yield causally coherent narratives, as I have argued earlier, but if they do, I know no absolute way in which to exclude them without supplying extra advice about permissible and impermissible goals in historical writing. We may allow the historian to choose his facts with eyes on all kinds of considerations, so long as he writes true and connected narrative.

After reaching this point we may still wish to ask whether there is a use of the phrase "superior history" which is exclusively that of the professional historian—the historian with a large "H"—a use which, when it is analyzed or clarified, will allow us to pick out some purpose or set of purposes that will distinguish his history from that of any truthful narrator. A number of preliminary things must be said before facing this question directly. The first is that professional historians write their histories about a limited class of things. Not *any* thing may be a central subject of a historian's history. Historians write histories of nations, civilizations, scientific societies, philosophical movements, revolutions, economies, religions. They usually do not write histories of planets, animals, stars, rocks, or galaxies. So we know that they are primarily concerned with the social behavior of human beings. However, the problem before us now is not that of defining the class of things or subjects *of which* historians with a large "H" may write a history. We are asking what features of a given subject should be mentioned in a history of that subject. And if we are seeking a *definition of the notion of what features should be recorded* by a professional historian, I do not think that any useful one can be supplied. At best we may say that what should be recorded are those features of the central subject which colligate the data and/or those which record items of interest and value to the historian. There is no rock of historical practice or usage on which to rest some more specific definition of what should be recorded. Historians may in one generation band together and by fiat rule out certain kinds of histories as nonhistories, but they cannot provide some clear notion of what should be recorded which supposedly flows from the nature of history as a discipline. That is why it is so strange that E. H. Carr should think that he has extracted the essence of history "properly so-called" when he suggests that the test of historical importance is revelance to the future triumph of the masses in Asia and Africa.[20] He is of course entitled to think that only such facts are worth recording, but not to think that he is delivering the essential truth about history as a discipline. Once again we are faced with a variety of essentialism, but this time it is essentialism concerning the concept of history or the office of historians. Yet historians, of all people, should realize that the logic of historical narration has no more room for the essences of offices than it has for the essences of individuals.

When faced with such an argument, some historians might insist that they certainly agree that we cannot extract a criterion for admissibility to a chronicle by reflecting on what it is to be a historian, but that nevertheless historians as a group do think that it is more important to write a history of the changes in forms of power in the United States than it is to write a history of changes in women's clothing.[21] And it has been argued in the same vein that a biography which concentrates on Marx's economic theories and political activities will be generally regarded as superior, other things being equal, to one which concentrates on his carbuncles, his Jewish origins, and his felicitous domestic life.[22] One may grant both of these points, however, and still assert that the choice of basic chronicle in both cases, the choice of what aspects of the United States or of Marx's life should be recorded in a history, cannot be defended simply by the argument that all the statements in the basic chronicle represents superior colligations of data, or that all of them "explain" more than all of those in the rival basis. The point is that the selection of at least some of the basic facts is determined by the historian's values and by his notion of what is interesting.[23] Most historians may believe that it is more important for the world to know about Marx's political ideas than it is to know about his carbuncles, and that it is more

[20] E. H. Carr, *What Is History?* (New York, 1962), p. 176.
[21] Lee Benson, "On 'The Logic of Historical Narration'," in *Philosophy and History*, ed. Hook, p. 270.
[22] Sidney Hook, "Objectivity and Reconstruction in History," in *Philosophy and History*, p. 270.
[23] See Popper, *The Open Society and its Enemies*, ch. 25.

important for the world to know about changes in the forms of political power in America than it is for the world to know about changes in women's clothing, but these are value-judgments even if they are generally shared. William James remarks that "the preferences of sentient creatures are what *create* the importance of topics";[24] and while there may be some uses of the word "importance" that are not linked to such preferences, certainly some are, and they underlie certain selections of historians.

However, as I have suggested, it is one thing to say that such judgments of importance are value-judgments or that they rest on the preferences of sentient creatures, and another to maintain that they do not command consensus. Therefore, I want to emphasize that many fundamental judgments of importance do not command the same degree of consensus as do descriptive judgments which are supported by historical evidence. Although most historians might agree that a history which concentrates on Marx's political activity and economic ideas is superior, other things being equal, to one that concentrates on his carbuncles, there are other extrahistorical judgments of importance on which historians are not in agreement. Take, for example, the notion advanced a half-century ago by James Harvey Robinson that history should be dominated by scientific motives and that the trouble with historians from Thucydides to Macaulay and Ranke was that they had examined the past with an eye to "amusing, edifying, or comforting the reader." Robinson was not accusing them of trying to amuse, edify, and comfort the reader by lying about facts or causal connections. It would be more accurate and more illuminating to say that he thought such historians formed the bases of their chronicles under the influence of extrahistorical purposes of which he disapproved. By contrast to these historians, Robinson thought of himself as a "scientific historian," and he summarized the shift from prescientific history to scientific history in the following way: "To scan the past with the hope of discovering

[24]William James, "The Importance of Individuals," in *The Will to Believe and Other Essays in Popular Philosophy* (New York, 1898), p. 261.

recipes for the making of statesmen and warriors, of discrediting the pagan gods, of showing that Catholic or Protestant is right, of exhibiting the stages of the self-realization of the Weltgeist, of demonstrating that Liberty emerged from the forests of Germany never to return thither—none of these motives are scientific although they may go hand in hand with much sound scholarship. But by the middle of the Nineteenth Century the muse of history, *semper mutabile,* began to fall under the potent spell of natural science. She was no longer satisfied to celebrate the deeds of heroes and nations with the lyre and shrill flute on the breeze-swept slopes of Helicon; she no longer durst attempt to vindicate the ways of God to man. She had already come to recognize that she was ill-prepared for her undertakings and had begun to spend her mornings in the library, collating manuscripts and making out lists of variant readings. She aspired to do even more and began to talk of raising her chaotic mass of information to the rank of a science."[25]

When Robinson spoke of history falling under the spell of science, in part he meant that it was beginning to tell us, with Marx and Darwin, how things had come about—*wie es eigentlich geworden*—in addition to telling us with Ranke how things were —*wie es eigentlich gewesen.* But how would Robinson have the historian choose those basic facts that were to be explained and whose effects were to be recorded in a narrative? Presumably in a "scientific manner." And yet when one turns to *The Development of Modern Europe,* written by Robinson in collaboration with Charles Beard and published in 1908, the same year in which the above-quoted words were published, one discovers there that it was Robinson's and Beard's "ever-conscious aim to enable the reader to catch up with his own times; to read intelligently the foreign news in the morning paper; to know what was the attitude of Leo XIII toward the Social Democrats even if he has forgotten

[25] James Harvey Robinson, *History* (New York, 1908), p. 14; the essay is reprinted in revised form under the title, "The History of History," in Robinson's *The New History* (New York, 1912), where the passage appears on pp. 43–44. See also my *Social Thought in America,* pp. 28–29.

that of Innocent III toward the Albigenses," and that they had "consistently subordinated the past to the present."[26] But this implied the judgment that the historian should include in his chronicles statements about the present or recent past, which should then be causally connected with other statements in the chronicle; and this judgment is just as extrahistorical and extra-scientific as the notion that the historian should report facts that amuse, edify, or comfort the reader. In other words, the idea of Robinson and Beard that historians should "consistently subordinate the past to the present" was dependent on a value-judgment which all historians do not share even though they might all be more interested in Marx's politics than in his relations with his wife. Therefore, one moral of our reflection on the writing of Robinson and Beard in 1908 is that even when some historians profess to be scanning the past with "scientific" motives in mind, they may be scanning it under the influence of a value-judgment, for example, the judgment that it is more important to know the attitude of Leo XIII toward the Social Democrats than it is to know the attitude of Innocent III toward the Albigenses. Any superiority which their histories may have over those of historians who scan the past with the hope of discovering recipes for states-men and warriors, or of discrediting the pagan gods, or of showing that Catholic or Protestant is right, is a superiority which is extra-historical in character. Historical evidence as usually conceived does not show us that one such purpose in writing a history is superior to another, and we cannot appeal to the essence of the historical enterprise in order to justify writing history with one purpose rather than another in mind.

Just as historians may disagree as to whether they should make their selections with an eye to explaining the present, so they may disagree as to whether they are obliged to describe the typical or the best features of a given period. Richard Hofstadter has said

[26] James Harvey Robinson and Charles A. Beard, *The Development of Modern Europe* (New York, 1907–8), I, iii. See also my *Social Thought in America*, pp. 48–49.

that while he, in his *Age of Reform*, is interested in the typical thought of the Progressive Era, other students of the period are interested in the best thought that it produced.[27] So far as I can gather, this is not asserted in criticism of the effort to chronicle the best thought, but some historians, if not Hofstadter, seem to think that those who describe ideas about day-to-day political, social, and economic developments in a period are concerned with the *really* historical aspects of the intellectual life of the period. They seem to think that historians should be concerned with that aspect of what happened rather than with more high-brow features of the period, and hence that their decision to record this aspect is objectively preferable. But I do not think that this decision can be defended on historical grounds alone, however many professors of history may make it at a given time. In short, I think that both evaluation, which may lead to the conclusion that certain features of a period are the best, and colligation, which may lead to the conclusion that certain features of a period are typical, may play a part in the formation of a chronicle. And often two historians of the same subject will form two different chronicles when they disagree about values and cannot resolve their disagreement in any way that could be called historical.

EXPLICIT AND IMPLICIT VALUE JUDGMENTS

Having said this, however, I should make a distinction between two ways in which the historian's values may affect the formation of his chronicle. He may be able to make explicit the standards on the basis of which he decides to include a given event, person, or philosophical idea in his chronicle; or he may not be. If he is a very self-conscious historian of the United States, he may be able to see that as a Jeffersonian he has on a number of occasions included events in his chronicle just because they are examples of the Jeffersonian tradition at work and because he values that tra-

[27] Richard Hofstadter, *The Age of Reform, From Bryan to F.D.R* (New York, 1956), p. 6.

dition in American life. If he is a historian of European philosophy wth a low opinion of Scholasticism, he may be able to make clear to his reader why his discussion of the Middle Ages is sketchy. If he is an intellectual historian of America, he may be conscious of the fact that has written the history of American thought from the 1880's to the First World War as if it were a record of liberal social philosophy in which the names of John Dewey, Justice Holmes, Thorstein Veblen, and Charles Beard predominate. In such cases a historian may be able to separate the facts that he records and the evaluative grounds on which he chooses them so that his readers, if they be Federalists in the first case, Catholics in the second, and conservatives in the third, may see that he has written histories that they would not have written. If, to take another example, T. S. Eliot had written a history of England and had prefaced it with an announcement that he was fond of the classical in literature, sympathetic to the royalists in politics, and Anglo-Catholic in religion, his readers who disagreed with him on these issues would know why their chronicles might be very different from his. In all of these cases the value orientation is explicit. The historian has a set of values of which he is conscious, and which he knows he has employed in some of his selections. Everything is aboveboard, and his critics, even if they disagree with his values, may be able to understand why, given his point of view, he has made so many proclassical, proroyalist, pro-Anglican entries in his chronicle. They can also see that if they were minded to sum up an age by reference to *the* man or *the* idea of the hour, they would not have chosen the same man or idea.

However, we all know, if we have tried to write history, that we do not sit back after every singular statement we make in a chronicle and ask ourselves, "Now, let me see. I know that James II did that, and that Dryden wrote that, and that Archbishop Laud said that, but are those the facts to record in my history of England?" Similarly, those of us who read histories do not always find ourselves giving two distinct grades, one for truth and the other for memorability or worthiness to be recorded. The two assessments are often made in a total way and are not explicitly joined by logical conjunction. Under such circumstances we find ourselves making a blended judgment which is based on a simultaneous estimate of truth-*cum*-memorability. We feel that the author has written a narrative which, in the light of our acquaintance with the facts and our estimate of their importance, is on the whole good, and yet we cannot apportion its merits under two different headings. We look at his history in a total way, and this is more likely to be the case the longer and the more complex the narrative. We approve of it because he seems to look at the central subject with eyes and values like our own, and yet we are unable to specify what values we share with him so that we can say to him something analogous to what we say to a man who sees the same figure as we do in a Rorschach inkblot, "You and I both see that as a ——— because we both love ———'s." In such a case there may be a similar value-orientation, but it is not explicitly formulable. Here our judgment of the history is like the judgment we make when we admire a portraitist. The painter has seen his subject as we do because, in some cases, he has valued or despised in the subject what we value or despise in him even though we cannot say explicitly what that is. Not all entries in a chronicle are made and evaluated in this way, using this sort of double vision, but some are. And when they are, we can understand why historians can approve of each other's chronicles without being able to render two separate reports, one on the truth of the statements and another on the value of the things they record.

PLURALISM AND THE DISTORTION OF HISTORY

In arguing that value judgments play a part in determining what truths a historian will record, I am not defending the right of the historian to warp and distort history in the interests of a political goal like the aggrandizement of a dictator or the denigration of a deposed political leader. The pluralist need not yield to anyone when it comes to criticizing false history. If a historian deplores political and religious tyranny and seeks to explain how they came about, he does not automatically twist the facts in the interest of his politics or religion. Nor does he do so by making value judgments within his history about past figures. He need not tie his hands nor debar himself from criticizing such distortion any more than a physician, who deplores the fact that his patient has a disease and who tries to find out how it came about, inevitably distorts the facts of the patient's medical history.

It must be remembered that the pluralism I have advocated does not permit a statement in a chronicle to be false, nor does it permit a causal statement in a history to be false. And there can be no doubt that a great deal of politically tendentious history is simply false. For example, in one of Stalin's writings on the October Revolution in Russia one finds the following passage in the chronology of events:

Oct. 24 (Nov. 6, New Style)—Lenin arrives at Smolny in the evening. Stalin briefs him on the course of political events.

Oct. 24–25—Lenin and Stalin lead the October uprising.[28]

If an historian has evidence that Trotsky was also a leader of the uprising, then clearly he is in a position to refute the second entry. It is a case of a chronicler misleadingly and mendaciously telling a partial truth and not a case where we may tolerantly say that, like any chronicler, he could not tell the whole truth and therefore had to be content with telling only part of it. There are occasions on which a partial truth is seen to be a falsehood when one reflects on the question that the chronicler is trying to answer. If we bear in mind that the sentence "Lenin and Stalin lead the October uprising" is used by Stalin to assert what would be more clearly expressed by the sentence "Lenin and Stalin were *the* leaders of the uprising," we see that Stalin has falsely answered the question "Who were *the* leaders of the uprising?" And then when we discover that Stalin systematically tried to wipe out all of the evidence

[28] Quoted in Bertram D. Wolfe, "Operation Rewrite: The Agony of Soviet Historians," *Foreign Affairs*, October, 1952, p. 47.

that was damaging to his answer, we see that he deliberately gave a false answer. It has been shown by students of the Russian Revolution that "mountains of books, newspapers, pamphlets, decrees and documents had to be consigned to the 'memory hole,' mashed to pulp, or brought out in 'corrected editions,' in order to substitute for *Lenin-Trotsky* a new duality-unity, *Lenin-Stalin*."[29] Therefore, Stalin's distortion cannot be defended on any of the grounds that an honest historian might offer in defense of his selection of a certain true statement as the statement to be made about one time in the career of the subject whose history he is writing. There is nothing in pluralism as I conceive it which provides a cloak of philosophical respectability for lying.

We cannot leave this topic without dealing with the contention that a historian may distort even though every statement in his chronicle is true, though every causal statement in his history is true, and though he may not be speaking falsely even by implication. A historian of the United States who sees it primarily or exclusively as liberal and who presents his chronicle and history accordingly, may not assert or imply false propositions, and yet he might be accused of distortion by someone who was moved to see the central subject differently. It is, however, more illuminating to think of the Federalist as reflecting his own value-orientation, his conviction that the central subject should be seen differently because he regards another tradition as superior or more worthy of attention. The situation is somewhat analogous to what goes on when two men look at the duck-rabbit of Jastrow and Wittgenstein,[30] and one man sees it as a picture of a duck while the other sees it as a picture of a rabbit. Can one of them say to the other that he is viewing the figure in a distorted way?

There are, of course, other kinds of variability or relativity in perception, but this one is peculiarly relevant here because it is a case where no Tiresias-like third party can say that both of the

[29] Ibid., p. 44.
[30] See Joseph Jastrow, *Fact and Fable in Psychology* (Boston, 1900), p. 295; also Ludwig Wittgenstein, *Philosophical Investigations* (Oxford, 1953), p. 194.

arguing observers are wrong and partial, on the ground that the figure is to be seen at one and the same time as *both* a rabbit and a duck. The point is that one cannot see it simultaneously as both. At a given moment one sees it either as a duck or as a rabbit, and there is no irenical solution which would consist in saying that one should describe it as a hybrid called a "ruck" or a "dabbit." And just as the viewer of the duck-rabbit must at a given moment see it as either a duck or a rabbit, so there are some historians who are presented with a similar option that cannot be resolved by presenting a "Feffersonian" or a "Jederalist" history. Herbert Butterfield wisely says that "we do not gain true history by merely adding the speech of the prosecution to the speech for the defence".[31] For a related reason, two chronicles of the same thing may not overlap and the two chroniclers may treat each other as understandingly as the two observers who see the duck-rabbit differently may treat each other. In other words, two different historians of the same subject may see it in different ways without one's concluding that the other is viewing it in a distorted way. The analogy with the duck-rabbit is closer than it is with more conventional illustrations in the theory of perception, for example, the penny which may be seen as an ellipse or as a circle. For there is a tendency to say that the penny is *really* round even though seen as elliptical from certain points of view, whereas there is no temptation to say that the duck-rabbit is *really* a picture of a rabbit or *really* a picture of a duck once one sees that it may be regarded as either. There is even a tendency to say that normally, when asked "What is that?" people will give what Aristotle calls the "individual essence" of *that*, as expressed in what James called its "commonest title," its "vulgarest name,"[32] whereas neither the phrase "picture of a duck" nor "picture of a rabbit" may be called *the* commonest title or vulgarest name of the figure above.

There is one other respect in which the analogy with the duck-

[31] Herbert Butterfield, *The Whig Interpretation of History* (New York, 1951), p. 7.
[32] *Principles of Psychology*, II, 334; see also Mill, *System of Logic*, Bk. I, ch. VI, sec. 3.

rabbit is more illuminating than that with the shape of the penny and the essence of the individual. In the case of the penny, one observer can usually tell another how the other can come to view the penny as the first one does. He can tell him to look at it from a certain angle. And William James was peculiarly adept at telling people in what frame of mind they had to be, or what interests they would have to have, in order to see an object as either a piece of paper, or a combustible thing, or an object whose dimensions were 8½ inches by 11 inches, and so on. But one peculiarity of the duck-rabbit that brings it close to the historian's situation is that one finds it hard to give the analogous instructions. At least I find it hard to describe what I do when I change from rabbit-seeing to duck-seeing, and I think that the historian who wishes to give similar instructions about shifting from a Jeffersonian to a Federist "slant" will have similar difficulties.

VII

History, Ethics, and
Free Will

So far our concern with the role of value judgments in historical investigation has led us to focus on those that may determine what true historical statement a historian should make. Should he say in his history that A is the cause of C, or should he say that A' is? Should his chronicle include one true statement about the central subject or another? Such decisions, I have argued, may rest on value judgments that may or may not be made explicit, that may remain behind the arras or that may be brought into the open. But now I wish to turn my attention to the sort of moral judgment that the historian explicitly makes about the actions of those with whom he deals, quite apart from whether the making of such judgments determines what true statements will appear in his chronicle or history. We all know that historians do engage in such explicit moral evaluation and judgment, but many historians and philosophers of history have protested against this practice. Croce, for example, says: "Those who on the plea of narrating history bustle about as judges, condemning here and giving absolution there, because they think that this is the office of history . . . are generally recognized as devoid of historical sense. . . . Such judgments somehow grate upon us: we feel their vanity and incongruity, almost as though we saw a boxer attacking a statue which, of course, would not move or exchange its expression."[1] And more recently Herbert Butterfield has held that it is wrong to direct ethical judgments "against actual people in respect of an action once that action is done".[2]

Many arguments, both good and bad, have been offered in behalf of the view that historians should not pass moral judgment, and I do not propose to survey them here. Many of them are not worth our attention. But there is one that is certainly worth our attention in spite of its hoary history, and that is the argument that the making of moral judgments is incompatible with the principle of determinism. Reflection on this argument will, I think, show that sometimes the question whether the historian should engage in moral judgment is itself a moral question, and that where it is, his linguistic practice is itself governed by a moral principle about the conditions under which it is correct to pass judgment, and not by a principle that may be called metaphysical or logical in character. In coming to this conclusion we shall see that the historian's values affect more than his answers to the questions "What happened?" and "What is the cause of what happened?" They also affect the extent to which he is prepared to criticize the actions he does record, and they may therefore be expressed in his most fundamental convictions.

It has often been maintained, particularly by historical relativists, that the historian's conceptual framework—the set of fundamental principles that he brings to history—is affected by his values, and I think there is a sense in which this is true. I use this guarded way of expressing my agreement with this point of view

---

[1] Benedetto Croce, *History as the Story of Liberty* (London, 1941), p. 47.
[2] Herbert Butterfield, *History and Human Relations* (London, 1951), p. 106.

because, as the reader will soon see, I come to it by a route very different from that traveled by many historical relativists. I arrive at it by an analysis of the connection between a moral judgment passed on an action and the belief that the action is free or voluntary, a connection which, as I have said, is itself moral rather than logical in character. This connection is based on the moral principle that no one should judge an action as right or wrong unless he thinks it is voluntary, a moral principle which, I shall argue, is a component of our conceptual framework but a component which is more detachable, so to speak, than its logical components. The historian who causally explains a given action is morally, but not logically, obliged to withold certain moral statements about the action; and this sort of moral obligation rests on a principle that may be accepted by some cultures while it is rejected by others. It is a metamoral moral principle which is less compelling than most logical principles. It is not a mere grammatical truth[3], as some philosophers might say.

In order to establish this conclusion I shall begin by critically examining the opposite point of view, one which I think rests on a misconception of the connection between certain moral judgments of actions and statements that those actions are voluntary. That misconception is evident in the following faulty argument: Since determinism is true, every human action is caused and therefore no human action is voluntary; but if no human action is voluntary, none can be morally praised or blamed. When contraposed, this argument may also be used as a supposed refutation of determinism, and it will be more convenient to examine it carefully in that form. So construed, it is supposed to show that since the historian does make singular moral judgments like "It was wrong (or right) of Brutus to have stabbed Caesar," the historian is logically required to abandon determinism. Both of these arguments operate on the false assumption that belief in determinism and belief in

---

[3] I have argued similarly in my review of Isaiah Berlin's *Historical Inevitability*, repr. in my *Religion, Politics and the Higher Learning* (Cambridge, 1959), pp. 75–84. In this chapter the argument is corrected and strengthened.

certain moral judgments about actions are logically incompatible, and therefore neither of them may be used as premises in a proof.

My aim in showing that this principle is moral or practical is related to an old tradition in philosophy, one that was represented by Locke when he said in his *Essay* that no practical principle— for example, the Golden Rule—is self-evident. In that place— though not everywhere in his writings—Locke says that only speculative and logical principles like "It is impossible for the same thing to be and not to be" are self-evident.[4] And in the same spirit I wish to argue that the principle that "wrong" implies "can" is practical, that is to say, moral, in character.

Having said this, however, I must add that I do not think that one can make a clear and sharp distinction between analytic truths and synthetic truths and blithely say that all so-called logical truths are analytic, whereas all practical or moral principles are not.[5] The closest we can come to asserting something like this is to assert that *by and large* logical principles and statements like "Every bachelor is unmarried" are among those truths that we are extremely reluctant to surrender, whereas by comparison, practical principles are not. I do not wish to exclude the possibility that we are extremely reluctant to surrender *some* practical principles, and therefore I do not wish to say that as soon as we classify a principle as practical we *ipso facto* remove it from the charmed circle of permanently protected truths. But once we show that a principle *is* practical, we establish a presumption in favor of its being surrenderable and hence a presumption against its being used as a principle underlying a logical proof. My aim, therefore, is to show that the principle underlying the inference "*a* is wrong, therefore *a* is voluntary" is practical or moral, and that once this is seen, any effort to *prove* the falsity of determinism by means of a chain of logical argument containing this link ought to be abandoned.

---

[4] For a discussion of Locke's view see my essay "Original Sin, Natural Law and Politics," the epilogue to the Beacon Press paperback edition of my *Social Thought in America* (Boston, 1957), esp. pp. 266–71.

[5] See my *Toward Reunion in Philosophy* (Cambridge, 1956), especially Pt. IV.

In discussing this problem we must bear in mind that there are many kinds of moral judgments and many conceptions of voluntary action, and that a full discussion of the question whether *all* moral judgments logically imply that the actions judged in them are voluntary would involve an examination of all sorts of moral judgments. But here I shall limit myself to one kind of moral judgment and one notion of voluntariness as applied to actions. I shall be concerned with those moral judgments in which it is either asserted that a past action is right or that it is wrong. Therefore I shall not be concerned with the doctrine that "ought" implies "can," but rather with its sister doctrine that "right" and "wrong" imply "could have done otherwise."[6]

In order to discuss the main issues more concretely, I shall use two statements as examples. My first illustrative example is:

(a) Booth's action in shooting Lincoln was wrong.

I shall construe (a) as equivalent to "Booth acted wrongly when he shot Lincoln" and to "It was wrong of Booth to have shot Lincoln." Statement (a) is not merely a report of the fact that Booth performed a kind of action *said to be* wrong or in fact proscribed at the time: it is a moral judgment of Booth's action that may be made by a historian of the United States, or by anyone for that matter, who wishes to blame Booth. And now the question is whether this statement logically implies the statement:

(b) Booth's action in shooting Lincoln was voluntary,

where by "implies" and by "voluntary" the speaker means things that would allow him to *prove* that voluntary actions exist, and to conclude from the fact that voluntary actions exist that determinism is a false doctrine. In other words, the question is whether he can argue successfully as follows:

---

[6] The major part of what follows in this chapter is reprinted from my "Moral Judgment and Voluntary Action," which appears in the volume honoring Harry Austryn Wolfson, *The Wolfson Jubilee Volume,* ed. Saul Lieberman *et. al.,* © 1965 by The American Academy for Jewish Research.

(a) Booth's action in shooting Lincoln was wrong.
Therefore,
(b) Booth's action in shooting Lincoln was voluntary.
Therefore,
(c) There are voluntary actions.
Therefore,
(d) There are uncaused choices.
Therefore,
(e) There are uncaused events.
Therefore,
(f) It is not true that all events are caused.
Therefore,
(g) Determinism is false.

I do not think this is a valid proof because I think that even if it be proper to say that (a) implies (b), the sense of "implies" here is not such as to allow us to say that we can prove (b) by deducing it from (a), and therefore the so-called chain of proof breaks down between (a) and (b) quite apart from whether every other link is strong. Some philosophers have been willing to let the step from (a) to (b) go unchallenged but have challenged the step from (c) to (d), for they deny that being voluntary in the relevant sense logically implies that the agent's choice is uncaused. My course is different. I argue that even if one were to grant that the action's being voluntary logically implies that there are uncaused choices, the statement (a) does not *logically* imply that there are voluntary actions, and therefore the putative proof breaks down at the very start.

In order to show this, the statement that Booth's action was voluntary must be elaborated. There are two main interpretations of it in the literature which takes its point of departure from the contention that (b) conveys the fact that Booth could have done otherwise. In other words, "Booth could have done otherwise" has been held to be ambiguous. It may mean:

(b_1) If, just before shooting Lincoln, Booth had chosen not to shoot Lincoln, he would not have shot Lincoln, or it may mean:

> (b₂) If, just before shooting Lincoln, Booth had chosen not to shoot Lincoln, he would not have shot Lincoln; *and*, moreover, Booth could have chosen not to shoot Lincoln.

It will be observed that (b₂) is logically stronger than (b₁); it implies (b₁) and something else. The stronger interpretation of voluntariness is usually employed by philosophers who wish to insure the validity of the "therefore" leading from statement (c) to (d) because they hold that the statement "Booth could have chosen not to shoot Lincoln" [the second conjunct of (b₂)] implies that Booth's choice—if he made one—to shoot Lincoln was uncaused. On the other hand, those philosophers who wish to accept all the steps from (a) through (c) but reject the rest that lead from (c) to (f), favor (b₁) as the correct interpretation of (b). The point made by this second group of philosophers is that if all you logically imply when you say that it was wrong for Booth to have shot Lincoln is that he could have done otherwise in the sense of (b₁), you are not logically committed to any view on whether Booth could have *chosen* not to shoot Lincoln; hence you do not imply that Booth could have chosen otherwise; hence you do not imply that he was bound to choose as he did, if he did choose; hence you commit yourself to nothing that contradicts the statement that all events, including choices, are determined. For all you know, his choice may have been caused even though his action was voluntary.

Now the fact that (b₂) is a conjunction of (b₁) and another statement means that if (a) does not logically imply (b₁), it does not logically imply (b₂) either. In other words, if the statement "It was wrong of Booth to have shot Lincoln" does not logically imply "If just before shooting Lincoln, Booth had chosen not to shoot Lincoln, he would not have shot him," then, a fortiori, it will not logically imply "If just before shooting Lincoln, Booth had chosen not to shoot Lincoln, he would not have shot him; *and*, moreover, Booth could have chosen not to shoot Lincoln." It will therefore suffice for my purposes to show that (a) does not logically imply (b₁) in order to show that the putative "proof," given above, of the falsity of determinism breaks down. After showing this I will try to say more positively why the connection between (a) and (b) is itself moral in character, whether (b) is interpreted as equivalent to (b₁) or to (b₂). Granted that we can say truly that the statement "Jones is a bachelor" logically implies the statement "Jones is unmarried," or that the premises of a syllogism logically imply the conclusion, or that the statement "This is scarlet" logically implies the statement "This is red," I do not believe we can say that the relation between (a) and (b₁) is the same relation of implication. None of the usual tests that some philosophers apply with confidence in these standard cases give the usual results in the case of (a) and (b₁). Conjoin (a) and the denial of (b₁) and you do not seem to "involve yourself in contradiction." Nor is it easy to see that (b₁) expresses "part of the meaning" of (a). Moreover, I am not aware of any other test that will do the trick. Note also that it is possible to say truly of a man who has done something wrong, "It was wrong of him to do it, but he could not help doing it." And when we say this, we are not normally accused of contradicting ourselves, even though we are conjoining statement (a) and a denial of voluntariness in the sense of statement (b₁).

Next, I wish to offer an argument which is most easily expressed in logical terminology. If (a) were to imply (b₁), the denial of (b₁) would imply the denial of (a). But some moral philosophers hold that the moral judgment which is a denial of (a)—namely, "Booth was *not* wrong in shooting Lincoln"—also implies (b₁). And if they construe both of these implications as logical implications, they are committed to the view that the denial of (b₁) logically implies both the denial of (a) and the denial of the denial of (a). This in itself indicates that something queer is going on.

Lastly, I mention an argument which I find less convincing than some philosophers might find it, but it is worth mentioning in a general airing of this subject. If a moral statement like (a) implies a statement of voluntariness like (b_1), and if you construe a statement of voluntariness like (b_1) as what some philosophers call an "is"-statement about an action, then you must conclude that the denial of an "is"-statement implies the denial of a "wrong"-statement. It is plausible to suppose that those philosophers who think that moral statements are not deducible from "is"-statements would also say they are not deducible from "is not"-statements. In that case, as I have said, this argument should carry weight with them. My own hesitation about using this argument (as opposed to mentioning it) stems from doubts about its basic general assumption—about the nondeducibility of moral statements from "is"-statements. But it is certainly an argument that should move the minds of those who think there is something called the naturalistic fallacy.

Once again it is relevant to express my grave doubts about certain traditional efforts to define, analyze, explicate, or give criteria for the notion of an analytic statement—for example, that according to which to be an analytic statement is to be true solely by virtue of the meanings of the statement's terms, or that according to which an analytic statement is one whose contradictory is self-contradictory. But on the chance that my difficulties with such analyses of analyticity may be removed by some future philosopher, I wish to say now that I do not see how any reasonable interpretation of "analytic"—by which I mean one that at least preserves something of our present convictions about how it is to be used—could allow a philosopher to say that statement (a) contains as part of its meaning what is asserted in (b_1), or that a man who asserts (a) and denies (b_1) involves himself in self-contradiction.

Under the circumstances, a philosopher who has learned that not all so-called logically necessary connections can be glibly called analytic, might be tempted to seek aid from another quarter. He might argue that the voluntariness of an action in the sense of statement (b_1) as construed earlier is a *presupposition* of statement (a) in the sense of P. F. Strawson. Strawson says that it is the relation which holds between a statement like "All of Queen Elizabeth's children are asleep" and the statement that Queen Elizabeth has children.[7] The former does not logically imply the latter; therefore, the denial of the latter does not logically imply the denial of the former. This encourages an analogous view of the relationship between our statements (a) and (b₁). On such a view of the relationship between them, the voluntariness of the action would be presupposed and not implied by the moral statement, the point being that if the action in question were not voluntary, the question of the truth or falsity of the moral statement about the action would not arise.

I believe that this is a step in the right direction, but it should not be allowed to obscure a cardinal difference between presupposing that the children of Queen Elizabeth exist when you state that all of them are asleep, and presupposing that an action is voluntary when you state that it is wrong. This difference must be seen if we are properly to understand the relationship between our statements (a) and (b₁). Before trying to describe this difference, I want to say that from the point of view of my argument, one of the chief virtues of construing the relationship between (a) and (b₁) as presupposition is that it shows why we cannot *prove* that there are some voluntary actions merely by asserting a true moral statement about an action and then deducing that the action about which we make the statement is voluntary. Even if Queen Elizabeth's having children is a necessary condition for making true-or-false statements by the use of the sentence "All of Queen Elizabeth's children are asleep," we cannot *prove* that she has children by deducing their existence from this supposedly true statement. To show that she has children, we must engage in biological investigation, and no amount of metalinguistic assertion can take its place. In the same way, to show that Booth's action has the characteristic of voluntariness expressed in our statement (b₁), we must engage in a kind of investigation that cannot be replaced by

[7] P. F. Strawson, *Introduction to Logical Theory* (New York, 1952), pp. 175-79.

a deductive argument of the kind previously considered.

Having said that the relationship between our statements (a) and (b₁) is that of presupposition rather than logical implication, I now wish to describe what I have called a cardinal difference between the two examples of presupposition considered so far—the one in which we presuppose the voluntariness of an action and the other in which we presuppose the existence of Queen Elizabeth's children. To see this difference, it is well to consider the difference between saying that our statement (a) presupposes the *voluntariness* of Booth's shooting of Lincoln and saying that the the same statement presupposes his *shooting* of Lincoln. I am assuming, of course, that there is a difference between performing (or failing to perform) an action and performing (or failing to perform) it voluntarily. On this assumption it would be proper to say that Booth shot Lincoln even if he had been hypnotized into shooting him, in which case we would say that although he shot Lincoln, he did not shoot Lincoln voluntarily.

What I want to bring out here is that a truism underlies the statement that "Booth acted wrongly in shooting Lincoln" presupposes Booth's having shot Lincoln, whereas no such truism underlies the statement that "Booth acted wrongly in shooting Lincoln" presupposes Booth's having shot Lincoln voluntarily. The truism which underlies the presupposition of the existence of the action, as in the case of the existence of Queen Elizabeth's children, is that you cannot make a statement that is true-or-false if there is nothing for it to be made about. But I do not think it truistic to say that you cannot make a moral statement like (a) about Booth's action, if his action is not voluntary in the sense expressed in statement (b₁) above. When Strawson is considering the illustration of a man who uses a sentence like "All of Queen Elizabeth's children are asleep", Strawson says it would be "incorrect (or deceitful) for him to use this sentence" unless (1) he thinks he is referring to some children whom he thinks to be asleep, (2) he thinks that Queen Elizabeth has children, and (3) he thinks that the children he is referring to are Queen Elizabeth's.[8] But there is no reason to suppose that it would be *deceitful* for a man to use our sentence (a) if he did not think our statement(b₁) was true. Would it be "incorrect"? Here I am inclined to say that it *would* be "incorrect," but only according to certain moral codes. In other words, it seems to me that underlying the presupposition of our statement (b₁) by our statement (a) is a nontruistic moral conviction on the part of those who speak in a certain way; while underlying the presupposition of "Queen Elizabeth's children exist" by "All of Queen Elizabeth's children are asleep" is something that might more properly be called a logical truism.

When an action has been performed, the question can arise whether it is true-or-false to say that it is right, whether it is true-or-false to say that it is wrong. And this may be conceived as the question whether that action is susceptible to moral judgment. But I think that the question whether an action is *subject* to moral judgment or *susceptible* to moral judgment is the question whether we are morally right in passing moral judgment on the action. Corresponding questions in more theoretical cases are different. If you think, for example, that you cannot predicate colors of numbers, you might express this too by saying that a number is not *subject* to color-predication, that sentences like "7 is brown" cannot be used to make true-or-false statements. But you would not say that it is not morally right for a number to be called violet, blue, green, yellow, orange, or red. And this is crucial for the understanding of my point. In our case the question is the moral question whether the judged man should be morally judged. And that is one reason why I think there is a crucial difference between the dictum that you cannot make a true-or-false statement like "All of Queen Elizabeth's children are asleep" unless certain things exist, and the dictum that you can't make a true-or-false statement of rightness or wrongness about nonvoluntary actions.

One further consideration: In an illuminating philosophical exchange, G. E. Moore was once persuaded by A. C. Garnett that Moore in his book *Ethics* failed to realize that it is not sufficient in

[8] Ibid., p. 175.

the case of an action to be judged morally that the action merely be one which the agent would have not done if he had chosen.[9] Garnett argues that a person with a certain disease which prevents choice might fail to do something (and a failure is here construed as a kind of action), in which case it would be true to say that he would not have failed to do it if he had chosen otherwise. The trouble was that he couldn't *choose* otherwise. Now, when Moore is prevailed upon to acknowledge that his original characterization of actions subject to moral criticism was deficient, and that he must add that the person must be able to choose, I submit that he is being moved to see that it would be morally wrong to criticize this diseased person.

My main conclusions are: that a moral judgment like (a) does not logically imply a statement of freedom like (b₁), and that although it is illuminating to say that (a) presupposes (b₁), we should not be misled by the latter formulation into neglecting the fact that the *basis* of our presupposition is a moral conviction. I think that we can imagine a society in which people do not accept the principle that "wrong" presupposes "voluntary," so to speak. Moreover, I think that there are people in our own society who do not really accept it, who make moral judgments on others for performing what they (the judges) think are nonvoluntary actions. Such people punish wrong-doers who act nonvoluntarily, and they often go through the same procedures as we do for testing their judgments of right and wrong, even though they do not think that they can judge only agents who have acted voluntarily. Therefore it seems parochial to *define* moral judgment as that which logically implies belief in the voluntariness of the action judged. One may try to advocate to such people a more enlightened way of engaging in the process of moral judgment, of deciding who should be visited with pain and who should be treated to pleasures; but one should realize that such advocacy is large-scale moral advice rather than logical or metaphysical instruction.

It is not my intention to assert that a moral code is simply a

---

[9] *Philosophy of G. E. Moore*, ed. P. A. Schilpp (Evanston, 1942). See Garnett's essay and Moore's reply to it.

glorified legal code, and therefore the argument I am about to offer should be construed as no more than analogical. It will probably be granted that from a legal point of view the rules which fix responsibility are not logical in character. If a code says that a man is legally responsible only if he is a sane adult not acting under duress, it does not base this on some logical assertion to the effect that being legally responsible *logically implies* satisfying this condition, or that we would contradict ourselves if we said that a man was legally responsible but did not satisfy the condition. Of course, we might say this *after* we had promulgated a rule of this kind, but we would not *justify* its promulgation by citing a pre-established logical implication or connection between the statement that the man is legally responsible and the statement that he is a sane adult who is not acting under duress. Morever, we may debate the moral wisdom of such a convention just as we debate the moral wisdom of setting the voting age at twenty-one. Why, then, should the situation change so radically when we come to an analogous issue involving *moral* responsibility? Why should we think that the connection between our statements (a) and (b₁) is fundamentally different from that between the statements (a'), "Booth acted illegally when he shot Lincoln," and (b'), "Booth was a sane man who was not acting under duress when he shot Lincoln"? Behind the notion that there is a fundamental difference, there may lie a parochialism about the nature of moral judgment which we have managed to outgrow in our thinking about the law.

Some philosophers might wish to argue that within logical theory itself one can find issues that are very much like those that surround the acceptability of the dictum that "right" and "wrong" presuppose "voluntary." According to logicians who operate with the conventions of modern mathematical logic, a statement of the form "All S is P" is *true* if there are no things to which the predicate S applies. In other words, they do not adopt the dictum regarding presupposition which is used by Strawson. The decision of the mathematical logician to treat "All S is P" as true where S does not apply to anything, is intimately connected with his construal of "All S is P" as equivalent to "For every x, if x is S, then x is P," where the connective "if-then" is in turn construed in such a way that a conditional statement is true if its antecedent is false. And part of the motivation for this decision concerning the use of "if-then" is to avoid what have been called "truth-value gaps." It is desirable from a mathematical logician's point of view that he should be able to attribute truth or falsity to every statement of his language, and therefore he calls a conditional statement with a false antecedent true, even though in ordinary language we might refuse to call it true-or-false. It follows that he must call a universal statement like "All S is P" true when nothing is S.

Now it might be said that these considerations adduced by the mathematical logician in defense of his departure from ordinary linguistic practice are similar in kind to those which might be adduced by a society that wished to justify its abandonment of the dictum that our statement (a) presupposes our statement (b_1). And, of course, representatives of such a society might argue that the whole language of moral judgment becomes less complicated when one says that a statement of rightness or wrongness is true or false irrespective of whether the action judged is voluntary. They also might appeal to the linguistic advantages of eliminating all truth-value gaps where statements of right and wrong were concerned. But my point is that they might, and probably would, defend their divergence from *our* practice—assuming that we *do* treat (a) as presupposing (b_1)—by giving arguments of a kind that might be better construed as moral. That is to say, they might defend the *moral* worth of regarding it as true-or-false that an action is right, quite apart from whether this action is voluntary in the sense of (b_1). Their mode of attributing rightness and wrongness, they might say, leads to certain desirable social consequences or to conformity with the moral attitudes of their own people, and not merely to smooth-running logical accountancy. They might argue, for example, that their "language game" diminishes the amount of frustration which is characteristic of ours, because we must check our natural impulse to condemn in moral language those who have ostensibly done wrong and our natural impulse to speak praisingly of those who have ostensibly done right, in order to be sure that they have acted voluntarily.

I cannot see why any philosopher would wish to deny that an alternative linguistic situation of the kind I describe might exist. I realize, of course, that he might be tempted to say that people who make moral judgments in my imaginary society do not "use" the words "right" and "wrong" as we do, or that they do not conceive the activity of moral judgment as we do. But everything will now depend on how we understand the crucial word "use" in this context and also on what we understand by the phrase "conceive the activity of moral judgment." The imagined situation is as I have imagined it, and if a philosopher chooses to say that I am picturing a group of people who do not use the words "right" and "wrong" as we use them, he may do so. But he should realize that in the situation I imagine, the words "right" and "wrong" could mean the same thing (in one sense of that difficult phrase) for my imaginary people as they mean for us. The difference between them and us would emerge, as it were, not in the interpretation of the *predicates* of the statement forms "*x* is right" and "*x* is wrong," but rather in the range of the variable. We would limit that range to voluntary actions, saying that the resulting sentences cannot be used to make true-or-false statements when we substitute the names of nonvoluntary actions; whereas the people of the other society would not be so restrictive. If it be said that an anthropologist who studied my imagined people would certainly not translate their moral predicates as "right" and "wrong" precisely because these people do *not* adopt our dicta of presupposition, I cannot agree. The anthropologist might describe it as a situation in which, meaning by the words "right" and "wrong" what we do, the people in question apply them in cases where we do not. And he could add that they, for moral reasons, do not adopt the same dicta of presupposition as we do concerning statements of right and wrong.

I can see that another philosopher might describe the situation under discussion by saying that those who do make moral judgments on actions where the actions are not voluntary have a different *conception* of moral judgment from those who do. He might say that one group means one thing by "moral judgment" while those who think and operate differently in this area mean another thing by it. But my quarrel with such a way of looking at the situation is that it tends to obscure the fact that one culture can influence another to adopt the other's presuppositions concerning moral judgment without thinking that it has persuaded the other culture to change the meaning of moral words, or to take up moral judgment as such. I find it difficult to imagine a conversation in which a representative of a culture which adopts the principle " 'Wrong' and 'Right' presuppose 'Voluntary'," saying to a representative of a culture which might not, "Why don't you start meaning by 'moral judgment' what we mean by it?" I should rather construe the dialogue as beginning, "Why don't you adopt the practice of morally judging only those actions that are voluntary?"

Those who cannot bring themselves to broaden their use of the term "moral judgment" may be asked what they shall call an activity which, in every other respect, is just like what they call moral judgment except for the fact that those who make the judgments do not feel obliged to limit them to voluntary actions. Surely we cannot deny that such an activity is conceivable. Many of us take ourselves to make moral judgments about actions whose voluntariness we do not in fact investigate. What are we doing? Surely something. Well, then, there might be societies in which it is morally permissible to do this thing. Such people would punish—that is, inflict pain—for wrong-doing. And if it be replied that they could not be said to punish when they do not think that the action punished is voluntary, because in that case their punishment would have no point, I say that it all depends on what you mean by "point." Call them savages, if you will, but not logical blunderers. We must not allow ourselves to be enticed into the view that people punish only with the alteration of the conduct of the punished person in mind. Some people punish in a spirit of vengeance. Shall we say that the judgment they make prior to punishing (viz., "This man acted wrongly") is therefore not a "moral" judgment? Shall we say that their infliction of pain for wrong-doing is not punishment? I think this would be absurd. It would be more plausible to say that they judge as wrong and punish actions that they should not so judge and punish.

Among the advantages of this view of the relation between moral judgment and voluntary action is the fact that it makes it easier to view the principle that "right" and "wrong" presuppose "voluntary" as one that need not be held by people who are capable of ratiocination. For I think it *is* logically surrenderable, not self-evident, probably not accepted by all cultures, or even by all members of our own. For that reason it is a very fragile link in supposedly knock-down arguments for the falsity of determinism. For the same reason, persuading people to accept it requires more than training them in logic. It will be recalled that those philosophers who try to derive the falsity of determinism from judgments of right and wrong often begin as follows. They argue that the statement "It was wrong of Booth to have shot Lincoln" logically implies "If just before shooting Lincoln, Booth had chosen not to shoot Lincoln, he would not have shot him; and, moreover, Booth could have chosen not to shoot Lincoln." I have concentrated on the first conjunct of the second statement and have shown, I hope, that *it* is not logically implied by the moral statement. In doing so I have shown that the conjunction is not logically implied. Moreover, although I have not discussed the relationship between the moral judgment and the second conjunct, "Booth could have chosen not to shoot Lincoln," the fact that it cannot be logically deduced from the moral judgment may be shown in essentially the same way. In any case, I think that the conjunction does not follow logically from the moral premise and that its connection with the premise is mediated, to use old-fashioned language, by a moral or practical principle.

Once again, therefore, we have discovered a moral judgment where we might not have expected to find one. That moral judgment takes the following form: *No one should judge an action as right or as wrong unless he thinks it is voluntary.* If a person judges an action which he knows or thinks is not voluntary, that person acts wrongly in so judging. Moreover, the fact that a man *makes* a moral judgment does not guarantee that the action he judges is voluntary. Of course, this formulation of the link between moral judgments like (a) and statements of voluntariness like (b) does not tell us how to interpret (b). It does not decide between (b₁) and (b₂) and therefore does not tell us whether we must think Booth was free in the weaker or the stronger sense in order to be justified in judging him. That is a separate question. But one thing is clear, and that is that if a person or a culture adopts the stronger interpretation, and if the statement that Booth could have *chosen* otherwise logically implies that Booth's choice to shoot Lincoln—if he made one—is uncaused, then a person who asserts that Booth's action was wrong is morally required to think that there are uncaused events, i.e., that determinism is false. The point is that if he is morally required to take Booth's action to have been voluntary, and if being voluntary logically implies being uncaused, then he is morally required to abandon determinism. Yet even though he is *morally* required to abandon determinism, that doctrine might have so much independent evidence supporting it or so much attraction for him as to place him in a quandary. Naturally, there is nothing new about this quandary, but there may be something new about our interpretation of it precisely because it is now seen to arise, in part, out of acceptance of the metamoral moral principle that no one should judge an action morally unless he takes it to be voluntary. And if, as I think, such a principle is not likely to be as basic to our conceptual framework as logical principles are, we have at least pointed to a way of eliminating the conflict between the belief in determinism and the making of ordinary singular moral judgments like "Booth acted wrongly in shooting Lincoln." I am not here advocating the abandonment of this metamoral moral principle, but I am intent on characterizing its role in the conceptual framework within which certain philosophers and perhaps most of us in our culture operate. The thinking man who feels compelled to give up determinism because he does not think it is cotenable with his making of moral judgments could solve his problem in another way, namely, by giving up this metamoral moral principle. Seeing that it is a *moral* principle may reveal a possibility that he had not seen before, and hence make the surrender easier.

In addition to providing this new way of looking at the dilemma of determinism, the recognition that the dictum " 'Wrong' implies 'Can' " is moral in character shows that the class of our basic beliefs, those that make up our world view, is not wholly logical in composition. Our world view is heterogeneous in make-up, and because some of its components are not what some philosophers call necessary truths, notably moral principles, it is more susceptible to change than some philosophers think. Moreover, such a conclusion lends considerable plausibility to the doctrine of "historical relativism" when it is formulated in an intelligible way. There may be doubt as to whether logic or arithmetic may vary from culture to culture, but it is hard to see why metamoral moral principles cannot. Even if a world view is *ours,* there is *some* room within it for alteration provided we are willing to pay the logical price. If we give up the moral principle that we should judge only actions thought to be voluntary, the pressure on determinism is diminished. Once we find ourselves in this fundamental part of our conceptual framework, we may *think* we are locked in by the language we *have* used in the past, but reflection can, as I have tried to show, soften the bars. If that be historical relativism, I feel no horror in accepting it. Moreover, our conclusion reveals at the level of the historian's very general principles what we have aleady seen in our discussion of explanation and narration—that value judgments may play an unnoticed role in determining what should be asserted. Just as some of our statements about what happened are made partly because we have certain values, and just as some of our statements about *the* cause of what happened are made partly because we have certain values, so some of our apparently logical statements turn out to be moral and relative in character. Once again we see the importance of *point of view* in an area thought to be determined exclusively by the facts—this time not the facts of life studied by the historian but the facts of language studied by the philosopher.

INDEX

ABOUT THE AUTHOR

MORTON WHITE is professor of philosophy at Harvard University. He is the author of *The Origin of Dewey's Instrumentalism* (1943), *Social Thought in America* (1949), *Toward Reunion in Philosophy* (1956), and, with Lucia White, of *The Intellectual Versus the City* (1962). He has edited *The Age of Analysis* (1955) and, with Arthur Schlesinger, Jr., *Paths of American Thought* (1963).

A native of New York, Professor White has taught at Harvard since 1948. He was graduated from the City College of New York in 1936 and received his Ph.D. from Columbia University in 1942. Before coming to Harvard, he taught at Columbia, CCNY, and the University of Pennsylvania. He was visiting professor at Tokyo University in 1952 and 1960.

Professor White was a member of the Institute for Advanced Study in Princeton, N. J., in 1953-1954 and 1962-1963; and a Fellow of the Center for Advanced Study in Behavioral Sciences in 1959-1960. He was a Guggenheim Fellow in 1950-1951 and a Fellow of the American Council of Learned Societies in 1962-1963. He is also a Fellow of the American Academy of Arts and Sciences.

Format by Katharine Sitterly
Set in Linotype Electra
Composed, printed and bound by The Haddon Craftsmen, Inc.
HARPER & ROW, PUBLISHERS, INCORPORATED